NATURE
·WATCHER'S·
DIRECTORY

NATURE
·WATCHER'S·
DIRECTORY

David Marsden

Hamlyn
London · New York · Sydney · Toronto

Foreword

The hallmark of a good naturalist is the respect he or she shows for all life, wild or otherwise. It would seem to be common sense that anyone who finds pleasure in seeing and watching wildlife will automatically strive to protect it, or at least do nothing detrimental to it, and most naturalists today are only too well aware of the damage that can be done by failing to observe the Country Code. But there are always those who are careless or neglectful, and there are far too many instances where wildlife enthusiasts have put birds off their nests needlessly, or trampled crops or damaged rare plants whilst taking photographs. Even worse are people who deliberately collect birds eggs, flowers or other wildlife. It is largely on account of this small minority that the whereabouts of some of our rarer species is kept secret and, with due respect to this secrecy, I have avoided giving away the locations of many of our most threatened species in this book. Even so, there will be those who will consider that I have given too much away. Personally, I regard too much secrecy as being rather negative. It is hardly reasonable to keep our wildlife behind 'locked doors' and then expect people to become concerned about its conservation. In writing this book, my aim has been to tempt more people to go into the countryside to see and enjoy our wildlife in the hope that they will be encouraged to join, and participate in, the growing movement towards conservation.   D.M.

Acknowledgements

Photographs
Biofotos II (top); VI; VII (top); X (bottom); Jim Flegg XI (top);
XII; Format Publishing Services: B. Edwards IV (top)/D. Hall
XI (bottom); Eric Hosking IV (bottom); David Marsden I; II
(bottom), III; V; VII (bottom); XIII; IX (top); Nature Photographers:
J.V. and G.R. Graham X (top)/David Sewell IX (bottom).

Line drawings by Phil Weare/Linden Artists

The publishers would like to thank particularly the following
for their valuable assistance and advice during the preparation of this book:

Jim Flegg (General consultant); Mike Busselle (Photographic consultant); Field Studies
Council; National Trust; Nature Conservancy Council; Royal Society for the Protection
of Birds.

Published by The Hamlyn Publishing Group Limited
London · New York · Sydney · Toronto
Astronaut House, Feltham, Middlesex, England
© The Hamlyn Publishing Group Limited 1984
First published 1984
First edition, second impression 1984

ISBN 0 600 30568 6
Printed in Italy

Contents

Introduction

The last few decades have seen a tremendous growth of interest in natural history and wildlife conservation. More and more people are spending their leisure time in the countryside watching birds and mammals, seeking out wild flowers and studying insects and other creatures. Evidence of this is not hard to find; the number of nature reserves and wildlife sanctuaries has grown apace in recent years, and the membership of our various natural history societies continues to increase in leaps and bounds. The shelves of our bookshops are stocked with a huge number of natural history books, especially those fieldguides which are designed to enable the naturalist to identify the various species of plants and animals which may be encountered.

This, indeed, is where most naturalists begin: by learning to identify our wild creatures and plants. Yet merely putting a name to an animal or plant is just the beginning. A keen naturalist will want to do much more than this. He or she will want to learn how animals live; to see with their own eyes something of the private lives of wild creatures; to understand why plants grow where they do; and to ensure that they have the right equipment for nature watching. The *Nature Watcher's Directory* is designed to help do just that, for it is intended to complement existing fieldguides and to provide a valuable source of reference for all the information needed by naturalists. In short, its aim is to help naturalists to get more enjoyment from wildlife.

For example, although many fieldguides briefly mention the distribution of the species they describe, they very rarely have room to give more than very general distribution maps, and certainly have no space to give specific locations. An important feature of the *Nature Watcher's Directory* is an extensive list of wildlife sites, including many nature reserves and sanctuaries. Each entry describes the main ecological and topographical features of the site, and catalogues the principal plants and animals to be found there, particular attention being drawn to any specialities or uncommon species. Details of access are also included for each site, including the precise location and, where appropriate, the addresses from which any permits may be obtained.

Another shortcoming of many conventional fieldguides is that, although they often state which habitat the various species may be found in, they are unable to elaborate on this or mention any other species which are also likely to be seen there. It would be a great pity, for example, to visit a lowland heath hoping to see nightjars or hobbies and yet remain totally unaware of the heath milkwort or marsh gentian growing among the heather, or to miss the chance of seeing a smooth snake or rare insect, and to this end the *Nature Watcher's Directory* also includes a section aimed at introducing the reader to the various wildlife habitats which exist in our country today, briefly outlining the ecology of each one and listing the most characteristic plant and animal inhabitants.

How to use this book

This book can be used in several ways. General information, such as which binoculars to choose, and how to watch birds, is given in the relevant chapters – in the examples here, in the chapters on Equipment and Nature watching respectively.

More specific information, such as the law relating to rare species, and addresses of the main conservation organizations, can be found in the Appendices at the back of the book.

As already mentioned, a major feature of this book is the list of sites and reserves where you can see wildlife. If you are on holiday, simply look up the relevant regional section to find out which habitats (and which species) are included in your area. You can then plan your trip, taking with you the necessary fieldguides and general equipment. Alternatively you can decide that you would like to see a particular plant or animal, and can then choose a location where, at the right time of the year, this species is likely to be present.

To simplify matters, only the English or common names of animals and plants are normally used. Latin names are included only where the species has no well-known English name.

The sites and reserves each have three sets of letters and figures. The first set refers to the regional location, and can be confirmed by looking at the map on page 59. The second set gives the number of the relevant Ordnance Survey map in the 1:50,000 Landranger Series on which the site is located. The third set is the location of the site using the National Grid referencing system. Atlases which use this system will provide explanations of how the system works, but basically Great Britain is divided into 100 kilometre grid squares, each of which is identified by two letters. Each square is then subdivided into 10 kilometre squares. These are numbered in an easterly and northerly direction from the south-west corner of the square. Thus: Lundy Island (SS1345) is located in 100 kilometre square SS, at the point at which 1.3 kilometres east and 4.5 kilometres north meet.

Equipment

Natural history is a pursuit which can be followed with very little equipment indeed. All you really need is plenty of enthusiasm and a keen sense of observation, although as your interests develop you will probably feel the need for a few accessories. Exactly what you will need depends on the branches of natural history you become most interested in: birdwatching, mammal watching, insects, botany or whatever.

Notebooks

One item of equipment you should have is a pocket notebook, preferably one with a hard back, and a pencil (a pencil is better than a pen since ink will run if it gets wet). You should get into the habit of writing down what you see, when and where you saw it, and any other observation you make. Such notes can come in surprisingly useful, particularly if you transfer them to some kind of permanent record at home – a card index or loose-leaf file arranged according to species is a good system. To illustrate the usefulness of notes, imagine that you see a grey heron flying overhead one day and note down the date, time and place and the direction of its flight. If you keep a permanent record of all such sightings, you may be able to plot the flight paths on an Ordnance Survey (O.S.) map and deduce the approximate location of the heronry. This may subsequently provide you with many happy hours of birdwatching.

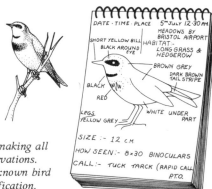

Fieldnotes are useful for making all kinds of on-the-spot observations. Here the details of an unknown bird are noted, for later identification.

8

Binoculars

Another very useful item of equipment is, of course, a pair of binoculars. Most people immediately associate them with birdwatching, but they are a very handy aid for all kinds of natural history study and can, for example, save you a lengthy walk by enabling you to identify a patch of wild flowers some distance away. Many people are tempted to buy a large and powerful pair in the belief that the higher the magnification the more useful they will be, but this is quite erroneous. A big pair are heavy to carry, cumbersome and difficult to hold still and often have such a tiny field of view that even finding your subject can be extremely difficult. A small pair which will slip easily into your pocket or are not too heavy to carry around your neck are the most suitable.

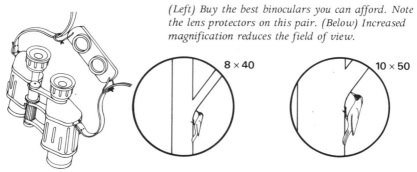

(Left) Buy the best binoculars you can afford. Note the lens protectors on this pair. (Below) Increased magnification reduces the field of view.

A pair of binoculars will have two numbers stamped on them, e.g. 8 × 30. The first number relates to the magnification. A magnification of 7 or 8 times is perfectly adequate for most uses. The second number refers to the size of the object lenses, and is expressed in millimetres. The size of the object lenses should be as large as possible in relation to the magnification, since this will give a brighter image. If you divide the diameter of the objectives by the magnification, the answer will give you an indication of the light-gathering power of your binoculars. This number should be as high as possible − at least 4 and nearer 5, which means that the best binoculars for nature watching will be those with numbers like 7 × 35 or 8 × 40 stamped on them.

Telescopes

If you wish to do long-distance watching − working on estuaries for example − you will probably need a telescope. Using a telescope requires considerable practice, however. It is virtually impossible to hold one still without a tripod, and the field of view is usually so restricted that it can be very difficult to find your subject. Perhaps the best solution to this problem is to buy a zoom telescope in which the magnification can be increased − perhaps from about 20 to about 60 − without losing the focus, so that you can find your subject on low power and then 'zoom in'.

A modern alloy instrument with an objective of about 60 mm, and a zoom range from about 15 or 20 to 60 is ideal. Some astronomical telescopes have a much higher magnification than this, but they are quite useless for natural history work because of the problems of holding them still and of finding the subject.

Handlens

Another item of optical equipment which is extremely useful, particularly for botanists, is a small handlens of perhaps 8 or 10 times magnification. If you take a special interest in mosses, liverworts or other small plants, a low-power binocular microscope is much more convenient to use although you cannot, of course, take it with you into the field.

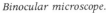

Binocular microscope.   *Vasculum.*

 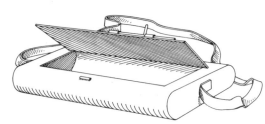

Vasculum

Although plant collecting is not recommended, it is sometimes necessary to take specimens home. This should only be done providing that the plant in question is present in some quantity, that it is not growing on a nature reserve or other protected area, and that you have positively identified it as not being rare. The best way to transport plant specimens is by means of a vasculum; this is a metal case which is partially filled with sphagnum moss or damp newspaper to keep the specimens fresh, and carried by a shoulder strap. A cheap substitute for a proper vasculum is a rigid plastic box, still containing moss or damp newspaper.

Torch

Enthusiasts will probably find a torch with a red filter useful for watching nocturnal animals such as mammals. A powerful handlamp is best, and the red filter can easily be cut from a piece of thin perspex or transparent plastic.

Traps for mammals

If your interest is in small mammals – such as mice, voles and shrews – you may find a Longworth mammal trap useful, although they are not cheap. These small metal traps are baited with cereals, etc. and are left out in likely places, preferably by the runs of small mammals. A small amount of grass or

Longworth mammal trap: cutaway (left); in position (right).

straw for bedding should also be provided, and traps should be checked at least once a day, and preferably more often. Shrews especially can die within hours if left to go hungry.

Equipment for insect-watching

If you develop an interest in insects or other invertebrates a few items of more specialized equipment will be useful.

Nets

The best-known of the entomologist's tools is the butterfly or kite net. Despite its name, however, it can be used for catching many other insects besides just butterflies. Nets can be bought from entomological suppliers, but a perfectly serviceable one can be made at home. The framework should consist of heavy-duty wire, bent into a triangular shape about 18 in (46 cm) along each side and taped securely to a short wooden handle. If you are mainly interested in catching butterflies the net itself should be made of soft cotton, dark in colour and about twice as long as the opening. If you intend to use the net for sweeping – that is, brushing the vegetation to collect dislodged insects – a white linen bag is better. Many enthusiasts have one of each type.

A scissors net is a more selective way of trapping individual insects.

Beating tray

Use a beating tray for collecting insects from trees. This is simply a light-coloured piece of cloth which is held beneath the tree whilst the collector beats the branches with a heavy stick – an action which dislodges many insects, causing them to fall on to the beating tray where they can easily be seen. An old sheet spread on to the ground will suffice, but a more convenient design consists of a piece of material a yard or so square which is supported underneath by four wooden spars which run from the corners of the cloth to the middle where they are hinged together so as to form a collapsible cross.

11

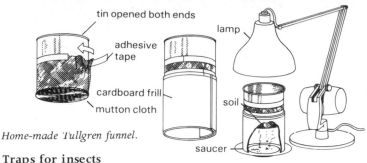

Home-made Tullgren funnel.

Labels in figure: tin opened both ends, adhesive tape, cardboard frill, mutton cloth, lamp, soil, saucer

Traps for insects

Ground-living insects, including many beetles, can be caught by miniature **pitfall traps**. These are easily made by sinking an empty can or plastic cup into the ground, up to its rim. In order to prevent rain water from collecting inside, cover the trap with a tile or piece of slate which is supported on three or four stones. This will also keep mice and other small mammals out. Punching a few holes in the bottom or placing one or two largish stones inside are added precautions against flooding, and a little moss will provide cover for the occupants until you are able to inspect the trap – which you should do at least once a day. It is sometimes profitable to bait the trap with meat or fruit.

The best way to collect moths is by means of a **mercury vapour trap**, available from certain biological suppliers. This consists of a circular box with a transparent conical top and a special mercury vapour lamp.

A much cheaper and more portable alternative is to use a Tilley lamp and an old white sheet. The sheet is either spread out on the ground and the lantern placed in the centre, or is hung over a branch or fence, etc. and the light placed in front. Another alternative is simply to leave a room light on all night with the windows slightly ajar. Keep the door to the room closed or the moths will need to be collected from all over the house!

Soil organisms can be collected by using a Tullgren funnel. Again, this can be obtained from some biological suppliers, although you can easily make one yourself. This is a large metal funnel with a sieve or grid about half way down. A small amount of soil or leaf litter is placed on the sieve and a light bulb is suspended above. The heat from the bulb forces any small creatures present to burrow into the soil and then to fall through the sieve and into a receptacle beneath.

Catching aquatic creatures

Aquatic creatures may be collected by means of a dredge net. This is essentially the same as the kite net described earlier, but with a rather stronger frame and longer handle. If you intend to make one yourself, bolting silk is recommended for the bag since it does not rot easily and has the correct mesh size to allow mud and sand to pass through without letting larger animals do so. Another way to catch pond life is with a grapnel. Again, this is easy to make yourself by bending four pieces of stout wire, each about 1ft (30 cm) long into hook shapes, inserting them into a small piece of lead piping and hammering it flat. (The lead piping is also important as weight.) A long piece of cord is attached, and the grapnel is thrown into the pond and hauled out again, hopefully with a mass of water weeds and their attendant fauna attached. Use this equipment with care: it can be very destructive to the habitat if repeated dredgings are made. Always sink the dredged weed back after inspection.

Clothing

If you are nature watching in the lowlands during the summer you are unlikely to need any special clothing. Problems arise, however, when you are visiting places where you are likely to get either cold, wet or both – especially in the hills or on the coast. The problem is aggravated by the fact that too many clothes cause the wearer to become overheated. When climbing a mountain, for instance, you can become very hot and start to perspire heavily in no time at all, yet sit down to study a pair of ravens or photograph an alpine flower and within minutes you can be shivering. The only answer is to wear several layers of clothes which can be peeled off or added to as required, and carried in your rucksack when not needed.

An anorak or oilskin-type jacket is the best investment for wet or cold weather. The warmest kinds are those which are belted around the waist and have button-down flaps over the zips. Most kinds have hoods, but these have the disadvantages of cutting off your lateral vision and impeding your hearing, so perhaps a hat or balaclava is better. Thick woollen trousers are probably the best kind since they are both water repellent and warm. If a skirt is worn whilst nature watching, choose a thick one. Long socks are infinitely preferable to stockings or tights.

Boots are generally recommended for visiting places which are off the beaten track since they help to keep your feet dry and provide ankle support. A sprained ankle is a problem anywhere, but high on a mountain or on some remote coast it can be a veritable disaster. Leather boots are to be recommended since they allow the feet to breathe, although wellington boots are obviously the order of the day on estuaries, marshes and other wet places.

Try to avoid clothing which rustles, since it not only alerts any animals to your presence but can also prevent you from hearing them. Remember also that your clothes should be an inconspicuous colour – preferably brown or olive – although it is wise to carry at least one brightly coloured garment which can be used as a signal in case of accident.

Maps and miscellaneous items

In remote places you should also carry a whistle, a compass, an O.S. map of the area, and some food. Dried fruit, nuts and chocolate are all recommended, and can be an extremely welcome 'pick-me-up' on a cold mountain top. O.S. maps are indispensable in remote areas, but they are very useful anywhere and can show you much more than just roads and footpaths. Most of our main wildlife habitats are shown on O.S. maps, too, including heath and scrub, marshes and bogs, open water, saltmarshes, mudflats, sand dunes, cliffs, various types of beaches, mountains and woods – although the current series of metric maps do not, unfortunately, distinguish between deciduous and coniferous woods like the older 1 inch maps did. In more built up areas they will also show you features such as disused railway lines and quarries, both of which can be worth visiting.

If botany is your main interest you might also find that large-scale geological maps are useful, too. Different rocks give rise to different soil.

Other useful items include a waterproof mat for sitting on, a rucksack for carrying your equipment, spare clothing and packed lunches, etc. Finally, you may decide you want to build a hide. Instructions for this are given on pages 52 and 53.

Fieldguides

You will also probably need at least one guide book, depending on where your main interests lie. Many fieldguides offer a good coverage of one group of animals or plants. This is fine if your main interest is in one particular group, but if you are an 'all rounder' you can find yourself having to carry a veritable library around with you, unless you opt for one of the general guides which cover a variety of wildlife. Their shortcoming is that they can never be nearly as comprehensive in their coverage as can the more specific guides. If you decide to visit, say, the mountains, however, there is no point in taking a comprehensive fieldguide to birds which will include garden birds, seabirds and woodland species, since you will not see any. On the other hand you might come across some interesting alpine flowers or mosses and wish you had brought your flower guide. For this reason you might consider buying a range of the fieldguides which cover habitats rather than biological groups. In any case, you can always keep a more comprehensive library at home and consult it using the information in your notebook to identify any species of which you are unsure.

As regards fieldguides illustrated by photographs rather than artwork, there is really little to choose, apart from what you consider to be the best coverage of the subject. Both styles of treatment have their merits, some people preferring one, and some the other.

Sound recordings

There are several recordings of bird calls and other sounds of nature which are available from certain organizations and from record libraries. They are an invaluable way to learn how to identify these species without actually seeing them, and of course they provide useful clues for locating wildlife.

Nature watching

It's quite a mystery to many people just how naturalists manage to see so much wildlife. Most people, especially those who live in cities, can stroll through the countryside and see nothing but fields, hedges and trees whilst others, more familiar with the ways of nature, are able to see so much more. They spot that tiny gap in the hedge through which the hares and foxes regularly pass; they are constantly aware of the singing skylarks as they perform their melodious aerobatics high above; and they notice the vetches and speedwells where other people only see a green field.

It is this awareness, of course, which sets naturalists apart from other people. They are constantly alert to the natural world around them. Their eyes are always on the look-out for an uncommon flower or subtle field sign, and their ears are constantly listening to the songs of birds and the calls of other creatures.

Many of these skills are, of course, born out of interest and fostered by observation and patience, and cannot very well be expressed in words. However, the techniques for studying wildlife – locating unusual flower species, recognizing field signs, watching mammals and so on – are easier to describe, and this chapter is designed to do just that.

Nature watching at home

You can even begin to develop your nature-watching techniques at home by providing a bird table. The best foods are cooked potatoes, cheese crumbs and rinds, raw pastry, chopped bacon rinds and all kinds of nuts, seeds and fruits. Peanuts and fat are also good.

Having decided to start a bird table, however, there are two rules which you should remember. Rule one is to keep the supply of food regular. In winter, when natural food is scarce, many birds will come to rely almost totally on you for food and to suddenly stop putting food out – even for one day – can be fatal. Rule two is to reduce your feeding in spring and summer when the birds are likely to be rearing young. The nestlings will develop far better on natural food.

Not only do birds need food, they also need water, for both drinking and bathing, and a bird bath will increase the attractiveness of your garden to wildlife enormously. An upturned dustbin lid sunk into the ground makes quite a good bird bath.

You will see even more activity if you encourage your local birds to nest around your home, either by judicious pruning of any hedges so as to provide a maximum number of potential nest sites, or by erecting nest boxes. There are many designs which you can either build yourself or buy. Details of the various kinds, and the birds for which they are suitable, can be obtained from the British Trust for Ornithology. The R.S.P.B. also supplies various well-proven types of nest box.

You can also try encouraging mammals, too. Bats, for example, can be attracted by erecting bat boxes or by allowing them access to your attic by making a small slot – about $\frac{3}{4} \times 2-3$ in ($20 \times 50-75$ mm) long will be sufficient – in the soffit boards next to the wall. Hedgehogs can also be encouraged to visit by putting milk and scraps out each evening.

Birdwatching

The most important items of equipment for birdwatching are a pair of binoculars and a good fieldguide. It is a good idea to jot down a description and make a rough sketch of any doubtful species in your field notebook so you can check these against your identification guides later, at home. And

It is essential to know the terminology used in fieldguides to describe birds.

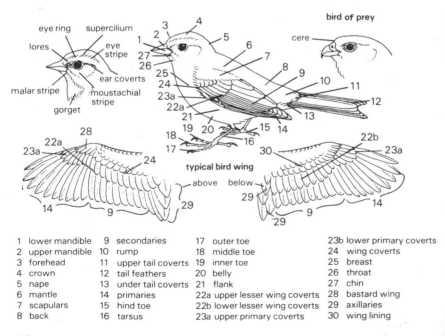

1	lower mandible	9	secondaries	17	outer toe	23b	lower primary coverts
2	upper mandible	10	rump	18	middle toe	24	wing coverts
3	forehead	11	upper tail coverts	19	inner toe	25	breast
4	crown	12	tail feathers	20	belly	26	throat
5	nape	13	under tail coverts	21	flank	27	chin
6	mantle	14	primaries	22a	upper lesser wing coverts	28	bastard wing
7	scapulars	15	hind toe	22b	lower lesser wing coverts	29	axillaries
8	back	16	tarsus	23a	upper primary coverts	30	wing lining

forget to use your ears. Bird songs are almost impossible to describe ⌐ paper but there are plenty of records and tapes available and these are a superb way of getting to know the various songs and calls.

Counting small numbers of animals does not present any great problems, but estimating the size of large congregations requires a special technique. The principle is to count ten individuals and notice what sort of 'area' they occupy. The next step is to count how many times that area will fit into the whole congregation and multiply up. Larger groups can be estimated by counting in 100s rather than in 10s.

Birds spend very little time 'doing nothing'. A great deal of activity can be seen by simply standing or sitting still and watching through binoculars. The keyword, of course, is patience, and remember that the best time for seeing wildlife is usually very early in the morning. Take care not to make any sudden movements or noises whilst watching.

There is a limit to how close you can get to any bird before it flies off, and there are also limits to how much you can see from a distance. Therefore if you want to watch at close quarters you will need some kind of hide. In certain circumstances you may be able to conceal yourself by using naturally available cover, but normally you will have to provide some cover yourself. You can, of course, use a photographic hide (as described in the chapter on nature photography), or you can improvise on the spot, making use of whatever natural materials are to hand.

You can encourage birds to your hide by putting down bait or by siting the hide by a known bird haunt. Good baits include eggs – which are greatly prized by magpies; rabbit carcases, which will bring magpies, crows and, if you are in the right sort of place, perhaps ravens and buzzards; and pieces of marrowbone or suet, which will attract woodpeckers. Regularly throwing a little wheat or split maize into a pond is a sure way of attracting waterfowl.

An alternative to baiting is to locate your hide at a known bird haunt. Natural feeding and watering places such as ponds and muddy river banks are often worth trying, but one of the most exciting places to use a hide is an estuary. During the winter and at migration periods many thousands of birds may be seen on our estuarine mudflats, but because estuaries can be quite large, the birds are thinly spread and difficult to see. Also there is no cover available to aid you in stalking them. In any case, it may be dangerous to even try to do so on account of quicksands and in-coming tides. Using a telescope is one way of studying estuarine birds but a far more exciting way is to visit a high-tide roost. At high tides the mudflats become flooded and the birds are forced to move, and at most estuaries there are traditional roosting places where vast numbers of waders and wildfowl congregate until the tide turns. The higher the tide is, the greater area of mudflats it will cover and the more birds will be displaced and forced to concentrate in a smaller area, so it follows that you should time your visit to coincide with the highest tide. Local tide tables will tell you both the height and time of

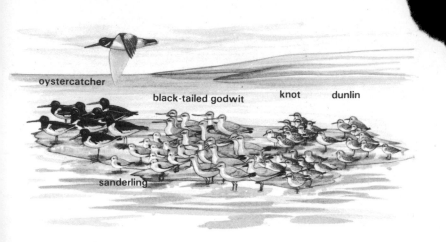

High-tide roosts are important places to look for birds on estuaries.

the tide and you should get into position and settled down at least a couple of hours before the tide is due to peak. Check tide times and heights so that you avoid being cut off.

Watching birds at the nest can be particularly rewarding, but with *any* nest watching great care is needed to avoid upsetting your subjects, and remember that it is actually illegal to disturb several uncommon species whilst they are breeding (see Appendices).

Nest locations may be found either by simple searching, or by more indirect means such as studying bird behaviour. For instance if you see a bird carrying nesting material or food, and you can see approximately where it is going, this will help to guide you towards the nest.

Some species perform a distraction display by feigning an injury in order to lure potential predators away from the nest site, and seeing this will indicate that a nest is nearby. Nests in hedges are often easiest to find early in the season before the leaves are out. If you get down low and view the hedge against the light, the bulk of a nest can easily be spotted in silhouette.

Species such as eagles, peregrine falcons and ravens which build their nests on upland crags can often be spotted from a distance by the white droppings which accumulate beneath them. Their nests are most often found occupying easterly or south-easterly aspects where they will catch the rays of the early morning sun. Such species as these are perhaps best watched through a telescope, however, since they are both rare and shy.

One precaution you should take when using a hide in an open place where the birds can clearly see you – on an estuary for instance – is to either settle down inside it before dawn, when your quarry is still roosting, or to take along an accomplice to act as decoy. If the birds see you both go into the hide, and then your friend leaving, they will be convinced that it is safe to return. (It is sometimes said that birds can count, but only up to one!)

Mammals

Looking at mammals is rather more difficult than birdwatching. With the exception of bats, mammals cannot fly away to avoid their predators, and so they have developed other means of doing so. Hedgehogs solve the problem by rolling themselves into a prickly ball and squirrels rely on their amazing agility in the trees, but most mammals have come to depend on remaining hidden and undetected, which explains why they are generally difficult to find.

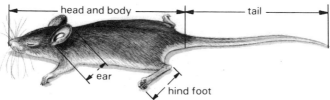

The measurements used in fieldguides to describe lengths of parts of the bodies of mammals.

You are unlikely to see very many — if any — wild mammals by just walking through the countryside, but you can often detect their presence by looking for tracks and paths, feeding signs, droppings and so on. Learning to 'read' these signs is the first step in mammal watching.

Tracks

Mammal tracks can be hard to find unless they have been made in mud, wet sand or snow. However, once spotted, they can tell you much about the animal that left them.

Fox prints are commonly seen, but care must be taken not to confuse them with those of dogs. Both have four toes, but the prints of dogs are wide and have much larger pads than those of foxes. Mustelids — the group which includes badgers and otters — have five toes. So do shrews although these are, of course, much smaller. Most rodents, including squirrels, mice, voles and rats, have four toes on the forefeet and five on the hind, whilst the tracks of rabbits and hares are very distinctive on account of the relative positions of the four imprints: those of the two forefeet being arranged one in front of the other and behind those made by the hind feet, which are side by side.

The prints left by animals with cloven hoofs are not usually mistaken for those left by other animals, but practice is needed to distinguish between those of deer and sheep.

Droppings

Individual sheep droppings are more or less spherical, although they often occur in adherent, cylindrical shaped masses: the individual faeces being squashed into angular or pyramidal shapes. Deer droppings, or fewmets,

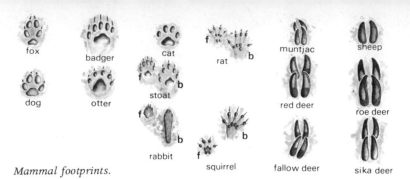

Mammal footprints.

are short and cylindrical, distinctly pointed at one end and either concave or rounded at the other. Stags generally produce the former type whilst the latter are more typical of hinds. Red deer droppings have a diameter of 13–18mm, whereas those of fallow deer are much smaller – about 9–12mm – and those of roe are smaller still – between 7 and 10mm.

Fox droppings are easy to spot because they are intentionally deposited in conspicuous places – on tussocks of grass, tree stumps, etc – to help advertize their owner's territory. They are more or less sausage-shaped, $3\frac{1}{2}$ in (9 cm) in length and often have a spirally twisted point at one end. Their colour varies from black, if the animal has been mainly eating berries, to chalky grey, which is caused by an abundance of bones in the diet.

The trails of mammals such as foxes, badgers and hares often pass through hedges or under fences, and following such a trail will show you how to recognize such regularly used pathways. Where the trail passes under a barbed wire fence or thorny vegetation, the animal may leave small tufts of hair behind and this can be another clue to the identity of the culprit.

Other signs

Other signs to look for are the remains of partially eaten food. In conifer woods for example, you will often find the remains of partly eaten cones, especially spruce, pine or larch, and if they occur in some quantity it is a sure sign that there are squirrels about. Single cones hidden beneath vegetation or elsewhere have probably been eaten by mice or voles. You may also find the remains of hazel nuts. If these have been split neatly into two halves, you can be fairly sure that this was also the work of a squirrel, but many other creatures, both mammals and birds, also eat hazelnuts and each has its own distinctive way of opening them. If there is an untidy hole in the side, a magpie is likely to be the culprit whereas a neat hole is more probably the work of a mouse or vole – if you look closely you can often see tiny toothmarks around the periphery of the hole. Great spotted woodpeckers tackle hazelnuts by wedging them into cracks in trees and chipping a hole in the side, and quite a large pile of empty shells can accumulate beneath – a so-called woodpecker workshop. Nuthatches sometimes do the same except that they rarely return to the same place twice, and so a solitary nut wedged into a crevice is more likely to be the work of a nuthatch.

Following the trails of burrow-dwelling mammals such as badgers, rabbits and foxes should eventually lead you to their homes. You may also stumble across the burrows by accident, of course, so it is useful to learn how to distinguish between the various kinds. Rabbit holes are much the smallest of the three mammals mentioned above – 6 in (15 cm) in diameter – and may either occur singly or in quite large numbers. A badger sett is easily recognizable, not only by the sheer size of the entrance holes – about 14 in (35 cm) in diameter – but also by the large amounts of soil which are dug out of them. A fox den or earth usually has only one entrance – about 8 in (20 cm) in diameter. A den can usually be recognized by its distinctive 'foxy' smell and by the remains of prey items (bones, etc.) by the entrance.

Mammal watching

Once you have established what mammals are present in an area and have found some of their haunts, you can set about observing them. Try and choose a site where you know there is plenty of activity – for example by a well-worn path, a known feeding site or a badger sett. Squirrels can be watched successfully at any time of the day, but most mammals are generally active in the early morning or in the evenings and you should bear this in mind when planning your expeditions. Most important of all, however, is to ensure that you remain unseen, unheard and unsmelled. The safest way to avoid the problem is to get off the ground so that even if your scent is blown towards your quarry, it will pass harmlessly over its head. Climbing a tree is the simplest answer, and in any case, this will also help you to remain unseen – ground-living creatures rarely look up.

You can often encourage your animals to linger by putting down bait. Foxes will be attracted to almost any kind of meat including fish and eggs; a rabbit carcase is a good type of bait. Badgers are omnivorous and will come to cereals, peanuts, vegetables, honey and bread as well as to the fox baits mentioned earlier. Not surprisingly, rabbits are attracted to proper rabbit pellets and deer can often be attracted by salt licks.

Stoats and weasels will also come to bait although they leave few field signs, and finding them in the first place is largely a matter of luck.

Droppings and other signs of the presence of mammals.

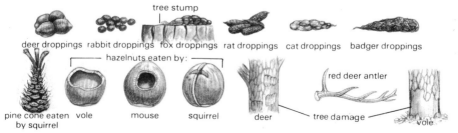

deer droppings rabbit droppings fox droppings rat droppings cat droppings badger droppings

hazelnuts eaten by:

pine cone eaten by squirrel vole mouse squirrel deer red deer antler tree damage vole

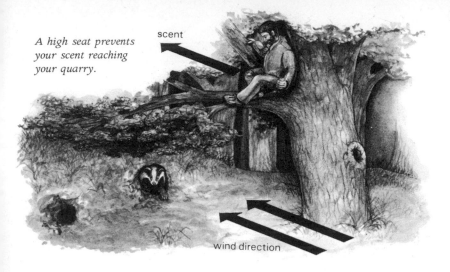

A high seat prevents your scent reaching your quarry.

scent

wind direction

One of the most interesting of our upland mammals is the red deer, Britain's largest wild land animal. Red deer occur in the New Forest, on Exmoor, in the Lake District and in southern Scotland but are seen at their best in the Scottish Highlands and Islands.

You may also occasionally find cast antlers, especially in spring; whilst during August and September, when the stags are cleaning their new antlers, you may find saplings which have been frayed, usually about 4ft (1.2 m) above the ground. During the rut in October, the stags can be heard bellowing over a considerable distance and you may also find wallows – peat haggs with much evidence of trampling and often a great deal of hair.

The animals themselves are not difficult to see, especially during the winter and early spring when they come down to lower ground, but getting close to them usually requires a lengthy stalk. Deer stalking is a profession in itself, and requires a great deal of practice. The essentials, as with all mammal watching, are to remain unseen, unheard and unsmelled. It is useless to even attempt to stalk deer if they are upwind of you, and a professional stalker will think little of making a five, or even ten mile detour in order to reach the right starting point. The next priority is to keep completely out of sight of the deer by keeping hidden behind the contours of other cover. The best time to stalk deer is during the rutting season in October, but remember that in some areas they are hunted between the 1st of July to the 15th of February so both for your own safety and to avoid disturbing a professional stalker, you should get permission before venturing on to deer forests during this period.

The same principle, of course, applies to watching wildlife wherever you go. Always get permission before visiting private land and, having done so, take the utmost care not to damage crops, stock, trees or any other property. Always follow the Country Code, and never put your own wildlife watching interests before the plants or animals.

Habitats

The different habitats which exist in our country today can be divided into six main categories, namely woodlands, lowlands (including farmland and heathland), wetlands, coastal habitats, mountains and moorland, and urban environments. Furthermore, each of these principal types can be sub-divided. For example woodlands can be split into oakwoods, beechwoods, pinewoods and so on. Each kind has its own characteristic species of plants and animals. Let us now take a look at each habitat in turn and see something of its structure and its inhabitants.

Woodlands

Although there are about 35 different kinds of trees native to the British Isles, only seven of these ever formed natural woodlands of any size. Oak is by far the commonest woodland type, and without man's intervention oakwoods would have covered almost all of our country except for the northern and southern extremities and smaller pockets elsewhere when particular ecological conditions favoured one of the other woodland types such as beech, pine, birch, alder or ash.

Oakwoods

There are two quite distinct types of oakwoods. The English or pedunculate oak is the principal tree of the British Lowlands and, although it grows best on deep heavy loams, it is really quite at home on a wide variety of soil types. In the hilly northern and western areas where the higher rainfall has leached many of the nutrients from the soil, however, the oakwoods are more likely to be dominated by the sessile or durmast oak. The two species

Britain's two most common types of oak: English or pedunculate (left); and sessile or durmast (right).

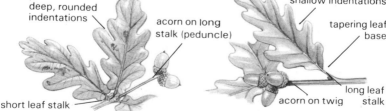

deep, rounded indentations

acorn on long stalk (peduncle)

shallow indentations

tapering leaf base

short leaf stalk

acorn on twig

long leaf stalk

23

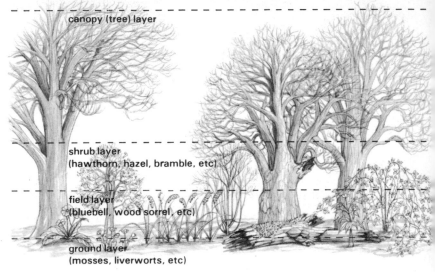

canopy (tree) layer

shrub layer
(hawthorn, hazel, bramble, etc)

field layer
(bluebell, wood sorrel, etc)

ground layer
(mosses, liverworts, etc)

The four layers of a deciduous woodland.

hybridize freely, however, and the two types often merge into one another.

Of course there are likely to be many other tree species present besides just oaks, and a great many shrubs and herbs, too. In a typical wood we can recognize four distinct 'layers' of vegetation. The first is the **tree canopy** itself; lower down is a layer of **woody shrubs**; then there is the **field layer**, and finally, the **ground layer**, which consists of mosses, lichens and other tiny plants. In practice the four layers are rarely found growing together since they are, to a large extent, mutually exclusive. For example the shrub layer tends to shade out any herbs whilst a dense field layer would prevent any shrubs from becoming established. At least part of the shrub layer will be made up of tree saplings, but other common oakwood shrubs include hazel, holly, hawthorn and blackthorn.

The herb layer of an English oakwood can vary enormously from one wood to the next, depending on the soil type, topographical features, local climatic influences, etc. Some of the better-known and more typical species are lesser celandine, wood sorrel, wood anemone and violets. Less colourful, but often very common, is dog's mercury which has inconspicuous green flowers and separate male and female plants. All these species flower very early in the year, from about March to May, before the trees come into leaf and cast too deep a shade. Flowering slightly later are bluebell, vast sheets of which decorate so many of our woods, red campion, herb Robert and, particularly on wet ground, the attractive and strongly scented ramsons or wild garlic.

All the above species are characteristic of pedunculate oakwoods. In addition, in the sessile oakwoods of the north and west, you are more likely to find foxglove, bramble, bracken and other ferns.

24

This vegetation provides an ideal home for a wide range of animal life. Over 400 different kinds of insects have been found on a single oak tree, and so the total number of species in an oakwood must run into thousands. The mammals and birds are well represented, too. Perhaps the most conspicuous woodland mammals are squirrels, especially the grey squirrel which was introduced from North America and has now replaced the native red variety in much of the country. Hedgehogs are another well-known woodland occupant although they are by no means restricted to woods. Much more elusive species include smaller mammals such as the yellow-necked mouse, dormouse, bank vole, common shrew, pygmy shrew, stoat and weasel. Foxes and badgers often make their homes in oakwoods, too, especially around the edges. Several species of deer spend their days lying up in woods, particularly the native roe deer and the introduced muntjac and Chinese water deer, although the latter two are restricted to parts of central and southern England.

Apart from squirrels, most woodland mammals are principally ground dwelling, whereas birds are also able to colonize the shrub layer and tree canopy as well. (A few species nest on the ground, of course, including woodcock, wood warblers and willow warblers.)

The shrub layer attracts a great many birds such as chiffchaffs, garden warblers, blackcaps, dunnocks, greenfinches, chaffinches, bullfinches, goldfinches, blackbirds, song thrushes and long-tailed tits, whilst tree canopy specialists include tawny owls, sparrowhawks, carrion crows and rooks.

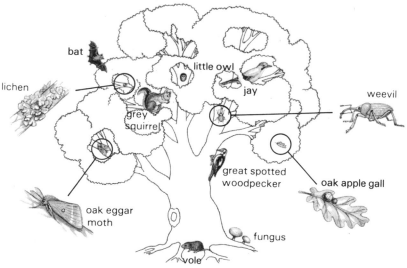

Even a single oak tree can support literally hundreds of species of plants and animals.

Many other species nest in holes or other natural cavities and these include woodpeckers, redstarts, nuthatches, blue tits, great tits, marsh tits, willow tits and pied flycatchers, the latter species being more characteristic of sessile oakwoods in the north and west.

Beechwoods

In the slightly drier and warmer climate of southern England, and especially on well-drained and well-aerated soils such as those found on chalky slopes and some sandy and gravelly soils, our oakwoods have been largely replaced by beech. One of the most important features of a beechwood is that the canopy is so dense that scarcely any light can pass through, and this means, of course, that few other plants can grow. Yew and holly are the commonest beechwood shrubs, and it is interesting to note that they are both evergreens and so able to use what little light is available during the winter months when the trees have lost their leaves. Many beechwood herbs are also evergreen for the same reason, and these include stinking hellebore and spurge laurel. Yet others are saprophytic, which means that they do not depend on light at all but derive their nourishment from the organic remains of dead plants. Two such species are yellow birdsnest and birdsnest orchid – which, incidentally, are quite unrelated despite their similar names.

So beechwoods do not support nearly the floral diversity of an oakwood and, in consequence, the fauna is relatively impoverished, too. Few plants means that there is both little food available and very few nesting sites or hiding places. It also means that the wind can pass more freely through a beechwood, and this has the effect of drying out the fallen leaves and arresting their decay so that even the soil flora and fauna are impoverished. Despite this, however, a mature beechwood is one of our most attractive habitats, and the rarity and interest of many of its specialized inhabitants make up for their lack in number.

Pinewoods

At the opposite end of the country other kinds of woodlands may be found. Once, sessile oaks probably extended well into the glens of southern Scotland, but on the hillsides and further north the conditions are more suited to the growth of Scots pine. In such places the soil is both very shallow and quite acid, and because of this the pines need a very extensive root system in order to support themselves and provide all the necessary nutrients. This means that the trees are often very widely spaced and plenty of light penetrates. In consequence, the flora of such woods is often very luxuriant although the number of species involved is limited to those which can tolerate the impoverished soil. Birch and juniper are the most frequent other tree species, whilst the lower layers are usually dominated by ericaceous plants including ling, bell heather and bilberry. Other noteworthy species are crowberry, the delightful little twinflower and the

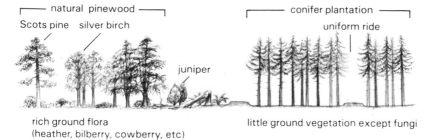

natural pinewood
Scots pine   silver birch
juniper
rich ground flora
(heather, bilberry, cowberry, etc)

conifer plantation
uniform ride
little ground vegetation except fungi

Natural pinewoods are quite rich in other flora, but conifer plantations have little but fungi.

saprophytic coralroot orchid, the latter two species, alas, being quite uncommon. Pinewoods are also noted for their variety of fungi.

Typical animals of pine forests include the enormous capercaillies, crossbills, crested tits, redpolls and siskins. Perhaps the most distinctive mammal is the pine marten, and although it is still a rare animal it definitely appears to be on the increase. Martens will feed on almost anything they can catch, including mice, voles, rabbits and hares, although their preferred food is probably the red squirrel. Although these have disappeared from most of our country, they seem to be holding their own in our remaining pinewoods.

Birchwoods

The native pine forests once covered very extensive areas of Scotland, although on high ground and in the extreme north their place was taken by birch scrub. The main species was probably downy birch with lesser amounts of silver birch. Like the pines the trees would have been widely spaced, but the number of plant species growing among them would have been limited because of the poor soils and exposed position. Rowan and juniper are frequent associates, with bilberry, tormentil, heath bedstraw, wood sorrel, greater wood-rush, common dog violet and several acid-loving grasses such as wavy hair-grass, common bent and sweet vernal grass found in the herb layer. Common birchwood ferns include hard fern and lemon-scented fern, and bryophytes and fungi are also common.

Birch trees are often the nesting sites of sparrowhawks, and when they decay they often provide nest-holes for woodpeckers, redstarts and tits.

Ashwoods

The two types of natural woodland which we have not yet mentioned are ash and alder, both of which have a rather more limited distribution.

Ash is quite markedly a calcicole (lime-loving plant) and so, without man's intervention, would have occurred mainly on limestone and chalk.

27

Because its leaves are pinnately divided, the ashwood canopy allows a great deal of light to filter through, and this encourages a most luxuriant flora to develop. Hawthorn, blackthorn and whitebeams are frequent ashwood shrubs, while the herbaceous flora may be immensely varied, and includes many kinds of interesting calcicoles. Examples include lily of the valley, herb Paris, spurge laurel, pale St John's wort, green hellebore, fingered sedge and dark red helleborine, but there is often an abundance of calcicole mosses, too.

Alderwoods

Alder is a tree which likes to have its roots in water or waterlogged ground, and so it forms woods on marshy ground, in fens and near to lakes and rivers, although it shows a preference for lime-rich water. Alderwoods are usually referred to as carrs and, predictably, the flora of carrs is dominated by plants which prefer wet ground. Sallows and willows are often present along with common blackthorn, red currant, marsh marigold and a variety of sedges.

Of course the majority of our native woodlands have now disappeared, having been cleared to make way for pasture and arable land, and most of the woods which exist today have either been greatly modified or artificially planted in their entirety. The wildlife of such woods is not always as rich and interesting as that of natural woodlands. Many of today's woods include a variety of foreign trees which do not necessarily provide the right sort of food for native British animals.

Fortunately, many of the remnants of natural woodland which have survived are protected as nature reserves, and several of these are listed in the section on places to visit.

Woodlands are worth visiting at any time of year. Spring is a particularly attractive time with the ground flora in flower before the canopy shades them out. Mammals and reptiles are stirring after hibernation and birds are actively rearing young. Autumn is the best time to look for fungi. Even in winter many species of insects, birds and mammals can be found in woodlands.

Lowlands

Farmland

In our country, almost all farmland is man made, having been created by the removal of the natural forests. The term 'farmland' covers a very wide range of different habitats, however, some of which are far more interesting to naturalists than others. For example arable farmland, that is land which is regularly ploughed up and re-sown with cereals or other crops, has very limited value from the wildlife point of view, whereas other areas, such as long-established hay meadows, pastureland or chalk downland, can hold a wealth of interest. These so-called 'permanent grasslands' include an extremely wide range of floral communities.

Neutral grassland

Neutral grassland is very widespread, especially in lowland Britain, but in recent years farming techniques have changed dramatically and the acreage of old established grassland is rapidly declining. Many meadows were once cut for hay, the first crop being taken in about July, by which time many of the wild flowers of the meadow had shed their seed ready for the next year. Haymaking is rapidly becoming an activity of the past, however, and is being replaced by silage manufacture. In this method the grass is cut much earlier in the year, much to the detriment of the wild flowers. Many other grasslands are being ploughed up, perhaps for the first time in centuries, and re-sown with modern improved strains of grass, particularly nourishing rye grass, and the large scale application of fertilizers and other chemicals is also having a detrimental effect.

Conservationists are doing their best to acquire some of the best examples of rich, ancient grasslands and to manage them on traditional lines so as to maintain their rich floral diversity. Such grassland areas obviously contain a wide variety of grasses such as timothy, cocksfoot, meadow foxtail and many others, whilst other plants include clovers, vetches, trefoils, buttercups, thistles, and docks. Many other species are scarcer and more localized, for example meadow saffron, great burnet, twayblades, green-winged orchid and snakeshead fritillary. The wildlife of grasslands is not restricted to plants, however, and many animals have also made farmland their home. Rabbits and hares are perhaps the first grassland animals to spring to mind, and both are favourite prey of foxes. Long-tailed fieldmice, harvest mice and short-tailed voles are hunted by stoats, weasels, kestrels and both little and barn owls. The mole is another grassland dweller, and although it is rarely seen, its tiny hillocks are a well-known feature all over the countryside. Familiar farmland birds include lapwings, partridges, skylarks, yellowhammers, corn buntings, rooks, crows, magpies, jackdaws and, in winter, fieldfares and redwings.

Calcareous grassland

The next type of permanent grassland is the very interesting sward which develops on basic soils; in other words in chalk and limestone areas. The North and South Downs, the Chilterns and parts of the Pennines are the best-known areas, but there are many other smaller pockets scattered throughout the country wherever outcrops of limestone or chalk occur. In many of these areas the soil is simply too shallow or the terrain too steep to allow ploughing, and the principal use of such grasslands is for sheep grazing. This is, in fact, very necessary since without it many shrubs and bushes can quickly become established and the area will revert to scrubland. Typical plants of chalk and limestone grasslands are wild thyme, bloody cranesbill, carline thistle, and fragrant and bee orchids. Rare and localized species include chalk milkwort, the delightful pasque flower and several orchids such as frog, burnt, spider, man, musk and butterfly.

Most of the animals which inhabit neutral grasslands are also found on these basic swards, especially rabbits, and partridges and quail seem to be particularly fond of chalk areas. The attractive chalk-hill blue butterfly is also a noted inhabitant of downland, where its caterpillars feed principally on horse-shoe vetch.

Heathland

A heathland will tend to develop on soils which are sandy and consequently well drained and poor in nutrients. Heaths are very widespread in Britain, and can be divided into lowland and upland types, the latter being included in the next section. Lowland heaths are mainly found in the south of England and parts of East Anglia and, although they were once regarded as agriculturally worthless, modern fertilizers and farming techniques are allowing many of them to be turned into much more productive, but far less interesting, grasslands. Heaths, in fact, are probably the fastest disappearing wildlife habitat in Britain today, which is a pity since they are fascinating places.

The layers of a heathland soil.

thin top soil ——————
dry peat ——————
iron salt pan ——————
subsoil ——————

The dominant plant of heathland is ling, which is specially adapted to living in conditions of dry soils and desiccating winds, although it cannot stand a very prolonged drought. Other ericaceous shrubs are usually present, too, including bell heather and, in slightly wetter areas, cross-leaved heath. Two other types of heather are Dorset heath and Cornish heath, both of which are very restricted in distribution, although not quite as restricted as their names might imply. Gorse is often a conspicuous member of the heathland flora, too – particularly common gorse. Our two rarer species, dwarf gorse and western gorse, are sometimes present as well. Broom is another heathland species and birches often manage to establish themselves where the heather carpet has been broken for any reason.

The tiny blue flowers of the heath milkwort are another feature of heathlands, and in places you may be lucky enough to find marsh gentian or the even rarer heath lobelia.

Reptiles feature prominently in the fauna of our heaths. Common lizards, sand lizards, adders and slow worms can all be found here, and there are several bird specialists, too, including stonechats, whinchats, nightjars and stone curlews. The red-backed shrike is another heathland species, albeit one which has declined rapidly during the last thirty years or so. Probably less than 150 pairs now regularly breed in our country. Rarer still is the Dartford warbler which has a very precarious foothold in Britain. It is our only non-migratory warbler, but unfortunately it seems ill adapted to cope with the very severe winters which occur from time to time and which invariably reduce its numbers. Only a handful of pairs still survive here, mainly on heaths in Dorset.

Finally, no introduction to heaths would be complete without a mention of the hobby; one of the rarest and most exciting of our birds of prey. There are perhaps just over 100 pairs of these elusive falcons left now, but it is well worth making a special effort to seek out and watch these spectacular birds. Indeed, the same could be said of much of our heathland wildlife.

Spring and early summer are the best times to visit downland, for many of the flowers are in bloom at this time. Late summer and autumn are also worthwhile times to visit heathland, since many of the animals will still be active, and now the heather comes into flower.

Mountains and moorland

Much of northern and western Britain is hilly or mountainous country and, in consequence, experiences a considerably higher rainfall than much of the lowlands. One result of this increased precipitation is that the soils in this more elevated half of Britain have lost a great deal of their minerals due to leaching, and the grasslands and heaths which have developed are rather different from their lowland counterparts.

Several different grades of montane grasslands can be distinguished depending on the degree of soil drainage. The better drained soils are often dominated by three species of grass, namely sheep's fescue, common bent and sweet vernal grass, all of which are readily eaten by sheep. If the area is overstocked with sheep, however, the continuous grazing pressure may so weaken these grasses that they are replaced by the less palatable mat grass and, indeed, vast areas of upland pastures are now dominated by mat grass.

Common herbs of these upland pastures include tormentil, heath bedstraw, heath milkwort, sheep's sorrel, heath speedwell, mountain pansy and several species of mosses.

In regions which are rather less well drained other grasses and sedges tend to become dominant. Purple moor-grass, tufted hair-grass and, especially in Scotland, deer grass − actually a sedge − are among these, whilst soft rush is often also present.

On even wetter soils, cottongrasses will flourish. Like the deer grass these are actually sedges, and there are two common species, the hare's-tail cottongrass, which has a single seed head resembling cotton wool, and the common cottongrass which has several seed heads.

Where the ground becomes totally waterlogged a bog flora will develop. Bogs are very common in hilly regions, although they are by no means

The layers of
a moorland soil.

thin top soil ——————
thick peat layer ——————
subsoil ——————

restricted to them, and they are dealt with more fully in the section on wetlands.

Britain's largest wild land animal, the red deer, is found on many of these upland pastures, especially on Exmoor, parts of the Lake District and the Scottish Highlands, where herds many hundreds strong may sometimes be seen. These impressive animals were thought originally to be woodland dwellers, but since the destruction of most of our woodlands, they have adapted to life on the hills. Another upland mammal is the mountain hare, a species which is more or less confined to Scotland, although there have been attempts to introduce them into parts of England and Wales, and some of these have been quite successful. Scottish wildcats also inhabit the mountains of the far north, whilst foxes are common in upland regions throughout the country.

Upland birds include curlews, golden plovers, meadow pipits, twites, wheatears, ring ouzels, hen harriers and short eared owls; for Scotland we can add hooded crows and the rare and elusive greenshanks.

Heather moors

Heather moors have a very similar vegetation to the heaths of the lowlands. Again, ling is the dominant species, and indeed, on many moors it is just about the only plant present. This is because the main use of heather moors is for grouse shooting, and the birds in question feed exclusively on the shoots of young heather. So in order to maintain an adequate supply of suitable food, the old heather is periodically burned so as to encourage the growth of young, vigorous plants. Apart from the grouse themselves, relatively few animals are likely to be encountered on such moors except perhaps the merlin, which likes to nest among the heather, and the occasional hen harrier.

Most of these heather moors are to be found in eastern Scotland, the Pennines and North Wales.

High tops

The altitudinal limit for both heather moor and upland pastures is slightly less than 3000 ft (915 m), depending on local conditions. Above this height there may be small amounts of bilberry or crowberry, but much of the ground will be composed of bare rocks and screes with rather limited patches of vegetation in sheltered hollows. That is not to say that mountains cease to be interesting above this height. Quite the contrary, in fact, for these barren mountain tops hold some of the most attractive and exciting plants and animals of all.

During the last Ice Age, which ended about 10,000 years ago, the climate of our country would have been much the same as it is today in parts of Scandinavia and the Alps, and the vegetation would have been very sparse and limited to those plants which are adapted to survive under such extreme conditions. As the Ice Age ended, however, the climate improved

Loch Scresort, on Rhum National Nature Reserve (see page 69).

(Above) Pine trees and heather at Black Wood, Rannoch.

(Below) Grey seals on the Farne Islands (see page 115).

and this tundra vegetation was gradually replaced by the developing forests. The only place where it managed to survive was on the very tops of our mountains.

These so-called arctic/alpine species are mainly found on north-facing crags where they are both shaded from direct sunshine and sheltered from the prevailing south-westerly winds, both of which have a desiccating effect on the plants. They also prefer sites which are inaccessible to browsing sheep, deer and feral goats.

Some arctic/alpines are quite widespread among our mountains whilst others are extremely rare or localized. Among the commoner species are roseroot, moss campion, mountain sorrel, mountain avens and a number of saxifrages such as purple mountain saxifrage, starry saxifrage and mossy saxifrage. The ferns are well represented, too, and include green spleenwort, parsley fern, holly fern, and lemon-scented fern. Rarer species include Snowdon lily (which, as its name suggests, has a very limited range in North Wales), Highland saxifrage, Highland fleabane and Scottish rush, all of which are restricted to Scotland. Purple coltsfoot, Scottish wormwood and diapensia are rarer still and are only known from one site each.

Animals of the high tops include ptarmigan, dotterels, ravens, peregrine falcons, and, of course, the majestic golden eagle.

It must be stressed that high areas, even in Britain, are potentially dangerous places, particularly in winter. The weather can change dramatically within minutes and swirling fog and cold winds can turn a pleasant nature trip into a potential disaster.

Always tell someone where you are going and when you expect to return. Carry a compass, map, whistle, adequate clothing, emergency food (such as chocolate) and, if possible, a bright coloured anorak. If a storm or foul weather should overtake you, try to shelter and keep warm until it subsides. Blow the whistle at intervals to let possible rescuers know where you are.

Coastlands

The British Isles is an archipelago which consists of almost 1000 islands. It has an aggregate coastline in excess of 5000 miles (8040 km), so it is hardly surprising that a great deal of interesting wildlife may be found living around our shores. Perhaps when most people think of the coast their minds conjure up visions of wide sandy beaches, but there are many other coastal habitats such as estuaries, sand dunes, shingle beaches, cliffs and rocky shores. Each habitat has its own distinctive wildlife.

Sandy beaches

Those wide expanses of sand which are so attractive to holidaymakers are relatively disappointing as regards wildlife, although low down on the beach the areas which are most frequently submerged by the tide can support an enormous number of worms, particularly lugworms, and molluscs.

Rocky beaches

Rocky beaches are far more interesting than sandy ones, and dabbling in rock pools is a must for any naturalist. Sponges, sea anemones (which are, in fact, animals and not plants), crabs, molluscs, starfishes and fishes are all frequent inhabitants of rock pools whilst barnacles, limpets and various species of seaweed often festoon the rocks between the pools. The most common seaweeds are the fucoids and the large, brown laminarians.

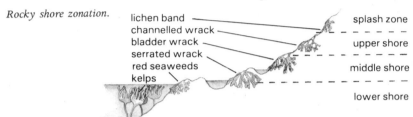

Rocky shore zonation.

lichen band — splash zone
channelled wrack —
bladder wrack — upper shore
serrated wrack —
red seaweeds — middle shore
kelps —
lower shore

Shingle beaches

A third kind of beach is that composed of shingle. Such beaches are most uninviting habitats for wildlife, because every time the tide comes in the shingle is rolled back and forth, effectively preventing anything from settling there. There are, however, a few shingle beaches which are above the level of most tides and which do manage to support a certain amount of vegetation. These vegetated shingle beaches are quite rare but very interesting, and their flora may include plants such as yellow horned-poppy, sea kale, sea pea, Nottingham catchfly and the rare southern hawksbeard.

Sand dunes

Although sandy beaches are not in themselves very exciting habitats, they often encourage the development of sand dunes and these, by contrast, can be full of interest. Dunes develop as a result of a sandy beach drying out during low tides, and some of the sand blowing shorewards in the sea breeze. Most of the sand is blown along very close to the surface so its progress is soon arrested by any small obstacles in its path, and a miniature dune will tend to develop around them. If the obstacle is a boulder or a piece of driftwood, the dune will grow until it reaches the top of the obstruction and no more. If it happens to be a plant, however, then the dune will continue to grow for as long as the plant does. Most plants, of course, are quickly overcome by a continuous accumulation of sand around their foliage, but marram grass is able to grow up through the sand until quite enormous dunes are formed. Indeed, some of the dunes at Braunton Burrows in Somerset are about 100 ft (30 m) high.

These marram-covered dunes are usually known as mobile dunes and, in addition to the marram itself, may hold several other plant species including sea holly, sea bindweed and the delightful little sea spurge.

Eventually the dunes become so completely overgrown with vegetation that the marram grass which was responsible for their formation in the first place is, quite simply, crowded out of existence and the dunes become known as fixed dunes. But the story is by no means over yet for, as time goes on, the sand undergoes subtle changes which have a profound effect on the vegetation. The first of these changes is that the lime is leached out of the sand by the rain. This is a long-term process, however, and two or three hundred years may elapse before the lime totally disappears – if, indeed, it ever does. The second change is that dead plant matter becomes incorporated into the sand, turning it into a proper soil, and eventually the dune flora changes to heathland flora with ling as the principal species. Even this maritime heath is not permanent, however, and in time this will also disappear and woodland will develop.

An interesting twist in the dune story is the formation of blowouts. If the vegetational cover of a fixed dune is broken for any reason, perhaps by excessive grazing or trampling for example, then the wind will soon get to work removing the exposed sand and creating a hollow or blow out which will continue to grow until the water table is reached. Such hollows often contain a pool or marsh at the bottom, and are then known as wet slacks. Wet slacks hold some of the most exciting wildlife of the entire dune system including early marsh orchid, southern marsh orchid, the extremely attractive marsh helleborine and round-leaved wintergreen. Wet slacks are also often the breeding places of the natterjack toad, Britain's rarest amphibian.

Eventually, however, wind-blown sand and plant litter accumulate in the blow out, and gradually the wet slack will change into a dry slack. Creeping willow is an important plant of dry slacks since, like marram grass, it has the ability to grow through accumulating sand. Its seeds need moist soil in which to germinate, however, and so it is quite unable to grow on mobile dunes.

Sand dune formation.

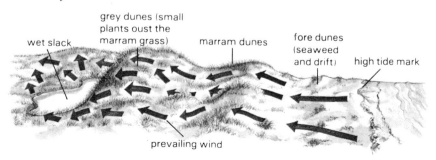

Many animal species may be found living among dunes. Some systems hold large colonies of both herring and lesser black-backed gulls, whilst others hold terns such as Sandwich, arctic, roseate and little. Ringed plovers and shelducks are also notable dune species, whilst the most frequently encountered mammals are rabbits and foxes.

Estuaries

The most interesting feature of an estuary must surely be its transient birdlife. Every year millions of waders and wildfowl migrate southwards from their breeding grounds in Siberia, Scandinavia, Iceland and Greenland to Britain. Many of them continue to continental Europe, merely resting here on route, but enormous numbers spend the entire winter here, living mainly on our estuaries. What entices them to stay are the myriads of tiny worms and molluscs which thrive in the estuarine mudflats, together with the security of safe roosting places far out on a sandbank or saltmarsh. The variety of these migratory birds is enormous and includes many species of waders (such as turnstones, plovers and godwits), ducks (such as wigeon, teal, mergansers and mallard), geese and gulls. These birds spend much of their time feeding far out on the mudflats, but when the tide starts to advance they are forced to move and seek out a safe roosting place. Some of these high-tide roosts can hold tens of thousands of birds, standing shoulder to shoulder and jostling for space as they wait for the tide to turn.

In areas where the mudflats are more stable and less frequently flooded by the tides the mud may become colonized by several plant species. Glasswort is one of the first plants to do this, and cord grass is another. These plants encourage the accumulation of mud around their stems and roots, stabilizing the flats still further so that other species are able to establish themselves. Sea purslane, sea aster, sea meadow-grass, sea-lavender and many others start to grow and before long, a saltmarsh is formed. Such marshes may extend for many square kilometres and provide a home for a range of animals. Many small mammals such as common shrews, short-tailed field voles and water voles may live here along with the predatory stoats, weasels and foxes. Nesting birds may include redshanks, oystercatchers, lapwings, snipe, common terns and mallard, whilst during the winter months they are joined by grey herons, water rails, hen harriers, kestrels, merlins and even peregrine falcons.

Cliffs

Some peregrines spend their summers on the coast, too, where they nest high on the sea cliffs. They are not alone in this of course, for many types of seabird are also cliff nesters. Indeed, we are extremely fortunate in this country to have the finest seabird colonies in Europe, if not in the entire North Atlantic. The reasons for this are, firstly, that we live among some of the finest fishing grounds anywhere in the world, and secondly, the British mainland has many smaller offshore islands, many of which, particularly those in the north and west, are small, uninhabited and cliff bound; ideal in fact for the vast populations of seabirds which nest on them each summer.

Gannets, fulmars, kittiwakes, guillemots and razorbills all nest on tiny ledges on the cliffs themselves, whilst black guillemots prefer the boulder scree below. The grassy slopes above the cliffs may be honeycombed with the burrows of puffins, shearwaters and petrels, and colonies of gulls and skuas often become established nearby. Cormorants, shags, rock pipits, rock doves and wrens add yet more variety to this most spectacular wildlife habitat.

Plants of the cliffs include thrift or sea pink, scurvy grass, sea campion, red campion and bluebell.

The advantage of seashores is that there is always something to see. The flowers and certain bird species have their seasons, but the invertebrate

Rocky cliffs and stacks are exploited by different nesting seabirds, each species choosing a particular site and elevation.

puffin

fulmar

gannet

razorbill

guillemot

cormorant

kittiwake

shag

and algal species are for the most part present all year round. It should be remembered, however, that the beach in winter can be extremely chilling, and adequate clothing must be worn. Remember also that the mood of the sea can change quickly, and special precautions should also be taken to avoid being cut off by the tide, particular in areas unfamiliar to you.

Wetlands

Strictly speaking the term 'wetland' refers to places where the ground is waterlogged; that is marshes, bogs and fens. For the sake of convenience, however, I have also included here a brief mention of rivers, lakes and ponds.

Lakes and ponds

There is no fundamental difference between a pond and a lake, although of course ponds are generally taken to be smaller than lakes and are frequently man-made, whereas lakes are larger and more likely to be natural. Many ponds were dug either as watering places for cattle or as marl pits, and they are a very common feature of much of lowland Britain, although their numbers are declining rapidly. Because they are mainly situated on fertile lowland farms, they are constantly topped up with nutrient rich ground water draining from the surrounding fields, and so are often very fertile habitats. The same is true of many lowland lakes, although many of the lakes in upland Britain are, by contrast, very low in dissolved nutrients and correspondingly less fertile. These nutrient-starved upland lakes are said to be **oligotrophic**, as opposed to more fertile lowland ones which are known as **eutrophic**, but there is, of course, a continuous gradient from one to the other.

Much of the plant life in a lake will be concentrated around the margins where the water is shallow enough to enable plants to take root in the mud. In eutrophic lakes and ponds this waterside vegetation may include reed maces, rushes, especially the soft rush, bur-reeds, the attractive yellow flag and arrowheads. Quite extensive reed beds may become established which provide an ideal nesting habitat for reed warblers, coots, great crested grebes, dabchicks, a variety of ducks and possibly mute swans.

Oligotrophic lakes and lochs are more likely to have stony or peaty bottoms and do not, as a rule, support nearly such a wide variety of plant life. Many of the species they do hold are relicts of the Ice Age, such as water lobelia, quillwort, shoreweed, awlwort and the curious pillwort. Common sandpipers are one of the few birds which nest by these upland waters, although in Scotland both red-throated and black-throated divers may be found, together with the rare and localized Slavonian grebe.

Rivers

The differences in fertility between upland and lowland lakes are also shown by rivers. Nearly all rivers can be traced back to a source in the hills where they usually appear as a spring. These springs often take the form of a 'wet flush', that is a place where water wells up from the ground and saturates the soil before running away as a tiny rivulet. Being so well watered the vegetation of wet flushes is often very lush, and they can frequently be discerned simply due to their 'greenness'. Golden saxifrage is a frequent occupant of flushes, as are several types of liverworts.

The tiny rills which are born in these flushes soon join up to form a stream, but mountain streams are generally too fast flowing to allow much wildlife to establish itself. Dippers somehow manage to find enough freshwater shrimps and mayfly nymphs to enable them to live here, and grey wagtails may sometimes be found nesting nearby, but it is not until the stream reaches lower ground and starts to slow down that it is able to support much wildlife. Once this happens, nutrient-rich silt starts to accumulate on the bottom and plants such as water crowfoot, water milfoils, pondweeds and perhaps water lilies can take root. Alders and willows may come to line the banks and their exposed roots may hide the nests of moorhens and mallard. Kingfishers, sand martins and water voles often take up residence in waterside burrows, and here herons and even otters hunt their slippery prey.

Marshes

Around the edges of rivers and lakes, particularly in flat and low-lying areas, small areas of marshland may be found. A marsh is characterized by the fact that the soil is waterlogged, although there is no standing water as such. Marshes have their own distinctive flora, and can often be spotted from a distance by the bright yellow colour of marsh marigolds, or the abundance of lady's smock. A closer inspection might also reveal water forget-me-nots, water mint and golden saxifrages.

In time, a permanent marsh will often develop into a true fen. The underlying difference between fen and bog is the mineral status of the water. Where the ground water is rich in dissolved nutrients a fen will form, whilst if it is poor in minerals and acid, a bog will be the result. Once, huge areas of Cambridgeshire and Norfolk were covered in fen, but these were extensively drained during the 17th century to create farmland, and now only tiny remnants of fen still remain. Smaller patches of fen occur throughout the country, however, especially where nutrient-rich water drains from limestone.

Fens

Fens are often dominated by the sedge *Cladium mariscus*, which makes excellent thatching material and is specially harvested for the purpose in some areas. The frequency of harvesting has a profound influence on determining which other species will grow. If the sedge is cut every four years, which is often the case, it may come to totally dominate the fen to the exclusion of anything else. If the cutting is more frequent than this, other species start to invade, such as wild angelica, yellow loosestrife, hemp agrimony and milk parsley – which is the principal food plant of the rare swallowtail butterfly. If the fen is not cut at all it will gradually change into a carr with alder and willows as the dominant species, and eventually it may dry out altogether and an oakwood will result.

Bogs

Bogs are more characteristic of upland areas where the rainfall is higher. Small 'valley bogs' occur when water collects in poorly drained hollows. Other bogs may develop in places where the rainfall is simply so high that the natural drainage of the land cannot cope, and these 'blanket bogs' as they are called can cover enormous areas. Yet a third type is the 'raised bog' which usually develops from a valley bog which spreads upwards into a dome shape by the continuous addition of peat. The most characteristic plant of bogs is *Sphagnum* moss, but there are many others including insectivorous sundews and butterworts, sweet-smelling bog myrtle and bog asphodel.

Wetlands are varied habitats, and a visit is worthwhile at any time of the year. Spring, autumn and winter are best for waders. Summer is best for dragonflies and butterflies, and of course many ducks and other birds are also active at this time.

Wetlands are by definition wet places, and the correct footwear is essential. Remember also that they may be very boggy in places, and a long stick will act as a useful probe to test suspect places first. Where possible keep to higher parts of the ground; they are likely to be the driest spots.

Urban environment

Early man was a hunter and fruit gatherer and as such would have lived just as harmoniously with the environment as any other wild animal. It was not until primitive technology invented the plough and we started to build settlements that we started to change the world to suit ourselves, a process which has been accelerating ever since. As we have already seen, farmlands and heaths are man made, but there are many other artificial habitats including towns and cities and the attendant by-products such as quarries, canals and railways. Although many people would dismiss them totally as wildlife sites, many of these man-made habitats have their own interesting and unique flora and fauna.

Let us consider swallows, swifts and house martins, for example. Originally, they were probably cliff or cave nesters, but are now almost totally restricted to nesting on or in houses. House sparrows and house mice are aptly named, and you may also have bats in your attic and foxes raiding your dustbin. Any vacant ground will be quickly colonized by rosebay willowherb, groundsels and ragworts.

Railway embankments and cuttings are often surprisingly fertile, and

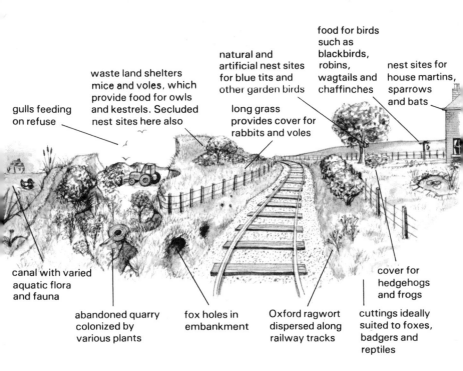

gulls feeding on refuse

waste land shelters mice and voles, which provide food for owls and kestrels. Secluded nest sites here also

natural and artificial nest sites for blue tits and other garden birds

long grass provides cover for rabbits and voles

food for birds such as blackbirds, robins, wagtails and chaffinches

nest sites for house martins, sparrows and bats

canal with varied aquatic flora and fauna

abandoned quarry colonized by various plants

fox holes in embankment

Oxford ragwort dispersed along railway tracks

cover for hedgehogs and frogs

cuttings ideally suited to foxes, badgers and reptiles

The urban environment is surprisingly rich in wildlife. A few of the places exploited are shown here.

frequently hold badger setts and fox earths as well as a variety of plant life. Any birdwatcher who has travelled by motorway cannot fail to have noticed the high populations of kestrels which feed on small mammals along the verges. Canals are also important reservoirs of aquatic wildlife – even more so in view of the rapidity with which ponds are disappearing.

Disused quarries can also be very interesting. Old sand and gravel pits may develop a flora similar to that of sand dunes, even though they may be far from the sea, whilst limestone quarries can hold a wealth of interesting calcicoles. Other waste tips may have their own characteristic flora. For example old lead workings and their waste heaps frequently support spring sandwort and alpine pennycress, both of which seem to be very tolerant of lead, whilst general rubbish tips are much visited by gulls and may hold all kinds of interesting plants.

Nature photography and sound recording

Choosing the right equipment

A quick glance through any photographic magazine will reveal a bewildering array of photographic equipment; not only cameras, but lenses, multipliers, close-up attachments, tripods, flash guns and all manner of gadgets and accessories each designed to tempt you to part with your money in the hope of taking better pictures. In actual fact the camera itself has very little to do with picture quality. It is the lens which governs the sharpness of the photograph, whilst its artistic merits depend solely on the skill of the photographer. You can save yourself a lot of money, and take just as good pictures, if you spend a little time in deciding exactly what you need before you buy.

Cameras

Clearly you need a versatile camera. Nature photography can include subjects as varied as a shy bird or mammal several hundred yards away to a close up of minute mosses or insects. To achieve this range you need versatility. The type of camera preferred by most wildlife photographers is a single lens reflex (SLR). The two most important features of such a camera are that firstly the lens can be unscrewed (or unclipped) from the camera body and replaced with others – perhaps a telephoto for shots of distant animals or close-up equipment for work with tiny plants or insects – and secondly, when you peer through your viewfinder, you actually look through the lens itself, whether it is a telephoto or close-up type. There are very many different SLRs available, however, so we must narrow the field.

One of the first decisions to be made regards format. SLR cameras fall into

Choose a versatile camera with a wide range of shutter speeds.

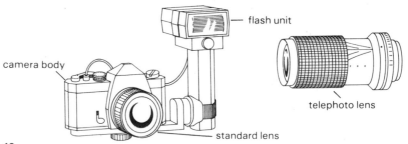

flash unit

camera body

telephoto lens

standard lens

two distinct categories: large format kinds which will produce a large photograph – often as big as 60 × 70 mm – and the smaller, so-called 35 mm models which actually produce pictures 36 × 24mm. The vast majority of SLRs belong to this second category because they are much cheaper and far more portable but, because they produce smaller pictures, and picture quality is always adversely affected during enlargement, the larger format cameras will deliver clearer and sharper photographs when enlarged.

Whichever format you choose to buy, one of the first features to look for is through-the-lens-metering (TTL). This means that the camera has a built-in light meter which actually measures the amount of light coming through the lens itself.

Another feature to look for in your camera is a wide range of shutter speeds. Some wildlife shots – a bird in flight for example – will need a very fast speed of perhaps 1/1000th second, whilst others, such as a toadstool which you might have found growing in the dense shade of a wood, might need an exposure of several seconds.

Now let us look at automatic cameras. Not long ago all cameras needed to have their shutter speed and aperture set manually. Recently, however, there has been a revolution in the development of automatic cameras. Modern electronics now enable manufacturers to produce cameras which not only measure the light level, but also automatically set their own controls, and all in the tiny fraction of a second which is needed for the shutter to operate.

Such cameras may be divided into three groups. Firstly there is the **aperture priority type**. This means that the photographer sets the desired aperture and the camera takes a light reading and automatically sets the appropriate shutter speed. This mode of automation is probably the most useful for all-round work, and is certainly the most popular, but if you are particularly keen on taking moving subjects, a **shutter priority type** may be more to your taste. In this type it is the photographer who selects the shutter speed whilst the camera chooses the correct aperture. The advantage of this sort of automation is that it makes the camera very easy to use; bear in mind, however, that neither kind will necessarily produce better pictures than a non-automatic type. They are merely quicker and more convenient to use.

The third kind of automatic camera is known as the **programmed type**, and here the camera chooses both shutter speed and aperture. However, because the photographer no longer has any control over either the depth of field or the shutter speed, such cameras remove a great deal of the creativity from photography. For this reason few professionals use them and, since they are often complex and expensive, they are not very popular with serious amateurs.

To summarize, probably the best tool for all-round wildlife photography is an SLR camera with TTL metering, a wide range of shutter speeds and, if you prefer it, either aperture or shutter priority automation.

Lenses

Whichever camera you choose it will almost certainly come with a standard lens; that is one which has roughly the same angle of view as your eyes. Such a lens will have a focal length of around 55 mm. As your photography develops, however, you will soon feel the need for other lenses; telephoto lenses for work with distant subjects, wide-angle lenses to take in a wider picture area or macro lenses for close-ups. Today, you can purchase a range of lenses manufactured by the same company that made your camera, as well as independently made lenses which will also fit.

Tripod

Another item of equipment which you are likely to want is a tripod. Many people seem to think that tripods are really a quite unnecessary refinement, and yet, if there is one item which will enable you to take sharper photographs, this is it. No matter how steady your arm, it is impossible to hold your camera perfectly still and even the slightest movement will result in some degree of blurring on the finished picture. When working with long focus lenses or close-up equipment the problem is even more acute since any blurring is literally magnified by the lens. You may sometimes be able to steady your camera by bracing it against an immovable object, if something suitable is to hand, but there is really no substitute for a good, solid tripod. Camera shake can be reduced still further by using a cable release or, if your camera has one, a self timer.

Flash

Flash equipment is also quite useful and has, perhaps, more uses than at first meets the eye. Its main function is obviously to provide light in situations which would otherwise be too dark, or to supplement existing light to enable you to use a smaller aperture and gain depth of field. It also has other uses, such as helping to isolate a subject from its background. This can be achieved by aiming the flash so that it illuminates the specimen but does not reach far enough to illuminate the background. Flash can also be used to arrest the movement of more active subjects.

The power of a flash gun – that is the intensity of the flash – is expressed by a 'guide number', but this is not an absolute unit and is measured in relation to the film speed. Most wildlife photography only requires the use of quite small guns and one with a guide number of about 100 ft at 100 ASA should be quite adequate for most purposes although if you intend to photograph badgers or other large animals, more powerful guns may be needed. (See the section on film for an explanation of film speeds and ASA units.)

With a basic, manual type of flash gun the intensity of the flash cannot be varied, and so to make sure of a correctly exposed picture it is necessary to measure the distance between the flash gun and the subject and to move the gun either closer or further away so as to ensure that just the right amount of light falls on to the subject. Needless to say, this can be very difficult when working with animals and probably the best answer is to use an automatic unit instead.

Even this system has its drawbacks, however. It works well if the flash gun is mounted on the top of the camera, but if you prefer to place it to one side (so as to provide better modelling) the amount of reflected light reaching the photocell in the flash unit and the film itself may not be the same. One answer to this is to buy a unit which has a detachable photocell. The cell itself is then mounted on the camera and connected to the gun by a lead. Another answer is to use what is known as a dedicated flash. This is an automatic unit but, instead of having its own built-in photocell, it actually uses the camera's own light meter, to which it is coupled, again by means of a special lead.

Film

The first choice you have to make is obviously between colour and black and white. Both are equally good, although some subjects lend themselves better to portrayal in one medium than the other. If you decide on colour your next choice is between colour prints and transparencies. The latter are both cheaper and produce better quality pictures but you need a projector to see them to their best advantage. If you intend to sell colour photographs, then transparencies are a must.

All film is sensitive to light, but the degree of sensitivity varies enormously, and is measured and expressed in ASA units; the more sensitive the film is, the higher its ASA rating. Less sensitive films are usually referred to as 'slow', and may be rated at perhaps 25 ASA. At the other end of the range, a 'fast' film may be rated at 400 ASA or even higher. Colour films are generally slower than monochrome films.

Many people imagine that, because a fast film is more sensitive, it will produce better photographs than a slow one, but this is wrong. Although a fast film will enable you to work in rather darker conditions, the sharpness and clarity of the finished pictures will be inferior to those taken on a slower one. If quality photographs are your aim, you should use the slowest film practicable.

Photographing plants

Flowers

One might think that plants are easy subjects to photograph. After all, they do not run, fly or crawl away the moment they are confronted with a camera. So it may come as quite a surprise to learn that movement is, in fact, one of the major problems of plant photography. On all but the very calmest days plants are in almost constant motion, gently swaying to and fro and nodding to themselves in the very lightest breeze. Tall flowering heads –

This simple arrangement helps to hold a swaying plant steady.

often the most photogenic feature – are particularly prone to wind movement and if a satisfactory picture is to be taken, some means of preventing this movement must be found.

The simplest way of overcoming the problem is to set up your equipment and wait for the right conditions. Even on quite windy days there is nearly always a lull sooner or later, although you may have to wait a long time for it and when it comes it may not necessarily coincide with ideal lighting conditions. One of the best ways to overcome the problem is to immobilize plants with long, top-heavy flower spikes by constructing wire supports. These can easily be made from a length of stout wire, one end of which is fixed to a clip – a spring type clothes peg or small bulldog clip for example – which is then padded with foam rubber (see illustration).

Some photographers have designed special wind-proof screens or even small polythene tents which are erected around their subjects, but in my experience such devices rarely work as well as one would like and are cumbersome to carry, awkward to erect and hardly worth the trouble.

Composition

Plant photographs often turn out to be rather disappointing because the picture is too cluttered with extraneous foliage or other distracting materials and these need to be removed, a process known as gardening. The object is to leave your specimen looking natural yet uncluttered and isolated from its surroundings. Achieving this needs practice. If you just tear away the surrounding vegetation your finished photograph will be most un-natural and even quite disconcerting to look at. Gardening should be a selective process, and one which involves a minimum of damage to the surrounding flora. It is often worth making a thorough search of the area before you begin rather than choosing the first specimen you come across. Some subjects require a great deal of gardening whilst others scarcely need any. Having chosen your subject begin by removing any dead remains from previous years. Even this requires considerable care if you are to avoid damaging your specimen. Next, look through the viewfinder and try to visualize what the finished photograph will look like. You can then decide what needs to be done. Whenever possible you should try to tie back any distracting plants rather than cut them down altogether, and you should always check for any uncommon species first. Pay particular attention to the background. There are few things more annoying than spending a long time carefully tidying the area around a plant, only to discover that the finished photo is spoilt by an out-of-focus tree branch cutting right across the background.

Some plants may be set in such an awkward or unattractive place that you will want to exclude as much of the surroundings as possible. One way to achieve this is to use a longer lens and work from a greater distance. The greater the focal length lens you use, the smaller will be the background area covered. Conversely a wide angle lens will take in a wide background area which can be very useful if you want to show the plant in its environment. Photographs of this kind can be very striking, especially for subjects such as alpine flowers which can be taken so as to show a spectacular mountain background or for maritime species with a backdrop of sea cliffs.

It is also possible to use a piece of coloured card as a background and, although the results are rarely as attractive as a natural one, the technique does have its uses.

There are still more ways of isolating a plant from its background. Getting down low and taking your photograph against the sky is one method, although if you do this it is a good idea to overexpose your photograph slightly. This is because your light meter will be more influenced by the bright sky than the plant itself, and if you are not careful you could end up with a perfectly exposed sky with very dark flowers silhouetted against it. It is impossible to know just how much overexposure is needed in any particular case, so the best policy is to 'bracket' the exposures; that is to take several shots, each one slightly more overexposed than the last.

Some plants have pleasing shapes, and will produce an attractive photograph when taken complete, whereas others are less photogenic. Many species, for instance, have their leaves clustered around the lower part of the plant whilst the flowers are produced on top of the stem. Such species are hardly likely to produce a well-balanced picture, so it is often a good policy to concentrate on just the flowering head. If this is taken so that it appears in the dead centre of the frame and bolt upright, however, it will result in a very 'posed' looking shot, and far better composition can be achieved by arranging the stalk so that it appears to come from near the bottom corner of the picture and ascends at a slight angle towards the flowering head in the centre.

Lighting

The best lighting conditions for plant photography occur on bright, yet overcast, days. Strong direct sunlight can make life awkward by producing very dark and unnatural looking shadows. The answer to this is to use either a small flash gun or a reflector to bounce some of the light on to the unlit side. A simple, but very effective reflector can easily be made by crumpling a piece of aluminium foil and gluing it on to a piece of card.

Some very effective photographs can be taken by using backlighting; that is with the light coming from behind the subject, shining through the petals and just glancing the foliage. When backlighting you should again overexpose your shots.

Non-flowering plants

Not all plants have flowers, but even non-flowering kinds can produce some very attractive photos. Mosses, for instance, can make attractive subjects. Of course their small size means that special close-up equipment will be needed. Many important optical accessories are described in the next section on insects, but other very useful gadgets are a **ground spike** and a **right-angle viewer**. The ground spike is simply a metal pin which is pushed into the ground and which attaches to the camera by a ball and socket joint. A right-angle viewer is a periscopic device which clips on to the viewfinder so as to allow the photographer to look downwards into his camera, rather than having to lie full-length on the ground. Liverworts and lichens can be photographed in much the same way.

Fungi are also interesting and again, since they mainly appear in autumn, they can be photographed when most of the flowering plants are dying down.

Trees

Trees offer a whole range of opportunities to the imaginative photographer. Simple portraits can be quite effective, although it is often surprisingly difficult to find good, well-shaped specimens which are accessible. Parks and arboreta are the best places to look, since these will not only have fine specimens but also often uncommon species, too.

Photographing animals

Insects

There are two distinct approaches to the subject of insect photography. One of these is to take your pictures in the field, the other is to take your specimen indoors and photograph it there.

Whichever technique you decide on, you will need to use special close-up equipment. The simplest close-up attachment is an **extension tube**. This is, quite simply, a tube which fits between the camera body and the lens so as to increase the lens-to-film distance, thus throwing a larger image on to the film. The degree of magnification depends on the length of the tube or tubes – they are usually sold in sets of three, each of a different length, so that by using different combinations of the three, it is possible to cover a wide range of magnifications. A refinement of this is a bellows attachment. This works in exactly the same way except that the length of the bellows can be varied continuously by turning a knob.

Extension tubes   *Bellows.*

An even better method of obtaining close-ups is to use a macro lens. Such lenses are specifically designed to give their best optical performance at very close ranges.

Outdoor photography

Outdoor work is fraught with difficulties. The problem of movement, scaring your 'quarry', setting up your equipment before the subject departs and background detail all have to be overcome. Several of these problems can be solved by setting up all the equipment in anticipation by, say, a *Buddleia* or similar plant attractive to insects. Quite often the only course of action, however, is to stalk the subject, approaching and setting up as quickly and quietly as possible. You will not of course be able to alter the background very significantly, nor are you likely to be able to change your own position very much if the subject isn't quite positioned as you would like. What you can do is use a longer focus lens to reduce the background area which will appear on the finished photo and use a large aperture (small f number) to throw the background out of focus. You can also use flash to illuminate your subject whilst keeping the background dark, aiming the flash from one side so as to prevent it from lighting up the background. This will also give more natural-looking lighting than holding the flash directly in front of the insect, but it requires either a second flash or a reflector to fill in the shadows on the dark side. This technique is described more fully in the section on studio work.

Indoor (studio) photography

The general idea is to build a small studio set which resembles as nearly as possible the natural habitat of the specimen. You then arrange the lights and other equipment and focus the camera on to a pre-arranged spot where, with luck, you can persuade your subject to stay until the session is over. Building sets can be great fun. The first step is to decide where you are going to place your specimen. This will often be a flower but it could equally well be a leaf, a grass stalk, a twig, a piece of bark, moss, a stone or almost any natural object.

Tall flowers or other vegetation can be supported by a piece of oasis, by means of plasticine or by simply standing them in a jar filled with sand – if you use a water-filled jar your specimen is almost guaranteed to take a nose dive into it – but you should ensure that whatever you use is kept out of the picture area. If you are planning to photograph a ground-living species you will probably need to point your camera downwards on to a piece of turf or a setting of sand or bark which will automatically provide a background, but if your subject is to be perched on a flower you will need to create an artificial backdrop some distance behind. This can either be a piece of plain coloured card, perhaps blue to represent the sky, or brown or green to suggest vegetation, or else you can build a more elaborate set-up from real vegetation.

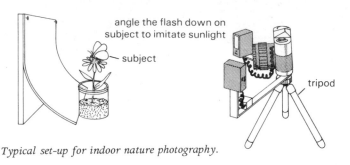

angle the flash down on
subject to imitate sunlight

subject

tripod

Typical set-up for indoor nature photography.

Having built your set, the next step is to prepare your camera equipment. You will almost certainly need to provide extra lighting, and this is best provided by means of flash. Don't position your flash gun directly in front of your subject, however, or you will get a very flat and unnatural looking picture. The best position is above and slightly to one side so that the flash gun imitates the position of the sun. This will give more natural looking lighting, but unfortunately it has the drawback of producing very dark shadows. To counter this, either use a second flash gun or a reflector to throw light on to the dark side and lighten the shadows. Be careful not to arrange your flash guns so that they throw shadows on to the background which, incidentally, can be separately lit, if desired, by another gun.

Eventually, when you have built the set and prepared all your equipment, you are ready to add the insect itself. If you are photographing insects for the first time it is wise to begin with some of the less mobile kinds. Caterpillars are ideal and have the added advantage that they are likely to be found already on their correct food plant. Ladybirds are also usually quite co-operative, especially if you can find a suitable piece of greenfly infested vegetation for them to feed on. Other good insects to begin with are lacewings, earwigs and most bugs. Butterflies and moths are perhaps more co-operative than you might imagine, but extra care is needed when handling them in order to avoid dislodging the minutes scales which cover their wings. Grasshoppers are rather temperamental; dragon-flies and damselflies, many beetles (especially ground beetles) and cockroaches are difficult, and flies and wasps border on the impossible.

Birds

There are two basic ways of going about bird photography. The first is by stalking, and the second is when the photographer keeps still and hidden and arranges things so that the subject comes to him or her.

Stalking

The stalking technique is very largely self explanatory. Having first located your quarry, you fix a long focus lens to your camera and gradually edge closer and closer, hoping to get a reasonable picture before your subject flies off. Many people use a shoulder grip type of support for their camera whilst using the stalking technique. It is a good idea to expose your first frame when you are still some distance away, gradually moving closer and taking more shots as you do so. If you wait until you are really close, there is a good chance that the bird will fly off before you can take your first picture.

Using a hide

Stalking birds can be great fun, and with practice you can achieve some very good results, but it has its limitations, and if you intend to do much bird photography you will soon find that you need to use a hide. A hide can also be used successfully when photographing certain mammals, too.

For many people the first introduction to hide photography can be at home, photographing birds at the bird table. You should set up your table close to a convenient window, that is at such a distance that you can expect to get a good sized image of, say, a blue tit in your viewfinder. Then, if you regularly put bait out the neighbourhood birds will soon find it and will become so used to people moving about in the house that they are hardly likely to notice when you start to photograph them through the window. If the window does not open make sure it is scrupulously clean, and position your lens up close so as to avoid reflections in the glass. Your pictures can be greatly improved if, instead of just photographing birds on the table itself, you add an attractive looking perch, arranging it so that the bird table is out of the picture.

It is surprising just what a wide variety of birds you can attract to your garden by putting out the right bait. Almost every bird table keeper knows that blue tits love peanuts, but it is perhaps not so widely known that nuthatches are attracted to hemp seed and Brazil nuts, robins to mealworms, woodpeckers to pieces of suet and marrowbones, and fieldfares to crab apples. Other good foods include all kinds of fruit, boiled rice, oatmeal, wheat, raw coconut, cheese, ants' eggs and a wide variety of wild seed, nuts and berries.

Many nature reserves and wildlife sanctuaries have hides which visitors are entitled to use and, although many are intended purely for observation, it is often possible to use them for photographic purposes, too. Some of the reserves which have hides are listed on page 61.

A car makes a very good mobile hide. In many rural car parks all you need to do is to throw a handful of crumbs out of the car window and you will immediately be surrounded by a multitude of small birds. Chaffinches are the first species to spring to mind, but many others may come down, too. To keep your camera steady you can either rest it on top of your half open window or, even better, use a special camera clamp, available from any photographic suppliers.

Do not simply toss your crumbs or other bait out of the window and on to the surface of the car park. If you do this you will neither have a very good viewpoint – since you will be looking down on to the birds – nor a very attractive background, and you will produce far better pictures if you do a little preliminary work first. You might, for example, be able to find a convenient log or other suitably attractive looking perch on to which you can place your bait. Even better, you can build yourself a small bird table and carry it with you. There are a great many variations on this idea. Parking close to a berry-laden bush in late summer will often prove to be rewarding. As will parking near to the edge of a pond which is a known haunt of wildfowl. Working in winter can be especially rewarding, since many smaller birds are only too eager for food at this time of the year.

But cars also have their limitations. Eventually you will want to use a hide. They can be bought, or you can make your own, which is cheaper.

Stages in building a hide.

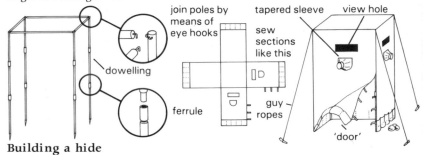

Building a hide

There are several designs, most of them being box shaped and about 5 ft (1.5 m) high and 3 ft (1 m) square. The four corner uprights can easily be made from pieces of dowelling about 6 ft (1.8 m) long. In most commercial hides these will be in two or three sections which slot together so that the hide can be packed up small. This is an advantage if you intend to carry it any appreciable distance but if you don't, there is no reason why you shouldn't make the uprights in one piece. Not only does this make construction easier but also adds strength to the erect hide. If you choose to make yours in sections, however, the easiest way is to use short pieces of aluminium or brass tubing to form a collar joint on each section. Sharpen the bottom of the uprights so they can be pushed into the ground; the top of the uprights are attached to a 3 ft (1 m) square framework. This can also be made from dowel, the joints being held together by screw hooks and eyes, or from pieces of aluminium. The main point to remember is that it should be easy to erect and dismantle in the field.

Having built your framework you next cover it with cloth. This should be of an inconspicuous colour, preferably brown or olive green, and quite opaque. Sacking and hessian are useless, since they are so loosely woven that your quarry will be able to see you moving about inside. Canvas is good, but it is both expensive and heavy. Probably the best compromise is dyed calico. If your hide has one-piece uprights you can easily tack the fabric straight on to these, remembering that the top framework should be left free so that it can be dismantled. For a hide with sectional legs you will have to make your material up as a separate bag which will slide over the frame. Incidentally, it is a lot quicker, and just as good, to glue the hide material, where necessary, with a latex adhesive, rather than sewing it.

Remember to include a door flap which can be closed either by means of tape ties, velcro or even buttons.

When the hide is finally erected the cloth should be held quite tightly to prevent it from flapping about. It is useful to sew large pockets around the bottom which can be filled with any heavy materials which are to hand since this also helps to prevent flapping. If the hide is to be left for any length of time, or if it is erected on hard or stony ground, it is also wise to secure it by means of guy ropes.

Finally, you will need both 'windows' and a hole for your camera lens. Your windows, preferably one on each side, need only be small — say 6 in (15 cm) by 2 in (5 cm) — and should be covered with a strip of dark coloured gauze. This will enable you to see out whilst making it very difficult for anything to see in. It is important that the fabric touching the lens does not transmit general wind movement to the camera, for blurred pictures may result. The solution to this problem is to make quite a large hole in the hide and fix on to it a tapered fabric sleeve. The lens fits through the small hole in the end of the sleeve which then acts as a buffer between the tightly stretched wall of the hide and the camera itself.

Having built your hide there are several different ways of using it. One way is to photograph birds coming down to bait in the same way as using a car, except that you can take your hide to more inaccessible places and leave it for longer periods to allow shy birds to get used to it before you start work. You could use a rabbit carcase to bait for ravens or buzzards, for example. Another very exciting way to use your hide is to pitch it on an estuary at a high tide roost an hour or two before the tide is due. You may well find yourself surrounded by thousands of waders and waterfowl just a few feet away — a good supply of film is recommended! Similarly you can pitch your hide overlooking a thrush's anvil or the plucking post of a bird of prey. Regularly used singing perches are also good sites and so of course, are nests, but here the law relating to certain species must be borne in mind (see Appendices).

Mammals

Mammals are one of the most difficult and time-consuming groups of all to photograph successfully. The only British mammal which can be described as easy to photograph is the hedgehog. Squirrels are also good species to begin with, especially the semi-tame variety which often frequent parks and gardens. They can be attracted by a variety of bait including nuts, especially filberts, chocolate, fresh fruit and raisins.

It is occasionally possible to take successful mammal pictures by stalking, using much the same technique as for birds. Deer, especially where they are found out in the open, are obvious candidates, but you must remember to keep downwind and out of sight. Grey seal pups, rabbits and hedgehogs are also suitable for stalking, but for most other mammals the best technique is to lie in wait near to a spot which you know is frequented by your quarry, making sure that you remain undetected.

Hares are perhaps easiest to photograph where one of their regular paths passes through a hedge – particularly during the main mating season in March and April when the jacks (males) especially, throw caution to the wind.

Forest-dwelling deer can be photographed from a high seat of the type used by stalkers, or by simply sitting in a tree close to a known haunt – a wallow perhaps. Again, the rutting season is a good time to choose since the animals are less cautious and the males will be fully antlered. Badgers and foxes can be photographed most easily by hiding close to a known sett or lair entrance, and waiting for the occupants to come out (see page 22).

Small mammals such as shrews, mice and voles are extremely difficult to photograph in the wild. If you encounter, say, a shrew on a woodland track, it may be worth returning at dusk to see whether it is using it as a regular trail. If your camera is set up ready with flash you may be lucky enough to get a shot.

Other wildlife

There are, of course, many other groups of animals and plants which have so far not been mentioned. Some of these can be photographed by using much the same techniques already discussed. Spiders, for example, can be treated in a similar way to insects, and some particularly attractive pictures can be obtained by photographing them on their webs outdoors, especially if you backlight your picture or take it early in the morning when the web is spangled with dew.

Aquatic life

It is possible to photograph life in shallow water such as ponds and rock pools by simply pointing your camera downwards into the water, although if you are not careful, surface reflections are likely to spoil your photograph. This problem is overcome by shooting vertically downwards into the water and using a polarizing filter. Shooting from directly above has its limitations however, and much greater versatility can be achieved by building yourself a simple periscope. This consists of a watertight tube with a mirror angled at 45 degrees, so that it looks out through a glass panel. The mirror end is immersed in the water and the camera pointed down into the tube so that you actually photograph the reflection of your subject in the mirror.

Another way of dealing with aquatic creatures is to transfer them to an aquarium tank and photograph them there. This technique is broadly similar to that used for the studio photography of insects. Your specimen

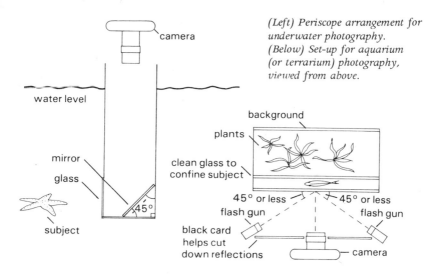

(Left) Periscope arrangement for underwater photography. (Below) Set-up for aquarium (or terrarium) photography, viewed from above.

can be confined by placing it between the front of the tank and a parallel sheet of glass placed a little way behind. The background can consist either of a piece of coloured card placed behind the tank, or can be an arrangement of aquatic plants or other natural objects. The best way to illuminate your set is from directly above so as to imitate the sun shining. If you aim your flash through the side of the tank instead, be careful that the flash does not cause reflections. To avoid this you should position your flash guns at an acute angle (about 45° or less) to the front wall of the tank.

Underground life

Now let us turn our attention from underwater life to underground life. At first thought, it might seem quite impossible to take pictures of earthworms or moles beneath the surface, but the techniques for doing so are really quite simple and consist of making a sandwich from two sheets of glass, filling the space between with soil and introducing your animal. The distance between the two panes obviously has to be chosen with some care and more soil can be packed behind the rear glass so as to provide a background. The set must be lit from in front, care being taken to avoid reflections in the glass.

Photographing nocturnal animals

Photographing nocturnal creatures such as badgers or foxes requires the use of larger flash guns than those needed for studio work. As always, two flashes are better than one, and ideally they should be arranged one on either side of where you expect your subject to be. You will, of course, either have to set them on tripods or clamp them to a convenient branch. Because some animals, especially foxes, are very nervous about strange objects, it is a good idea to place a couple of dummy flash heads in position a few days before you intend to start taking pictures, so that the animals will become used to them. Once you are sure the animals in question have accepted the dummies, you can substitute the real guns, set up your camera gear and wait, making sure, of course, that you remain undetected by your quarry.

It is also a good idea to focus the camera on a pre-selected spot where you know the animals will be — the entrance to a burrow for example — before dark. You may also put bait down to encourage the animals to go to a certain spot, but take care either to use the sort of food which the animals might find naturally, or else hide it under leaf litter to ensure that it is not obvious in the photograph.

The flash itself does not seem to alarm animals unduly, although the noise of the shutter and film advance mechanism may, so, if possible, use a blimp to cut down on such noises.

Sound recording

Sound recording is included here because it is becoming increasingly popular among wildlife enthusiasts, and collecting your own tape recordings of bird songs and other sounds of the countryside can be very satisfying. A small cassette recorder is perfectly adequate and should, of course, be battery operated to allow greater mobility. The type which can also be used with mains electricity by means of a separate transformer is obviously lighter to carry than one with the transformer built in. The standard microphones which are issued with such equipment are usually inadequate for wildlife work, however, since they tend to collect sound from a wide area. The problem can be solved by using a parabolic reflector which will collect the sound from one direction and focus it on to the microphone, thus both eliminating much of the background noise and producing a louder and clearer recording. Fitting a light fabric cap over the reflector will cut out a lot of wind noise.

Some subjects — grasshoppers, some birds and bees for instance — can be recorded by fixing a standard microphone to the end of a broom handle by means of a simple spring clip and then manoeuvring this into position near to them.

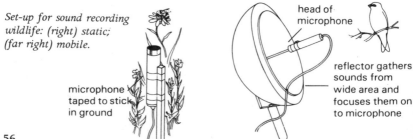

Set-up for sound recording wildlife: (right) static; (far right) mobile.

microphone taped to stick in ground

head of microphone

reflector gathers sounds from wide area and focuses them on to microphone

Seabirds nesting on the cliffs of Ailsa Craig (see page 95).

(Above) Leighton Moss R.S.P.B. reserve, viewed from the hide (see page 100).

(Below) Oystercatchers, redshanks and sanderlings roosting at high tide.

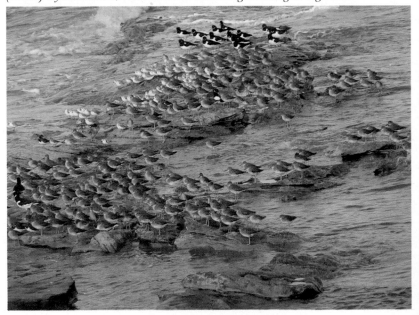

Places to visit

This chapter includes details of about 200 of our finest nature reserves, sanctuaries and other wildlife sites. The list is by no means comprehensive, of course, and in choosing which sites to include it has been necessary to be very selective. Nevertheless this should be a list of those sites which represent a broad cross-section of our main habitats, and which between them include a great variety of our wildlife. I have; through necessity, omitted a great many other good sites, especially those which are either too small or delicate to accommodate large numbers of visitors without risking damage to the wildlife they contain.

Wherever you live in Britain, there will certainly be other local sites which are noted for their wildlife, and one of the great pleasures in studying natural history is to discover and explore such places for yourself. A quicker way to discover local places of interest is to join your local or county natural history society or wildlife trust, many of which have their own local reserves.

It is important to point out that the species listed in the sites and reserves in this book are not necessarily the only ones to be seen at those places. Many habitats have a constant and characteristic assemblage of species which it would be repetitive to include at each similar site, and an impression of the more general species may be had by reading the chapter on Habitats. Remember, too, that the presence of a particular species can indicate that others favouring the same conditions may also be found.

It will be seen that some of the reserves are only accessible to permit holders. Generally speaking the permit system is designed to keep out casual visitors, large numbers of whom might damage, albeit unwittingly, the site and its flora and fauna, whilst at the same time allowing access to the genuinely interested. With a very few exceptions (for example if the site is dangerous or if delicate research work is being carried out there) permits are freely granted to anyone who takes the trouble to apply, and bona fide naturalists should have no hesitation about applying for permits. Addresses at which to apply are given in the text where appropriate. In other instances you should apply to the headquarters of the organization under whose management the reserve falls (see Appendices). Bear in mind also that certain sites may involve access across private land.

Map key

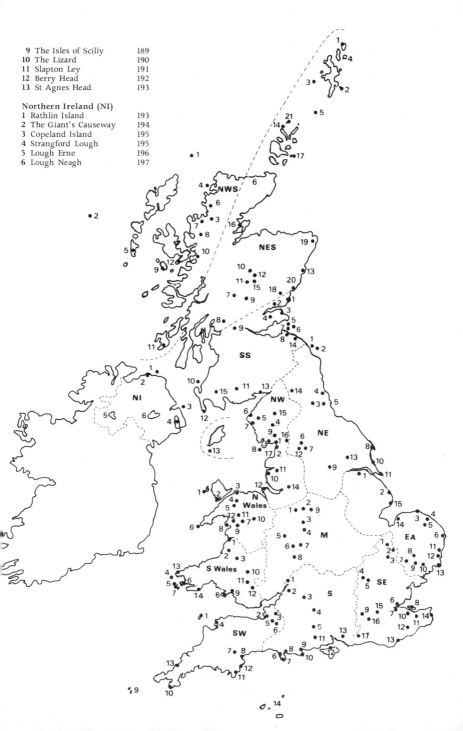

Checklist of habitat types

If you want to visit a particular type of habitat – say calcareous grassland –
simply look in the relevant part of these lists to find the reference numbers
to that habitat.

Woodlands

Pedunculate oakwoods
NW 3
NE 5
S 1
SE 5
M 7, 8

Sessile oakwoods
NWS 10, 11
NES 8
NW 3, 4, 16
N. Wales 11, 12
S. Wales 3, 9
SW 7
SE 10
M 1, 4, 6, 7, 8

Beechwoods
S. Wales 12
S 11
SE 6

Birchwoods
NWS 3, 6, 8, 12
NES 15
EA 9
M 4

Pinewoods
NWS 8
NES 10, 11, 12

Ashwoods
NWS 12
NW 2, 3, 9, 17
SW 3, 5, 6
NE 5, 6
M 2, 9

Alderwoods
NWS 11, 12
NES 16
S. Wales 9
M 4

Lowlands and heaths

Neutral grassland
S 3
EA 10

Calcareous grassland
NWS 7
NW 9, 16, 17
N. Wales 3

S. Wales 11, 14
SW 3, 5, 10, 12
NE 3, 7, 12, 14
M 2, 9
S 4, 5
EA 8, 9
SE 5, 12, 15, 17

Heathland
S. Wales 13
SW 9, 10, 13
NE 13, 14
M 4
S 9, 10, 11
EA 9, 14
SE 9, 16

Mountains and moorland

Upland pastures
   (Acid grassland)
NWS 5, 6, 8, 9
NES 1, 4, 11, 12
SS 15
N. Wales 7, 9
S. Wales 3, 11
NE 12, 14

Upland bogs
NWS 6, 8, 9
NES 7
SS 15
NE 7

Heather moors
SS 15
N. Wales 7
NE 12, 14

High tops
NES 9, 11, 12
SS 15
NW 5
N. Wales 4, 5, 9
S. Wales 10

Coastlands

Beaches
NW 8
SW 11
NE 11
S 6
EA 3
SE 13

Sand dunes
NWS 11
NES 6, 13, 19
SS 1, 3, 8
NW 7, 8, 10
N. Wales 2, 8
S. Wales 9, 14
SW 4

NE 1
S 10
EA 2, 3, 15
SE 14

Estuaries, etc
NES 13, 16, 20
SS 3, 8, 13
NW 3, 12, 18
S. Wales 1
SW 2, 8
NE 1, 11
S 2, 12, 13
EA 1, 3, 6, 12, 15
SE 6, 7, 8, 14
N. Ire 4

Cliffs
NWS 1, 2, 4, 6, 9, 11
NES 1, 2, 3, 4, 5, 6, 14,
    17, 21
SS 1, 5, 6, 10, 12, 14
NW 6, 13
N. Wales 1, 3, 6
S. Wales 4, 5, 6, 7, 8,
    13, 14
SW 1, 12, 13
NE 2, 8
N. Ire 1, 2

Wetlands

Lakes and ponds
NWS 5, 6, 7
NES 8, 10, 12, 18, 19
SS 1, 3, 4
NW 11, 14, 17
N. Wales 10
SW 12
NE 7, 9, 10
S 6, 8, 10

EA 4, 5
SE 1, 4, 11
N. Ire 5, 6

Marshes, fens and carrs
NES 8
NW 1, 3
S. Wales 9
NE 7

EA 4, 5, 11, 12
SE 2, 3, 11

Lowland bogs
SS 9
NW 3
S. Wales 2
S 11
SE 9, 16
M 3, 4

A list of reserves which have hides

Loch Garten NES 10
Loch of the Lowes SS 2
Morton Lochs SS 3
Threave Wildfowl Refuge SS 11
Eastpark Farm,
    Caerlaverock SS 13
Leighton Moss NW 1
Martin Mere NW 11
Llyn Vyrnwy N. Wales 10
Fairburn Ings NE 9
Slimbridge S 2

Arne S 9
Studland Heath S 10
Blacktoft Sands EA 1
North Norfolk Coast EA 3
Minsmere EA 12
Havergate EA 13
Ouse Washes SE 1
Wicken Fen SE 3
Castlecaldwell Reserve,
    Lough Erne N. Ire 5

North Rona and Sula Sgeir
NWS 1   OS map 8   HW 8132

These two remote islands lie about 50 miles (80 km) north-east of the Butt of Lewis, and are separated from each other by a distance of $12\frac{1}{2}$ miles (20 km). Both islands are included together as one National Nature Reserve, and are privately owned.

North Rona is by far the larger of the two, and is about 300 acres (120 ha) in extent and more or less cliff bound. Sula Sgeir, which lies to the west, is much smaller, a mere rock in fact about $\frac{1}{2}$ mile (approx. 800 m) in length and slightly over 200 ft (60 m) high.

Fauna

BIRDS The bird life of North Rona is very prolific. It includes one of Britain's biggest colonies of **greater black-backed gulls** – over 1000 pairs – and possibly the biggest British colony of **Leach's petrels**. **Storm petrels** also breed in large numbers and there are colonies of **puffins, kittiwakes, fulmars, great skuas** and a few **arctic terns**.

The island is also well situated to receive a good quota of migratory vagrants, too, **crossbills, jackdaws, woodpigeons, red-headed buntings** and **red-breasted flycatchers** being among the species which have been recorded on passage.

Sula Sgeir is dominated by its colony of about 9000 pairs of **gannets**. This is the only gannet colony in the British Isles which is still harvested. Every year in late summer, men from the township of Ness on the Isle of Lewis visit Sula Sgeir for two or three weeks to collect some 3000 or so young gannets, or 'gugas' as they are called. They are caught with the aid of a long pole with a noose at the end and are plucked, cleaned and salted there and then. This tradition is a very ancient one, and a special clause was included in the Protection of Birds Act so as to allow it to continue. In addition to the gannets there are **fulmars**.

MAMMALS The main mammalian interest lies in the enormous colony of **grey seals** on North Rona. Between September and December about one-seventh of the total world population haul out here to give birth to some 2500 pups. North Rona was once undisputedly the world's largest grey seal rookery, but it has now been overtaken by the Monach Islands.

Access

Unfortunately, getting to either island is both extremely difficult and expensive. There are no regular sailings there so the only means of reaching them is to organize your own expedition. The fishermen of Stornoway (Lewis) or Kinlochbervie (Sutherland) will sometimes agree to take people there, or alternatively it is possible to charter a boat. It is also possible to land on North Rona by helicopter although this is an extremely expensive exercise.

People intending to visit the islands should first request permission from the Nature Conservancy Council, 9 Culduthel Road, Inverness IV2 4AG.

St Kilda NWS 2 OS map 8 NA 1000

St Kilda is probably the best-known and most exciting of all the outlying Scottish islands. It boasts the highest cliffs and sea stacks in Great Britain and has some of the largest seabird colonies anywhere in the world.

The archipelago consists of four main islands and lies about 45 miles (72 km) west of the Outer Hebrides. It is owned by the National Trust for Scotland and leased by them to the Nature Conservancy who adminster it as a National Nature Reserve.

Hirta is the largest island, some 1600 acres (647 ha), and the only island on which landing is easy; the others are entirely cliff bound. It has the remains of an old village which was evacuated in 1930, and is studded with scores of tiny stone larders known as 'cleitean'. It also has a small military camp. The hill of Mullach Mor is capped by a radar station. Hirta also has Britain's highest cliff: the 1397 foot (425 m) high Conachair.

A little way to the north-west of Hirta is the islet of Soay, and to the south-east is the islet of Dun. Four miles (6.5 km) north-east is Boreray, whose cliffs are slightly lower than those on Hirta but far steeper and more impressive. Boreray is guarded by two enormous pillars of rock: Stac Lee (567 ft/172 m) and Stac an Armin (647 ft/196 m) the latter being the loftiest sea stack in Britain.

Fauna

BIRDS The world's largest colony of **gannets** is to be found on Boreray and the stacks. Almost 60,000 pairs nest here together with many thousands of **guillemots, razorbills, fulmars** and **kittiwakes**. The sight is awe inspiring.

Hirta also has its share of seabirds including many thousands of **guillemots, razorbills, kittiwakes, fulmars, storm petrels, Leach's petrels** and **Manx shearwaters**. There are small colonies of **black guillemots, shags, great skuas,** and **gulls** (including **herring, common, lesser black-backed** and **greater black-backed**). Also to be found are **oystercatchers, eiders, snipe, hooded crows, ravens, wheatears, twite, rock pipits, meadow pipits** and, perhaps most interesting of all, the unique **St Kilda wren**, a sub-species which is slightly larger and more vividly coloured than its mainland counterpart and which has a slightly different song.

Dun is the home of Britain's largest colony of **puffins**. Something in the region of 40–60,000 pairs nest here today, although this is far fewer than the three million reported in 1950.

MAMMALS The most distinctive mammal is the **St Kilda fieldmouse** which, like the St Kilda wren, is found nowhere else. Another unique mammal, the **St Kilda housemouse** became extinct shortly after the islands were evacuated.

The only other mammals are the **Soay sheep**, which is a very ancient breed not far removed from the ancestral moufflon and which has remained virtually unchanged on St Kilda for hundreds of years, and a small **grey seal** rookery which produces about a hundred pups annually.

Flora
FLOWERING PLANTS Much of the island is covered with acid grasslands with **white bent grass, fine bent, sweet vernal grass, red fescue, Yorkshire fog** and **mat grass**. Other areas are covered in **ling**, and **great wood-rush** is fairly common.

The cliffs have some rather more interesting species including **purple saxifrage, moss campion** and **bog rush**.

FERNS **Sea spleenwort** is found on some of the cliffs.

MOSSES AND LIVERWORTS Two members of the bryophyte flora are **woolly fringe moss** (*Rhacomitrium langinosum*) and the liverwort *Fossombronia angulosa*.

Access
Visitors arriving at the island on private vessels must report to the NTS/NCC summer warden. No camping is allowed without special permission being first obtained from the Nature Conservancy Council, 9 Culduthel Road, Inverness IV2 4AG.

Corrieshalloch Gorge   NWS 3   OS map 20   NH 2078
Corrieshalloch Gorge is a spectacular wooded ravine situated about 12 miles (19 km) south of Ullapool. The gorge is nearly 1 mile (1.6 km) long and has sheer walls which rise to about 200 ft (60 m) in places. It has been cut, through rather acid rocks, by water action and includes the Falls of Measach, a waterfall which may be seen to advantage from a nearby suspension bridge.

The National Trust for Scotland owns the site but it is also scheduled as a National Nature Reserve.

Flora
FLOWERING PLANTS The narrow strip of woodland which runs along the gorge consists mainly of **birch** with **oak, rowan, hazel, wych elm, beech, pine** and several other trees including some introduced exotics. Herbs of the reserve include **wood anemone, red campion, bitter vetch, meadowsweet, sanicle, primrose, yellow pimpernel, hedge woundwort, bugle, woodruff, common valerian, ramsons, great wood-rush, wood millet, opposite-leaved golden saxifrage, roseroot, mountain sorrel** and **stone bramble**.

FERNS **Fir clubmoss** is found here.

MOSSES AND LIVERWORTS The high humidity and poor light in the gorge have encouraged a good bryophyte flora which includes *Aphanolejeunea microscopica, Radula aquilegia, Tetraphis browniana, Plagiochila punctata, Calypogeia suecica, Sphenolobus helleranus* and *Tritomaria exsecta*.

Access

The gorge lies close to the main A835 from where it is easily accessible. No special permits are needed. The Gorge is dangerous and official routes only must be followed.

Handa NWS 4 OS map 9 NC 1348

Handa is a small island of 766 acres (310 ha) which lies $\frac{1}{2}$ mile (800 m) offshore and some 3 miles (5 km) north of Scourie, about 18 miles (29 km) south-west of Cape Wrath. It is a nature reserve of the R.S.P.B. and is mainly famous for its seabird colonies which occupy the 400 ft (122 m) high cliffs.

Fauna

BIRDS Recent counts have suggested that some 30,000 pairs of **guillemots** nest here along with about 9000 pairs of **razorbills,** 10,000 pairs of **kittiwakes** and about 2000 pairs of **fulmars.** The grassy slopes above the cliffs are riddled with the burrows of some 500 pairs of **puffins,** and the island also holds small colonies of **great skuas, arctic skuas, herring gulls, greater black-headed gulls** and **arctic terns.** A few **shags** and **black guillemots** may also be found, along with **ravens, rock doves, wheatears, twite, ringed plovers, oystercatchers, rock pipits, shelducks** and **eiders.**

Red-throated divers breed in most years and **merlins** have attempted to do so. **Peregrine falcons** may also be seen from time to time.

Flora

FLOWERING PLANTS Handa is not particularly noted for its plant life, but there are one or two notable species. These include **hybrid marram grass,** which is only known from two other British sites, and localized **water whorl-grass.** There is also some **crowberry.**

Access

The reserve is open from April to August (except Sundays). Boats are available from Tarbet and there is a small landing fee as well as the cost of the trip itself. Accommodation is only available to R.S.P.B. members. Contact R.S.P.B. 17 Regent Terrace, Edinburgh EH7 5BN.

Loch Druidibeg NWS 5 OS map 22 NF 7937

The National Nature Reserve of Loch Druidibeg lies on the island of South Uist in the Outer Hebrides. The entire island holds a wealth of interest for naturalists, and the Loch Druidibeg reserve lies in one of the richest parts. It embraces almost the entire spectrum of south Hebridean habitats including the fertile machair (low-lying sandy beaches) so characteristic of the Outer Isles, rolling moorland and a variety of lochan types which range from the peaty and acidic Loch Druidibeg itself to eutrophic (see page 38) machair lochs which began life as dune slacks.

The reserve covers a total of 4145 acres (1677ha).

Fauna

BIRDS The bird life here is extremely prolific, especially the waders and waterfowl. One of the principal attractions of the reserve is the breeding colony of **greylag geese** which is the largest in the country and currently includes about 70 pairs. The Nature Conservancy has built a viewing tower from which it is possible to observe the geese as well as the other breeding birds of the reserve. These include **tufted ducks, teal, eiders, red-breasted mergansers, dunlin, lapwings, ringed plovers, redshanks, oystercatchers, snipe** and **arctic terns. Grey herons** have a small colony on one of the numerous islands on the reserve and visitors include the occasional **red-necked phalarope.**

Flora

FLOWERING PLANTS The surrounding machair holds a large variety of common wild flowers including the **bulbous buttercup, kidney vetch, wild thyme, eyebright, yarrow, red fescue, Yorkshire fog, white bent, common reed** and **eared sallow.** A less common species is the **lesser meadow-rue.**

Loch Druidibeg itself is very peaty and markedly oligotrophic (see page 38), and holds species such as the **water lobelia** and **floating spike-rush.** Other lochans nearby are much more fertile and support a wider variety of plants including **alternate water milfoil** and **marestail.**

Access

The reserve lies alongside the main A865 road but a permit is needed to visit the reserve during the summer months. Permission should be sought from the warden at nearby Stilligarry or from the Nature Conservancy Council, 9 Culduthel Road, Inverness IV2 4AG.

Inverpolly NWS 6 OS map 15 NC 091188

Covering some 42 square miles (108 km²), Inverpolly is the second largest nature reserve in Britain. It lies about 15 miles (24 km) north of Ullapool, to the west of the A835 and includes mountains and moorland, numerous lochs and streams, areas of relict woodland and several miles of coastline; a true epitome of the Highlands.

The western part of the reserve is underlain with ancient gneiss while the east is composed of sandstone. This fact is, of course, strongly reflected in the botany of the area and there is also a small outcrop of limestone near Knockan where the Nature Conservancy has built a $\frac{3}{4}$ mile (1.2 km) long nature trail.

The attractive Loch Sionascaig lies at the centre of the reserve, and several small but interesting islands occupy the loch.

The highest point on the reserve is the 2784 ft (848 m) Cul Mor, and there are several other peaks over 2000 ft (609 m).

Fauna

BIRDS The birdlife of the reserve is very impressive and includes the following: **golden eagles, peregrines, buzzards, merlins, kestrels, ravens, black-throated divers, red-throated divers, red-breasted mergansers, ptarmigans, red grouse, black grouse, greenshanks, common sandpipers, golden plovers, snipe, curlews, woodcock, grey herons, ring ouzels, wheatears, stonechats, whinchats, twite, redpolls** and **snow buntings.**

Redwings have also been known to nest, while on the coast there are nesting **fulmars, shags, eiders** and one or two small colonies of **greylag geese.**

MAMMALS About 500 **red deer** inhabit the area along with **roe deer, wild cats, otters, pine martens, badgers, foxes** and **mountain hares.**

Flora

FLOWERING PLANTS Undoubtedly the most exciting plant here is the very rare **Scottish worm wood** which was discovered in this country as recently as 1952. Its main stronghold is on the twin sandstone peaks of Cul Mor and Cul Beag. Another speciality is the uncommon **Scottish rush.**

The western regions, where gneiss predominates, are generally wetter than the better-drained sandstones and have large areas of bog, while the higher ground holds several alpine species. Plants to look for are **least willow, small bladderwort, crowberry, Irish bladderwort, English stonecrop, bogbean, bog asphodel, slender-leaved sedge, moss campion, white beak sedge, alpine lady's mantle, bog sedge, golden saxifrage, many-stalked spike-rush, globe flower, alpine bistort, bog myrtle, pale butterwort, great sundew.**

There are several relict birchwoods scattered throughout the reserve, particularly in the north-west along the River Kirkaig and around Loch Sionascaig, where several other interesting plants may be found including the **melancholy thistle.**

The flora of the nature trail includes the rare **rock sedge, mountain avens** and **yellow mountain saxifrage.**

FERNS The ferns of the hills include **green spleenwort, hay-scented buckler fern, Wilson's filmy fern** and **lesser clubmoss.** The **lemon-scented fern** may be found growing among the birchwoods.

Access

There is one unclassified road which meanders along three sides of the reserve and passes over moors and through woodlands before eventually reaching the coast. Access to most of the area is on foot, however, over miles of moorland. You are requested to check with the wardens at either Knockan Cottage, Elphin, or Strathpolly, Inverpolly, before walking in the reserve.

There is a visitors' centre on the A835 about 3 miles (4.8km) south of Elphin from where a geological trail begins.

Inchnadamph NWS 7 OS map 15 NC 2719

Inchnadamph National Nature Reserve is perhaps better known to geologists and fossil hunters than to naturalists. It lies in limestone country at the head of Loch Assynt and has limestone pavements, cliffs and caves, one of which, Allt nan Uamh, has yielded bones of Late Pleistocene animals, including early man. The limestone also gives rise to a most interesting calcicole flora.

The reserve covers 5 square miles (12.9 km²).

Flora

FLOWERING PLANTS Among the more uncommon species which may be found here are the **Scottish sandwort**, **dark red helleborine**, **rock sedge**, the rare grass **Don's twitch** and **mountain avens**. There is also an extensive area of **willow** scrub which is dominated by the uncommon **whortle-leaved willow**.

FERNS The **holly fern** grows here.

MOSSES AND LIVERWORTS The bryophyte flora is quite rich and has a number of rarer calcicoles such as *Tortula princeps*, *Amblystegium compactum*, *Seligeria trifaria* and *Grimmia trichodon*.

Access

The reserve is adjacent to the A837 about 25 miles (40 km) north of Ullapool, but a permit is needed in order to visit. Applications should be addressed to the Nature Conservancy Council at 9 Culduthel Road, Inverness IV2 4AG.

Beinn Eighe NWS 8 OS map 19 NG 9560

Beinn (or Ben) Eighe has the distinction of being Britain's first National Nature Reserve, and was declared such in November 1951. It covers $16\frac{1}{2}$ square miles (42.4 km²) of wild mountain country with moorland, lochans, streams and bogs and includes about 330 acres (133 ha) of relict pine and birch woodland through which the Nature Conservancy has built a nature trail.

The reserve is situated at the south-eastern corner of Loch Maree about 3 miles (5 km) from Kinlochewe.

Fauna

BIRDS The birds of the hills include **golden eagles**, **buzzards**, **ptarmigan**, **ravens**, **black-throated divers**, **peregrine falcons**, **snow buntings** and occasionally **dotterels**. **Crossbills**, **siskins** and **twite** may be found in the forests.

MAMMALS A herd of about 150 **red deer** share the reserve with **wild cats** and **pine martens**. **Roe deer** are sometimes seen on the nature trails.

Flora

FLOWERING PLANTS A very wide range of habitats occur on the reserve, and the flora is correspondingly rich and varied. Some of the rarer species are **Highland saxifrage, limestone bugle** and **arctic mouse-ear** but there are many other interesting species including: **mossy saxifrage, purple mountain saxifrage, mountain sorrel, moss campion, purple hawkweed, roseroot, northern rockcress, alpine pearlwort, wild azalea, alpine meadow-rue, flea sedge, stiff sedge, Scottish rush, spiked wood-rush, great wood-rush, upland scurvy grass, least cinquefoil, thrift, ling, bearberry, black bearberry, crowberry, melancholy thistle, wild angelica, purple moor-grass, mat grass, tufted hair-grass, juniper, bog myrtle, common sundew, bog asphodel, alpine lady's mantle, least willow, globeflower, dwarf cornel** and **alpine bistort**.
FERNS **Holly fern, alpine lady fern** and **moonwort** are found here.
MOSSES AND LIVERWORTS The liverwort *Herberta borealis* which occurs on the hills here is only known from one other site in the world, and was only recognized in 1970. Other notable bryophytes include *Campylopus shawii, C. atrovirens* and *Pleurozia purpurea*.

Access

Access to the reserve is unrestricted. The nature trails start from the Loch Maree picnic site which is on the A832 some 3 miles (4.8 km) north-west of Kinlochewe. A much longer mountain footpath diverges from the trail and runs into the centre of the reserve and back to the road.

There is a visitors' centre at Aultroy, and a nearby attraction is the superb little deer museum at Torridon.

Rhum NWS 9 OS map 39 NM 3798

The entire island of Rhum, an area of 40 square miles (103 km²), is not only a National Nature Reserve but is also an enormous outdoor laboratory run by the Nature Conservancy. It lies about 15 miles (24 km) west of Mallaig and is a very rugged island with mountains rising to 2659 ft (810 m), windswept moors, bogs and some seabird cliffs. For many years it was known as the Forbidden Isle because its owners permitted very few people to land. Today the Nature Conservancy permits visitors, who are allowed to explore the area around Loch Scresort and wander along the nature trails.

Fauna

BIRDS Rhum is the home of Britain's largest colony of **Manx shearwaters**, over 130,000 pairs of which nest on the high slopes of Trollaval, Askival, and Hallival. A few **storm petrels** are also known to nest. The island is famous for its **white-tailed sea eagles** which the Nature Conservancy is attempting to re-introduce. In 1975 they released one male and three females on to the island. Several others have been released at intervals since, and they have now started to nest in other parts of the Hebrides.

Three or four pairs of **golden eagles** also nest, and other birds of prey include **peregrines, merlins** and **kestrels**. A variety of small passerines nest in the woodlands around Loch Scresort along with **woodcock**. Other notable birds are: **corncrakes, red-throated divers, ring ouzels, ravens, hooded crows, red-breasted mergansers, fulmars, shags, eiders, kittiwakes, arctic terns, razorbills, guillemots, black guillemots, puffins, twite, short-eared owls** and **long-eared owls**.

MAMMALS One of the main research projects being carried out on Rhum is a long-term study of the island's **red deer**. About 1600 of them occupy the island, sharing it with **feral ponies, feral goats**, and a variety of small mammals including the '**Rhum mouse**' (*Apodemus hebridensis hamiltoni*), **brown rat, pygmy shrew** and **pipistrelle bat**. The **otter** is also found here.

AMPHIBIANS **Smooth** and **palmate newts** are found here.

INVERTEBRATES The insect life has been well studied, in particular the Lepidoptera (moths and butterflies), and there are several species of note. The Irish sub-species of the **marsh fritillary** and the **dark green fritillary** have both been recorded, and there are also the **large heath butterfly, belted beauty** and **transparent burnet moth**.

Flora

FLOWERING PLANTS The island also has great botanical interest and the flora has been extensively studied by Nature Conservancy scientists. There are some attractive woodlands in the Loch Scresort area which were planted in the early years of this century and which hold a wide variety of both hard and softwoods. The Nature Conservancy has also embarked upon an extensive planting programme using native trees.

Among the more notable members of the island's flora are: **Scottish sandwort, starry saxifrage, lesser butterfly orchid, mossy saxifrage, bog orchid, mountain avens, small white orchid, cyphal, grass of Parnassus, alpine meadow-rue, purple saxifrage, northern rockcress, arctic saxifrage, alpine lady's mantle, lovage, floating bur-reed, Scottish asphodel, bog asphodel, pale butterwort, common sundew, great sundew, long-leaved sundew, moss campion** and **globe flower**.

FERNS **Alpine clubmoss, parsley fern, royal fern** and **Scottish filmy fern** are found.

Access

Visitors are welcome at Kinloch, at the head of Loch Scresort, from where two nature trails start. Anyone wishing to stay on the island must have prior permission from the Nature Conservancy Council at 9 Culduthel Road, Inverness IV2 4AG. Visitors may either camp or stay in Kinloch Castle, the former estate owner's home. Boats sail to Rhum from Mallaig about four times per week.

Allt-nan-Carnan NWS 10 OS map 24 NG 8940

Allt-nan-Carnan is a 1 mile (1.6 km) long gorge which has been cut through lime-rich schists near the head of Loch Carron. Because of its inaccessibility and the difficulty in extracting timber, the gorge contains some fine relict woodlands which are of such interest that it has been declared a National Nature Reserve.

The reserve covers 17 acres (7 ha).

Flora

FLOWERING PLANTS **Sessile oak, birch** and **ash** are the principal tree species but there are smaller amounts of others, too, including **rowan, holly, aspen** and **bird cherry**. An interesting feature of the gorge is that, although it is virtually at sea level, it holds a selection of montane plants such as **alpine lady's mantle** and **yellow mountain saxifrage**.

Opposite-leaved golden saxifrage, water avens, wild strawberry and **stone bramble** are also found here.

Access

The gorge lies adjacent to the main A896 just by Lochcarron village. No special permits are needed.

Islay NWS 11 OS map 60 NR 4550

From the natural history point of view, Islay is one of the most interesting of all the Inner Hebrides. It covers about 150 square miles (388 km²) and has a wide variety of habitats including cliffs, dunes and woodlands.

Fauna

BIRDS 110 species of birds are known to breed on Islay and over twice that number have been recorded. **Choughs** nest on the Oa peninsula at the extreme south of the island, one of their few Scottish breeding stations. Fortunately the colony there seems to be increasing. **Golden eagles** breed along the southern coasts and elsewhere there are **peregrines, buzzards, sparrowhawks, merlins, hen harriers, tawny owls** and **short-eared owls**.

Coastal species include **Manx shearwaters, fulmars, kittiwakes, shags, cormorants, guillemots, puffins, razorbills, oystercatchers, eiders, black guillemots, common** and **arctic terns, rock doves** and **shelducks. Scoters** occasionally nest.

Other nesting birds are **kingfishers, twite, redstarts, whinchats, black grouse, goldcrests, woodcock, red grouse, ravens, hooded crows, dippers** and **redpolls**.

The Loch Gruinart – Loch Indaal area is particularly well known on account of its wintering geese. These include 18,000 **barnacle geese** (one-sixth of the world population!), more than 2000 **white-fronted geese** and several hundred **greylags**, as well as **scaup, red-breasted mergansers** and **great northern divers**.

MAMMALS The mammal fauna includes **red, roe** and **fallow deer**, the last having been introduced to the south-east of the island. **Feral goats** are also present along with **mountain hares, long-tailed fieldmice,** a sub-species of the **short-tailed vole** (*Microtus agrestis macgillivraii*), a sub-species of the **stoat** (*Mustela erminea ricinae*) and a distinct race of the **common shrew.**

INVERTEBRATES Islay is not without interest for the entomologist either, and includes the Irish sub-species of the **marsh fritillary,** as well as **green hairstreak** and **speckled wood** butterflies.

Flora

FLOWERING PLANTS There are some interesting woodlands in the area around Claggain and Ardmore, at the extreme south eastern corner of the island. They are mainly of **oak** and **alder** with some **hazel, birch, sallow** and **rowan.** The other plants include **bluebell, primrose, wood sorrel, foxglove** and **tormentil.**

Elsewhere on the island you may find the **slender naiad, rock samphire, frog orchid, purple mountain saxifrage, oyster plant, sea holly,** and **pale butterwort.**

FERNS The Claggain – Ardmore Woods support **lady fern, hard fern, lemon-scented fern** and **bracken. Adder's-tongue** and **royal ferns** grow elsewhere on the island.

Access

Getting to Islay involves a car ferry trip from Tarbert, Kintyre to either Port Ellen or Port Askaig. There is an adequate road network on the island and plenty of accommodation.

Tokavaig Wood NWS 12 OS map 32 NG 6112

Tokavaig Wood is on the Isle of Skye, on the southern shore of Loch Eishort, and is a National Nature Reserve. Its great interest stems from the fact that it lies on a variety of rock types including sandstone, limestone and quartzite and that these different rocks support different floras. The woods are of particular interest to moss and liverwort enthusiasts, and a variety of birds and mammals may also be seen.

Flora

FLOWERING PLANTS The sandstone and quartzite areas are mostly covered with birchwood (**downy birch**) with some **rowan, holly** and **sessile oak. Bilberry** and **ling** are common shrubs and the **lesser twayblade orchid** grows in places beneath the **heather. Tormentil, great wood-rush, wood sage** and **wavy hair-grass** also occur.

The limestone areas are mainly of **ash** and **hazel**, with **wych elm, bird cherry** and **guelder rose.** Other flowers include **bluebell, primrose, wood anemone, frog orchid, sweet woodruff** and both the **tufted hair** and **slender false brome** grasses.

In some of the deep ravines which cut across the limestone you may find the **dark red helleborine, herb Paris, mountain melick grass, stone bramble** and **bearberry.**

Yet a third woodland type may be found in wetter areas where **alder** is the dominant species and the herbs include **opposite-leaved golden saxifrage** and **remote sedge.**

Common twayblade orchid and **melancholy thistle** may also be found in the woods.

FERNS The limestone gorges support **hartstongue fern, hard shield fern** and **green spleenwort.** Both **Wilson's** and the **Tunbridge filmy ferns** may be found growing on boulders in the woods.

MOSSES AND LIVERWORTS The bryophyte flora includes *Adelanthus decipiens, Bazzania trilobata, Ulota scutatus, U. vittata, Riccardia palmata, Hylocomium umbratum, Dicranum scottianum, Frullania germana, Harpanthus scutatus, Lepidozia trichoclados, Cephalozia catenulata, Trichostomum hibernicum, Tetraphis browniana, Fissidens celticus, Lophocolea fragrans, Plagiochila tridenticulata* and *Grimmia hartmanii.*

LICHENS *Sticta dufourii, Solorina saccata* and *Sphaerophorus melanocarpus.*

Access

The Isle of Skye may be reached either on the ferry from Mallaig to Armadale Bay, or on the sailing from Kyle of Lochalsh to Kyleakin. The woods are accessible via the A851 and the unclassified roads to Tokavaig itself, which pass through the woods.

The woods are privately owned, however, and permission should be sought from the Nature Conservancy Council at 9 Culduthel Road, Inverness IV2 4AG before wandering too far from the road.

Herma Ness NES 1 OS map 1 HP 6018

Herma Ness has the distinction of being the most northerly point of the British Isles. It lies at the extreme tip of the island of Unst in the Shetlands and consists of a headland which culminates in a series of 450 ft (137 m) high cliffs which provide a home for myriads of seabirds. The area is scheduled as a National Nature Reserve and covers $3\frac{3}{4}$ square miles (9.6 km²).

Fauna

BIRDS **Gannets** are one of the principal attractions and although the colony is not very large – about 6000 pairs.

In addition to the gannets there are many thousands of other seabirds. There are some 16,000 pairs of **guillemots**, about 2000 pairs of **razorbills**, and the grassy slopes above the cliffs are honeycombed with the burrows of 15,000 or so pairs of **puffins**. In addition, there are 8000 pairs of **fulmars** and 5000 pairs of **kittiwakes**. About 300 pairs of **great skuas** and 50 pairs of **arctic skuas** breed on the moorland, which also holds breeding **whimbrel, golden plovers, dunlin** and **snipe. Red-throated divers** occasionally nest on some of the lochans here. **Eiders** are found at Burra Firth (see below), and there are also **rock pipits** and **wrens**.

MAMMALS To the east of Herma Ness is the long inlet of Burra Firth where **grey seals** may be seen.

INVERTEBRATES The area is also noted for its Lepidoptera (butterflies and moths), among which are two rare moth species: **arctic northern arches**, and a dark sub-species of the **autumnal rustic** which is restricted to the Shetlands.

Flora

FLOWERING PLANTS Much of the headland is dominated by **mat grass** and **purple moor-grass**, but there is also some **ling, bilberry, heath rush, deer grass** and **cottongrass**.

The cliffs themselves have some interesting arctic/alpines including **lovage, roseroot** and **moss campion**.

Access

Access to Unst is via the Shetlandic car ferry network. From the end of the road (HP 613148) you have to walk some $2\frac{1}{2}$ miles (4km) over rough moorland, following a series of marker posts which take you to the warden's hut.

Noss NES 2 OS map 4 HU 5540

The island of Noss is one of the finest seabird breeding stations in the country. Indeed, it has been described by one distinguished ornithologist as 'the most spectacular island in Europe'. It lies a few miles east of Lerwick in the Shetlands and is a National Nature Reserve. It covers 774 acres (313ha).

Fauna

BIRDS About 4000 pairs of **gannets** head the list of seabirds, which also includes **guillemots, razorbills, puffins, kittiwakes** and **fulmars** as well as **great** and **arctic skuas**. Noss also has one of Britain's biggest colonies of **greater black-backed gulls**, which nest on the offshore stack of Cradle Holm. **Red-throated divers** and **eiders** also breed.

MAMMALS **Grey seals** are often seen in Noss Sound – the narrow straits which separates Noss from the neighbouring island of Bressay.

Flora

FLOWERING PLANTS Noss is not particularly noted for its plant life, but the grassy top of the island includes **red fescue, smooth meadow-grass**, several **bents** (*Agrostis* spp), **mat grass, purple moor-grass** and a certain amount of **ling, crowberry, cottongrass, deer grass** and **tormentil**. **Great wood-rush** and **chickweed wintergreen** have also been recorded.

Access

There are two ways to see Noss; either by taking a boat trip around the island, or by actually landing on it. Boat owners in Lerwick run several trips around Noss daily which are advertised locally and are well worth the cost. To land on the island you must first cross Bressay, a much larger island, which separates Noss from Lerwick. A ferry crosses Bressay Sound several times daily and you must then either walk or take a taxi the 2½ miles (4km) across Bressay to Noss Sound where the Nature Conservancy Council operate a ferry service, for which a fee must be paid. It may also be worth a visit to nearby Ullins Water — HU 521408 — which usually holds **red-throated divers**.

There is a small visitors' centre on Noss.

Foula NES 3 OS map 4 HT 9639

Lying 24 miles (38km) west of the Shetland mainland, Foula is probably the most remote inhabited island in the United Kingdom. A mere handful of crofters still manage to make a living there, but whereas the human population is tiny, the bird population is enormous.

Foula is also famed for its cliffs. The Kame of Foula is Britain's second highest, and rises to the dizzy height of 1220 feet (372m).

The island is not specifically managed as a nature reserve, but its prolific birdlife and remoteness make it a most valuable sanctuary.

Fauna

BIRDS 30,000 pairs of **guillemots** head the list of seabirds together with 25,000 pairs of **puffins**, 8000 pairs of **fulmars**, 6000 pairs of **razorbills**, 6000 pairs of **arctic terns**, over 3000 pairs of **great skuas** and about 250 pairs of **arctic skuas**.

There are also numerous **kittiwakes**, **shags**, **storm petrels**, Manx **shearwaters**, and colonies of **herring gulls**, **lesser black-backed gulls**, **greater black-backed gulls** and **common gulls**. Whimbrel, twite and **rock pipits** also breed here.

Flora

FLOWERING PLANTS Most of the island is covered with montane grassland which includes species such as **mat grass**, **wavy hair-grass**, **deer grass**, **heath rush**, various **fescues**, **stiff sedge** and **cottongrass**. There are also areas of **ling**, **crowberry** and **bilberry** and some **cross-leaved heath**. **Sea plantain** and **buckshorn plantain** are also found in places as are the **great wood-rush** and **least willow**. Two of the rarest species here are the **alpine bistort** and the **dwarf cornel**.

FERNS The uncommon **Scottish filmy fern** grows on some of the boulders here, especially in wetter parts.

Access

Access is, of course, very difficult and expensive and only the most dedicated naturalists manage to get to Foula. There are air and sea connections with the mainland of Shetland but no regular accommodation so visitors have to be prepared for camping. Intending visitors are advised to enquire at the Shetland Tourist Board, Lerwick, Shetland.

Fetlar NES 4 OS map 1 HU 6293

The island of Fetlar lies a few miles east of Yell in the Shetlands, and covers about 12 square miles (31km²). It was made famous in 1967 when the first snowy owls ever known to breed in Britain chose this attractive island to do so. Alas, the owls have not bred in recent years but at least one owl regularly summers there so they may resume breeding again in years to come.

The R.S.P.B. created a reserve at Vord Hill especially to protect the owls, but the whole island is sufficiently rich in birdlife to merit the status of a reserve.

Fauna

BIRDS The north side of the island has some seabird cliffs where **fulmars**, **kittiwakes**, **shags**, **puffins** and a few **black guillemots** breed. The headland of Lamb Hoga has some small colonies of **storm petrels** and **Manx shearwaters** on its western side – the Stack of Grunnigeo is a good place to see them.

The island is probably the main British stronghold of the **red-necked phalarope** and has one of the largest British colonies of **arctic skuas** –over 200 pairs.

Elsewhere on the island you may see **red-throated divers**, **great skuas**, **eiders**, **dunlin**, **redshanks**, **curlews**, **whimbrel**, **twite**, and, if you are lucky, **peregrine falcons**, **corncrakes** and, of course, **snowy owls**.

MAMMALS Otters are seen regularly on the island and there are **grey seals**, **common seals** and **porpoises** in the surrounding seas.

Access

Getting to Fetlar used to be a long and complicated process but now a regular car ferry makes frequent trips. There are one or two small guest houses or you may camp on the links – the causeway between the sea and Papil Water (HU 606905).

Fair Isle NES 5 OS map 4 HZ 2172

The famous Fair Isle is situated mid-way between the Orkneys and Shetlands and about 24 miles (38km) from either. Its location is all-important, for it lies on the main route of millions of migratory birds and, being the only land for miles, it attracts many thousands of them down to land and rest. This explains why its bird observatory has added more bird species to the British list than any other location. The observatory was founded in 1948 and has a fascinating history.

Fair Isle is owned by the National Trust for Scotland and covers about $7\frac{3}{4}$ square miles (20.2km²).

Fauna

BIRDS In addition to being a superb migration watchpoint, Fair Isle also has a good selection of breeding birds including 10,000 pairs of **guillemots,** 1200 pairs of **razorbills,** 15,000 pairs of **puffins,** 17,000 pairs of **fulmars** and 12,000 of **kittiwakes.** There are smaller colonies of **great skuas, arctic skuas** and **storm petrels.** A small gannetry has recently become established.

The list of migrants recorded by the observatory is extensive, but some of the more exciting species are **great bustards, bee eaters, hoopoes, Pallas's sandgrouse, honey buzzards, gyr falcons** and **golden orioles.**

Access

Fair Isle is usually reached from Shetland, either by sea – often an uncomfortable experience on the *Good Shepherd* – or by air.

Details of access and accommodation at the observatory are available from: The Warden, Fair Isle Bird Observatory, Fair Isle, Shetland ZE2 9JU.

Invernaver NES 6 OS map 10 NC 6960

Lying by the mouth of the River Naver on the north coast of Sutherland, Invernaver National Nature Reserve has some of the most interesting plant communities in the whole of Scotland. The habitats on this reserve include an area of moderately lime-rich sand dunes which gradually merge into the acid moorland behind. Also, because of the extremely exposed position, several arctic/alpines are found here, growing virtually at sea level. There are also small areas of saltmarsh, shingle and cliffs.

The reserve covers 2 square miles (5.5 km²).

Flora

FLOWERING PLANTS The flora of the dunes includes **mountain avens, bearberry, crowberry,** Scots **primrose** and some **juniper,** with **creeping willow, curved sedge** and **bog rush** in some of the slacks.

Some of the most notable arctic/alpines are **purple milk vetch, purple mountain saxifrage, yellow mountain saxifrage, alpine bistort** and **moss campion.**

Sea plantain and **chestnut rush** grow in a small area of saltmarsh and **sea pink** and **sea campion** grow on the cliffs.

MOSSES AND LIVERWORTS Invernaver is also well known on account of its bryophytes which include **shaggy moss** (*Rhytidiadelphus triquetrus*) and **mountain fern moss** (*Hylocomium splendens*). The rare moss *Brachythecium erythrorrhizon* has its only known British site here.

Access

Access may be gained from Invernaver village (NC 7060) which is off the A836. No special permits are required.

Rannoch Moor NES 7 OS maps 41 & 42 NN 3652

Rannoch Moor is one of the most extensive areas of blanket bog in Britain. It covers about 40 square miles (104km²) in all and about 4½ square miles (12.1km²) are managed as a National Nature Reserve.

Fauna

BIRDS Several interesting Highland birds regularly breed on the moor including **snipe, golden plovers, dunlin** and the uncommon **greenshank** as well as **black-throated divers** and **golden eagles**.

MAMMALS The most notable mammal is the **red deer** which occurs in fair numbers.

INVERTEBRATES The insect fauna is quite rich and the moor is noted for its uncommon **dragonflies** which include *Aeshna caerulea* and *Somatochlora arctica*, both of which are very localized species.

Flora

FLOWERING PLANTS The most distinguished member of the flora is the **Rannoch rush** which lives here in its only known British locality. All three species of **bladderwort**, the **small, greater** and **Irish**, can be found and there are also **great sundews**.

The **sedges** are well represented and include **bog sedge, slender-leaved sedge, white sedge** and **tall bog sedge**. Other species are **bog myrtle, dwarf birch** and **many-stalked spike rush**.

Access

The moor straddles the main A82 from Crianlarich to Fort William and is easily accessible from the road. The National Nature Reserve is best reached from Rannoch Station at the end of the A846.

Loch Lomond NES 8 OS map 56 NS 3598

In addition to being one of the most famous and picturesque of all Scottish lochs, Loch Lomond is also of great interest to naturalists, especially birdwatchers and botanists, and 1,028 acres (416ha) of the area have been declared a National Nature Reserve. The reserve includes part of the flood plain of the River Endrick, which flows into the south-eastern corner of the loch, and five small islands: Inchcailloch, Clairinsh, Torrinch, Creinch and Aber Isle.

Fauna

BIRDS Large numbers of wildfowl congregate on Loch Lomond in winter. About 1000 **greylag geese** gather here annually, together with over 100 **Greenland white-fronted geese**. **Whooper swans** are also frequent winter visitors, along with a wide variety of ducks such as **mallard, teal, wigeon, shovelers, tufted ducks, pochard** and **goldeneye**.

MAMMALS Several of the islands on the loch have small herds of **fallow deer**.

Flora
FLOWERING PLANTS The four larger islands all have some interesting **sessile oakwoods**. Torrinch Isle also has **aspen** and Inchcailloch has **alder**, and **willow** swamps with some **Scots pine**. Clairinsh has some particularly fine oaks, whilst the other plants include **common twayblade, early purple orchid, stone bramble, columbine** and **globe flower**.

Where the River Endrick joins the loch some large areas of marsh have developed, the most extensive known as the Aber Bogs. These bogs form a tapestry of **willow** carr, small pools, ditches and marsh. Among the characteristic plants which may be found here are **cowbane, bogbean, tufted loosestrife, yellow loosestrife, marestail, common skullcap, yellow flag, nodding bur marigold, greater reedmace, water mint, marsh willowherb, purple loosestrife, water forget-me-not, marsh marigold, bladder sedge, sharp rush, meadowsweet,** and **wild angelica**.

The **eight-stamened waterwort** is found in the loch itself and the rare **Loch Lomond dock** is also found in the loch.

FERNS Several of the islands hold the **Tunbridge filmy fern** and the **hay-scented buckler fern**.

Access
Only Inchcailloch is readily accessible to the public and may be reached by boat from Balmaha. A permit from the Nature Conservancy is needed to visit the mainland part of the Reserve. Applications should be addressed to the Nature Conservancy Council, The Castle, Loch Lomond Park, Balloch, Strathclyde.

Ben Lawers NES 9 OS map 51 NN 6240
Ben Lawers is a 3984ft (1214m) high mountain which is well known to lovers of arctic/alpine plants. It lies in the Breadalbane Hills about 8 miles (13km) north-east of Killin and to the north of Loch Tay, and is probably the best-known location for montane plants in the whole of Britain. About $11\frac{3}{4}$ square miles (30.3km²) of the mountain are managed as a nature reserve by the National Trust for Scotland in association with the Nature Conservancy Council. The National Trust for Scotland also run a visitors' centre and nature trail.

Fauna
BIRDS include **buzzards, peregrines, lapwings, curlew, ravens, wheatears** and **black grouse**.

INVERTEBRATES The mountain is not famed for its animal life, although the invertebrate fauna is fairly rich. The molluscs in particular are well represented, and the **mountain ringlet butterfly** is quite common.

Anyone who climbs up to the summit cairn might be interested to know that the moss growing upon it is the home of both an arctic and an antarctic species of Tardigrada; a type of tiny water-living creature.

Flora

The Breadalbane Hills, which extend eastwards from Tyndrum for about 30 miles (48 km), are composed of a calcium-rich schist which gives rise to a very fertile soil. Ben Lawers is by far the highest peak in the range, and the rich soil and elevation combine to support a most remarkable assemblage of montane plants. Seventy-five species of arctic/alpine flowers, some of them exceedingly rare, are known from the site along with several montane bryophytes.

FLOWERING PLANTS The **Breadalbane sedge** is only known in Britain from one boggy corrie here. **Alpine forget-me-not** is found in only two British sites – Ben Lawers and Upper Teesdale – and **drooping saxifrage** is restricted to Ben Lawers and Glen Coe.

Other rarities include **brook saxifrage, alpine gentian, alpine pearlwort, lesser alpine pearlwort, Highland fleabane, small jet sedge, rock sedge, two-flowered rush, chestnut rush, rock speedwell, rock whitlow-grass, plum-leaved willow, netted willow,** the rare grass **Don's twitch, Highland catstail** and **alpine sandwort.**

Other notable species on Ben Lawers include **alpine lady's mantle, moss campion, alpine meadow-rue, mossy cyphel, alpine scurvy grass, twisted whitlow-grass, alpine cinquefoil, globe flower, alpine mouse-ear, three-flowered rush, alpine willowherb, roseroot, purple saxifrage, mossy saxifrage, mountain avens, yellow mountain saxifrage, whortle-leaved willow, arctic saxifrage, downy willow, mountain pansy, northern bedstraw, mountain sorrel, alpine bistort, viviparous fescue, Scottish asphodel, alpine meadow-grass, hair sedge, bluish mountain meadow-grass, jet sedge,** and **russet sedge.**

FERNS Among the montane ferns found here are **mountain bladder fern, holly fern, green spleenwort** and the rare **alpine woodsia.**

MOSSES AND LIVERWORTS Included among the montane bryophytes are the moss *Aongstroemia longipes* and the liverwort *Fossombronia incurva*, both of which were discovered for the first time in Britain in 1964.

Access

The visitors' centre is situated just off the A827 at OS map reference NN 608379 and is well signposted locally. It is open from Easter to September. The nature trail and path to the summit both start at the centre.

Loch Garten   NES 10   OS map 36   NH 9718

Loch Garten must surely be one of the best-known nature reserves in Britain. It is a reserve of the R.S.P.B., and its great claim to fame are the famous ospreys which may be watched on the nest from a wooden hide. But this $3\frac{1}{2}$ square mile (6 km²) reserve has much more to offer than just ospreys, for it includes some fine natural pine forest where a variety of other birds may be seen.

Fauna

BIRDS In addition to the **ospreys** themselves there are **crested tits, crossbills, capercaillies, blackcock, buzzards, sparrowhawks** and **siskins.**

MAMMALS Mammals include both **red** and **roe deer, foxes** and, occasionally, **otters.**

Access

No permits are needed although the viewing hide is open only from mid-April to end August to avoid excessive disturbance of the ospreys.

The Cairngorms NES 11 OS map 36 NJ 0101

Covering about 100 square miles (259 km²), the Cairngorms National Nature Reserve is easily the largest nature reserve in Britain, and one of the largest conservation areas in the whole of Europe. Most of the reserve is extremely wild mountainous country with lochs, streams and bogs. The summit of Cairn Gorm itself is on the edge of the reserve but the summit of Ben Machdui, rising to 4296 ft (1309 m) – Scotland's second highest mountain – lies just within the boundary as do several other peaks over 4000 ft (1219 m). It is hardly surprising, therefore, that the mountain flora is extraordinarily rich. In fact, 77 species of montane vascular plants have been recorded here. In addition, over 2000 acres (809 ha) to the north of the reserve are occupied by Rothiemurchus Forest; the largest, and probably the finest relict pinewood in the whole of Scotland.

The reserve lies a few miles south of Aviemore in a region which is exceptionally rich in wildlife. The Glen More Forest Park (NES 12) lies nearby, whilst the famous Loch Garten (NES 10) and Craigallechie National Nature Reserves are only a little way to the north. Caenlochan National Nature Reserve lies a few miles to the south, although it is a considerable journey away by road.

Fauna

BIRDS Both the hills themselves and the pinewoods are outstanding bird habitats. The hills hold **dotterels, greenshanks, dunlin, red grouse, ptarmigan, ring ouzels, golden plovers, snow buntings, peregrine falcons, merlins** and **golden eagles**. A few pairs of the latter nest in trees in the forests. Other forest species include **crested tits, capercaillies, Scottish crossbills, siskins, woodcock, buzzards, sparrowhawks**, and the occasional **goshawk.**

MAMMALS **Red deer** are found throughout the reserve. **Scottish wildcats, otters, foxes** and **mountain hares** are all found among the hills, whilst **roe deer, badgers** and **red squirrels** prefer to live in the pinewoods.

INVERTEBRATES The invertebrate fauna is also very rich, and over 400 species of moths alone have been recorded including the rare **mountain burnet moth**. Rothiemurchus Forest has some fine colonies of **wood ants.**

Flora

FLOWERING PLANTS The Rothiemurchus woods are predominantly of **Scots pine** with some **birch, rowan, alder, juniper** and **willow**. The herbaceous flora includes several notable rarities including four members of the wintergreen family, namely **St Olaf's candlestick**, which is restricted to this area, **yavering bells, common wintergreen** and **greater wintergreen**. Another noteworthy plant is the delightful little **twinflower** which is also only found, in this country, in northern pinewoods.

Other notable plants include **purple saxifrage, creeping lady's tresses, yellow mountain saxifrage, lesser twayblade,** Scottish **asphodel, chickweed wintergreen, grass of Parnassus, cloudberry, alpine rush** and **dwarf cornel**.

The mountains also have their rarities, which include **alpine milk vetch**, which has only been recorded in Britain from three mountain ledges, and **brook saxifrage** which has its main British stronghold here. Other extreme rarities are **alpine foxtail, tufted saxifrage, mountain bog sedge, mountain oval sedge, rock speedwell** and **woolly willow**.

The following interesting, if less rare, species have been recorded from the mountains: **mountain avens, northern bilberry, netted willow, dwarf birch, whortle-leaved willow, curved wood-rush, downy willow, spiked wood-rush, least willow, alpine lady's mantle, purple saxifrage, alpine cinquefoil, starry saxifrage, least cinquefoil, rock whitlow-grass, arctic mouse-ear, alpine meadow-grass, Scottish rush, starwort mouse-ear, moss campion, alpine mouse-ear, northern rockcress, rock sedge, mountain speedwell, hair sedge, purple hawkweed, jet sedge, alpine azalea, sheathing sedge, bearberry, stiff sedge, crowberry** and **alpine bistort**.

FERNS Among the more interesting ferns of the hills are **mountain bladder fern, parsley fern** and **alpine lady fern**.

The pteridophyte flora of the pinewoods includes **oak fern, beech fern, fir clubmoss, alpine clubmoss** and **stagshorn clubmoss**.

Access

No special permits are needed to visit the reserve and the public are free to wander over much of the area at will, although it is unwise to venture too far into the hills without proper clothing and equipment.

An exceptionally fine nature trail wanders through the forest around Loch an Eilein (NH 895075).

Glen More Forest Park NES 12 OS map 36 NH 9709

The Glen More Forest Park covers about 18 square miles (47km²) and lies some 3 miles (5km) east of Aviemore, and adjacent to the Cairngorms National Nature Reserve (NES 11). About half of the park is wooded, the remainder being mountainous country which rises to the summit of Cairn Gorm itself at 4084ft (1244m).

The area has been well developed by the Forestry Commission to cater for the thousands of tourists who flock here all the year round. A caravan park, camp site and youth hostel are all clustered around Loch Morlich where angling, sailing and canoeing are permitted. There is also a ski school and the White Lady Chairlift is an easy way of ascending Cairn Gorm for both skiers and naturalists.

Fauna

BIRDS The woodlands hold **crested tits, crossbills, siskins, capercaillies, woodcock** and **redstarts** and you may be lucky and see the **ospreys** from nearby Loch Garten fishing in Loch Morlich.

The birds of the hills include **ptarmigan, black grouse, greenshanks** and **golden eagles**.

MAMMALS The most distinctive member of the mammal fauna is the herd of about a hundred **reindeer**. These were introduced from Sweden in 1952 as a possible source of meat, but are now a tourist attraction. Some reindeer are often seen at the half-way halt on the chairlift and the owners regularly take parties to see the main herd. These trips are widely advertised in the area. Sharing the hills with the reindeer are **red deer** and **wildcats**, and **mountain hares** and **roe deer** live in the woodlands.

Flora

Much of the forested area consists of planted exotics of relatively little interest to the naturalist, although in the immediate vicinity of Loch Morlich there are some remnants of native **Scots pine** forest.

Access

The park is reached by the unclassified road which leaves the B970 at Coylumbridge. Most of the area is freely accessible and there are several nature trails through the forest, details of which are available from the Loch Morlich campsite (NH 975097).

Ythan Estuary and the Sands of Forvie
NES 13   OS map 38   NK 0227

The River Ythan meets the sea about 13 miles (21km) north of Aberdeen. Its estuary, some 3 miles (4.8 km) long and $\frac{1}{4}$ mile (400 m) wide is a well-known wintering ground for some 11,000 waders and wildfowl. To the north-east of the estuary is an extensive area of sand dunes known as the Sands of Forvie, which is a National Nature Reserve of $2\frac{3}{4}$ square miles (70.4km²).

Fauna

BIRDS The list of wintering birds includes about 7500 **pink-footed geese,** 2000 **greylags** and smaller numbers of **bean geese,** all three British **swans, common** and **velvet scoters, eiders, scaup, wigeon, goldeneye, goosanders, divers, long-tailed ducks, pochard, red-breasted mergansers,** and several thousand assorted waders, principally **knot.**

During the summer the area is famous for its **eiders**. Over 2000 pairs have bred in recent years, the largest colony in Britain. In addition to the eiders there are **arctic, Sandwich** and **little terns**, and **black-headed gulls**.

Flora

FLOWERING PLANTS The Sands of Forvie is the fifth biggest, and also one of the least disturbed, systems of sand dunes in the country. It displays the various stages of succession from mobile dunes to heathland very clearly, and has several notable species including **creeping lady's tresses, heath rush, curved sedge, separate-headed sedge, lovage, crowberry, creeping willow, cross-leaved heath** and **sea wormwood**.

FERNS **Stagshorn clubmoss** is found among the dunes, and **sea spleenwort** may be found growing on some of the low cliffs in the area.

Access

Probably the best vantage point from which to see the birds is the A975 between Newburgh and the bridge over Tarty Burn. A footpath runs from this bridge across the sand dunes, but a permit from the Nature Conservancy Council, Wynne-Edwards House, 17 Rubislaw Terrace, Aberdeen AB1 1XE, is needed to leave it.

Noup Cliffs NES 14 OS map 5 HY 3950

Noup Head lies at the western extremity of the Island of Westray in the Orkneys, and has cliffs some 200ft (61m) high which support an immense colony of nesting seabirds. The cliffs also have an interesting flora and there is an extensive area of maritime heathland above them.

Much of the cliffs is a reserve belonging to the R.S.P.B.

Fauna

BIRDS The cliffs probably have one of the largest seabird colonies in the British Isles, with some 40,000 **guillemots** and 25,000 pairs of **kittiwakes**. There are also large numbers of **razorbills, fulmars** and **shags**, and a rather smaller colony of **puffins**.

Flora

FLOWERING PLANTS Some of the more interesting species which occur on the cliffs are **moss campion, alpine meadow-rue, slender bedstraw, twisted whitlow-grass** and **thale cress. Bog pimpernel, grass of Parnassus** and **common butterwort** grow in the wet flushes.

The maritime heath behind the cliffs is dominated by **ling, bell heather** and **crowberry**, and also has **spring squill, Scottish primrose** and **sea plantain**.

FERNS The cliffs are particularly abundant in pteridophytes, and support **sea spleenwort, wall spleenwort, black spleenwort, common spleenwort, common polypody, bladder fern** and **lady fern**. The **lesser clubmoss** may be found in some of the wet flushes.

Access

The island of Westray can easily be reached from Kirkwall via the Orcadian car ferry system. Access to the cliffs is gained from the Noup Head lighthouse road. No special permits are required.

Morrone Birkwoods NES 15 OS map 43 NO 1390

This 250 acre (102 ha) wood lies on the lower slopes of 2819 ft (859 m) Morrone Mountain near Braemar, at an average height of about 500 ft (152 m). It is a good example of a Scottish birchwood, and has been designated as a National Nature Reserve. Although noted for their plant life the woods support a variety of birds and mammals.

Flora

FLOWERING PLANTS The principal tree species here is the **downy birch** and there is also a little **juniper**. The ground flora is largely dominated by grasses including **bent grass, sweet vernal grass, wood fescue** and **mountain melick**, and there is also some **bilberry, ling** and **cross-leaved heath**. More notable plants include **common wintergreen, yavering bells, chickweed wintergreen, melancholy thistle, common valerian, water avens, wood cranesbill, dog's mercury** and the delightful little **twinflower**.

Perhaps surprisingly there are also a few montane species such as **alpine cinquefoil, alpine bistort** and **northern bedstraw**. In the fertile wet flushes there are the rare **alpine rush, three-flowered rush, Scottish asphodel, yellow mountain saxifrage** and **broad-leaved cottongrass**. FERNS **Variegated horsetail** and **holly fern**.
MOSSES AND LIVERWORTS *Tritomaria polita, Leiocolea gilmanii* and *Tayloria lingulata*.

Access

The wood lies about 1 mile (1.6 km) south-west of Braemar, and can be reached via the unclassified road which runs westwards from Braemar along the Dee Valley. No special permits are needed, but visitors are asked to keep to the marked paths.

Loch Fleet and Mound Alderwoods

NES 16 OS map 21 NH 7996

Loch Fleet is the name given to the estuary of the River Fleet, and it is situated a little way north of the Dornoch Firth roughly midway between Dornoch and Golspie. A road and rail embankment was built across part of the estuary during the early years of the last century, and this has had the effect of cutting off part of the upper estuary from the sea. This section has since been colonized by alder woodlands and is now a National Nature Reserve of 659 acres (266 ha). Loch Fleet itself is a reserve of the Scottish Wildlife Trust.

Fauna

BIRDS The estuary is important on account of the wildfowl which regularly winter there. These include quite large numbers of **mallard, teal, wigeon, goldeneye, eiders, red-breasted mergansers** and **shelducks,** and smaller numbers of **velvet scoters** and **long-tailed ducks.** The wintering waders include numerous **oystercatchers, ringed plovers, turnstones, curlews, bar-tailed godwits, redshanks, greenshanks, knot, dunlin, sanderling** and, occasionally, **ruff.**

Flora

FLOWERING PLANTS The woodland behind the embankment is dominated by **alder, willow** and **birch,** and is the largest woodland of its kind in Britain. The herbaceous flora includes **soft rush, jointed rush, common cottongrass, dwarf yellow sedge, star sedge, remote sedge, common spike-rush, lesser spearwort, marsh cinquefoil, meadowsweet, bog myrtle, purple moor-grass, brown bent, Yorkshire fog, marsh ragwort, marsh pennywort, marsh bedstraw, devilsbit scabious** and **red rattle. Scots pine** grows on some of the higher ground.

The embankment allows a certain amount of sea water to seep through, and so a brackish flora has developed nearby. This includes **chestnut sedge, slender spike-rush, sea arrow-grass** and **sea plantain.** There is also a small area of saltmarsh on the seaward side of the embankment which has **sea meadow grass, red fescue, few-flowered spike rush, chestnut sedge, knotted pearlwort, seaside centaury** and **eyebright.**

Access

Quite good views over the estuary can be had from the A9 and other nearby roads. The Mound Alderwoods themselves are only open to permit holders, however. Permits may be requested from the Nature Conservancy Council at 9 Culduthel Road, Inverness IV2 4AG.

Copinsay NES 17 OS map 6 HY 6101

Copinsay is a small sandstone island of 375 acres (152 ha) which lies about 4 miles (6.5 km) east of the Orcadian mainland. It is a reserve of the R.S.P.B. and is noted for its immense populations of seabirds, although there is also some floral interest.

Fauna

BIRDS The 150 ft (46 m) high cliffs on the south-east face of the island are home to about 30,000 pairs of **guillemots,** 10,000 pairs of **kittiwakes** and over 13,000 pairs of **fulmars,** 1000 pairs of **razorbills,** and smaller numbers of **black guillemots,** and **shags.** There is also a sizeable colony of **greater black-backed gulls** and a few **puffins, arctic terns, rock doves** and **rock pipits.**

Flora

FLOWERING PLANTS Much of the island is dominated by sheep pasture with **red fescue, Yorkshire fog** and the **tufted hair-grass** but the cliffs, especially those on the north side, have some more interesting plants such as **sea aster, sea pearlwort, sea spurrey** and **sea meadow-grass**. The uncommon **oyster plant** grows in some profusion on neighbouring Corn Holm Island, which is connected to Copinsay by a storm beach at low tide. FERNS **Sea spleenwort** may also be found on the northern cliffs of Copinsay.

Access

No special permits are needed to visit the island and it can be visited, by boat, from Skaill (tel. Deerness 252).

Loch of Kinnordy NES 18 OS map 54 NO 3654

The Loch of Kinnordy is a small eutrophic loch (see page 38) which covers about 163 acres (66 ha) and lies near to Kirriemuir. It is an R.S.P.B. reserve, and is mainly of interest on account of its wintering wildfowl.

Fauna

BIRDS The loch is used as a winter roost by up to 2500 **greylag geese** and smaller numbers of **mallard, teal, wigeon, tufted ducks, shovelers** and, occasionally, **whooper swans**.

Flora

FLOWERING PLANTS The surrounding reed beds hold **false bulrush, branched bur-reed, bottle sedge, marestail, bogbean** and **greater spearwort**, as well as **common reed**.

Access

The reserve is open only on certain days of the week, and visiting arrangements may change from time to time. Intending visitors are advised to check with the warden before planning their visit. The address is: The Warden, The Flat, Kinnordy Home Farm, Kirriemuir DD8 5ER. There is a small admission charge.

Loch of Strathbeg NES 19 OS map 30 NK 0759

This 500 acre (202 ha) lake is the largest wet slack in Britain. It lies between Fraserburgh and Peterhead and about $\frac{1}{2}$ mile (approx. 800 m) from the sea. An R.S.P.B. reserve, it is internationally important as a refuge for wintering wildfowl. The surrounding reed beds and dunes are also interesting from the botanical point of view.

Fauna

BIRDS The lake is used by about 8000 **pink-footed geese**, over 6000 **greylags**, over 2000 **mallard**, up to 2000 **tufted duck**, and smaller numbers of **pochard, teal, wigeon, goosanders, goldeneye, mute swans, whooper swans** and **Bewick's swans.**

Flora

FLOWERING PLANTS There are some extensive reed beds at the north-western end of the lake where the flora includes **common spike-rush, amphibious bistort, slender-leaved pondweed, fennel pondweed, perfoliate pondweed** and **shoreweed.**

The surrounding dunes are lime-rich and support **lovage, grass of Parnassus, field gentian, Baltic rush** and **early marsh orchid.**

Access

The reserve is open throughout the year but only by prior arrangement, so intending visitors must check with the warden first. His address is: The Lythe, Crimonmogate, Lonmay, Fraserburgh AB4 4UB. There is a small admission fee.

Montrose Basin NES 20 OS map 54 NO 6858

The Montrose Basin is the large estuarine basin of the River South Esk, and is immediately adjacent to Montrose itself. During low tides, the basin empties to reveal about 3 square miles (8 km²) of mudflats which attract many wildfowl. The basin is a local nature reserve, largely owned by the Scottish Wildlife Trust.

Fauna

BIRDS The Basin supports 6000 **pink-footed geese** and 1000–2000 **greylag geese** but there has been a serious decline in these numbers. The Scottish Wildlife Trust has recently protected the area, however, and it is encouraging to see the geese returning in their former numbers.

Up to 3500 **wigeon** still regularly use the site, along with smaller numbers of **pintails, eiders, teal, tufted ducks, shelducks** and **mallard.** Waders are also well represented and include **knot, oystercatchers, curlews, dunlin, redshanks, bar-tailed godwits, golden plover** and **ringed plover,** and up to 10,000 **common, arctic** and **Sandwich terns** gather here in autumn.

Access

Good views over the basin may be had from the A92 Montrose to Arbroath road and other surrounding roads. Observation hides are available to keyholders – details from the Scottish Wildlife Trust, 25 Johnston Terrace, Edinburgh.

North Hill (Papa Westray) NES 21 OS map 5 HY 4953

This is an R.S.P.B. reserve which lies on the island of Papa Westray in the Orkneys.

Fauna

BIRDS The main interest here is the enormous colony of **arctic terns** which

(Above) Part of the woodlands flanking Whitbarrow Scar (see page 106).

(Below) A wet slack at Ainsdale Dunes (see page 107).

Vertical face of Bempton Cliffs R.S.P.B. reserve (see page 118).

currently contains about 6500 pairs and is one of the largest British colonies. There are also about 90 pairs of **arctic skuas** and several species of cliff-nesting seabirds including densely packed colonies of **guillemots, razorbills** and **kittiwakes**.

The site is also of interest in that it was the last known breeding station of the now extinct great auk.

Access

The island is easily accessible on the Orcadian ferry network, but visitors are asked to contact the warden before entering the reserve, and preferably in advance of any visit. His address is: The Warden, c/o Gowrie, Papa Westray, Orkney KW17 2BU.

St Cyrus SS 1 OS map 45 NO 7464

The National Nature Reserve of St Cyrus lies on the east coast of Scotland a few miles north of Montrose and on the estuary of the North River Esk. Its 227 acres (91 ha) include sand flats, saltmarsh, sand dunes and some 200 ft (61 m) high cliffs.

Fauna

BIRDS Several common shore birds may be found among the dunes and saltmarshes including **redshanks, oystercatchers, ringed plovers, shelducks** and **eiders**. There is also a colony of **little terns** which is renowned for its year by year fluctuations. In 1974 it was the largest colony in Britain with over 100 pairs whilst in other years they may reject the site. Numerous **fulmars** nest on the cliffs.

Flora

FLOWERING PLANTS The sand dunes hold some interesting species such as **frosted orache, maiden pink** and **spring vetch**, while the uncommon **Nottingham catchfly, clustered bellflower, wild liquorice** and **rough clover** grow on the cliffs.

FERNS The curious **moonwort** grows among the dunes.

Access

The reserve may be found about 6 miles (10 km) north of Montrose and close to the main A92, from which it is easily accessible. No special permits are required.

Loch of the Lowes SS 2 OS map 53 NO 0443

Loch of the Lowes is set amid some attractive mixed woodlands and is managed as a nature reserve by the Scottish Wildlife Trust. Its main claim to fame is that a pair of ospreys regularly nest there, but there is much else to see besides.

The reserve covers a total of 242 acres (98 ha).

Fauna

BIRDS In addition to the **ospreys**, which may be watched on the nest from a public hide, you may see **sparrowhawks, buzzards, kestrels, great spotted woodpeckers, green woodpeckers, crossbills, siskins, redstarts** and **great crested grebes. Slavonian grebes** have nested on occasions.

In winter **greylag geese, whooper swans, wigeon, pintails, shovelers, goldeneye, red-breasted mergansers** and **goosanders** are all regular visitors.

Flora

FLOWERING PLANTS A variety of aquatic species grow in the loch itself and these include **water lobelia, bogbean** and **water lilies.**

The woodlands are mainly of **oak** and **pine.**

Access

The reserve lies just east of Dunkeld by the A923. There is a visitors' centre, which is open from April to September, and a public hide which offers good views over the area. Elsewhere on the reserve, however, access is not permitted except adjacent to the road on the southern shore.

Tentsmuir Point and Morton Lochs
SS 3 OS map 54 NO 5027

Tentsmuir Point lies on the southern bank of the Tay Estuary just across the river from Dundee. The mudflats and sandbanks just off the point are a notable haunt of wintering wildfowl and waders, and there is also an extensive system of sand dunes which are of interest to botanists. Both dunes and mudflats are included in the Tentsmuir National Nature Reserve which covers 2 square miles (5km^2).

A little way inland from the Point are three small pools known as the Morton Lochs and which are such a magnet to migratory birds that they, too, have been scheduled as a National Nature Reserve.

Fauna

BIRDS One of the main interests at Tentsmuir are duck, and autumn sees the build-up of a large flock of **eiders**, sometimes up to 15,000 strong. **Mallard, wigeon, scaup, common scoters, shelducks, red-breasted mergansers, goldeneye** and **long-tailed ducks** are also frequent winter visitors as are **oystercatchers, grey plovers, sanderling, dunlin, redshanks** and **ringed plovers. Terns** are frequently noted on passage.

About 150 bird species have been recorded from Morton Lochs. The most regular are **gadwall, pintail, teal, wigeon, shovelers, tufted ducks** and **mallard.**

MAMMALS Both **grey** and **common seals** are often seen in the area.

Flora

FLOWERING PLANTS The sand dunes at Tentsmuir Point comprise one of the fastest growing dune systems in Britain. Most of the habitats associated with dunes may be found here including mobile and fixed dunes, slacks and developing scrubland of **willow, alder** and **birch**. The area is not, unfortunately, particularly lime-rich, but despite this several notable species may be found including **lyme grass, purple milk-vetch, coral-root orchid, Baltic rush, grass of Parnassus** and **crowberry**.

Access

Both sites are best reached from Tayport. Morton Lochs lie near to the B945 about 1½ miles (2.5 km) south of Tayport and may be reached from the track which leaves the road at NO 453260. The lochs are overlooked by a number of hides, but these are only available to permit holders. Applications for permits should be sent to the Nature Conservancy Council, 12 Hope Terrace, Edinburgh EH9 2AS.

From Morton Lochs, the track continues through the vast Tentsmuir Forest and out on to the dunes. No special permits are required here.

Loch Leven SS 4 OS map 58 NO 1501

Loch Leven is an exceptionally fertile lowland lake which lies roughly half way between Perth and the Forth Road Bridge. The biology of the lake has been extensively studied. Several interesting food chains have been investigated here and numerous planktonic and benthic organisms have been recorded, but for most naturalists the main attraction of the loch is its wildfowl. Indeed, Loch Leven reputedly holds the largest population of breeding duck in Britain, and is famous among birdwatchers for the vast congregations of geese which winter here and use the lake as a stopover during their migrations.

The loch is designated as a National Nature Reserve which covers 6 square miles (15.9 km²) and the R.S.P.B. also maintains a sanctuary at Vane Farm on the southern shore of the loch.

Fauna

BIRDS The breeding wildfowl comprises mainly **tufted ducks** (over 500 pairs) and **mallard** (about 400 pairs) with smaller numbers of **gadwall, wigeon, shovelers, shelducks, teal** and **mute swans**.

The winter populations of wildfowl are enormous. Up to 12,000 **pink-footed geese** and 4000 **greylags** gather here towards the end of September before dispersing elsewhere. The wintering ducks include some 4000 **tufted ducks**, over 2000 **mallard**, 1000 **pochard** and smaller numbers of **teal, wigeon, goldeneye, shovelers** and **goosanders**. A flock of **whooper swans**, often in excess of 200, also winter here.

Access

Unfortunately, a great deal of the lakeshore is inaccessible, but there are four points from where the loch can be viewed. The best is undoubtedly the R.S.P.B. refuge at Vane Farm which is on the southern shore of the loch at NT 160990. The farm covers some 450 acres (182 ha) and has a splendid visitors' centre and nature trail.

The shore is also accessible at Kirkgate Park, Kinross (on the west side), from the A911, about 2 miles (3 km) north-east of Kinross.

Isle of May SS 5 OS map 59 NT 6599

The Isle of May is a National Nature Reserve lying about 5 miles (8 km) south-east of Anstruther in the Firth of Forth. It covers some 140 acres (56 ha) and is largely bounded by cliffs which rise to about 150 ft (46 m). It is a well-known watchpoint for migratory birds and has a bird observatory.

Fauna

BIRDS A wide variety of seabirds breed on the island, and these include about 12,000 pairs of **guillemots**, a similar number of **puffins** and 5000 pairs of **kittiwakes**. Rather less than 1000 pairs of **shags** also nest here and there are small numbers of **razorbills** and **fulmars**.

Both **herring gulls** and **lesser black-backed gulls** have large colonies here which have now increased to such a size that their numbers have to be controlled.

Other breeding birds here include a large colony of **eiders**, also **rock pipits**, and **oystercatchers**.

The list of migrant birds which have been recorded on the Isle of May is far too long to give in full, but among the more exciting species are **barred warblers, bluethroats, ortolan buntings, Lapland buntings** and **pine grosbeaks**. More frequently seen migrants include **arctic** and **great skuas, whimbrel, little stints, wrynecks, spotted redshanks** and **purple sandpipers**.

MAMMALS The mammals include **rabbits** and a large **grey seal** rookery which produces perhaps 600 pups annually.

Flora

FLOWERING PLANTS The island is not noted for its plant life, but there are one or two notable species such as **English stonecrop, lovage, early scurvy grass, thrift** and **sea campion**.

FERNS **Sea spleenwort** grows here.

MOSSES AND LIVERWORTS The liverwort *Frullania germana* may be found growing on some of the cliffs.

Access

Boats regularly sail to The May from Anstruther. No permission is needed for day visits and anyone wishing to stay at the observatory can obtain details from Mrs R. Cowper, 9 Oxgangs Road, Edinburgh E10 7BG.

Bass Rock SS 6 OS map 67 NT 6087

Bass Rock has one of the best-known and most easily accessible gannet colonies in the British Isles. It lies about 3 miles (5 km) from North Berwick, where the Firth of Forth meets the North Sea. It is not large, a mere 300 ft (91 m) high and less than $\frac{1}{2}$ mile (812 m) in circumference, but despite this it is a most spectacular island and its sheer rock walls are covered with an almost unbroken cloak of dazzling white gannets and many thousands of other seabirds.

Fauna

BIRDS The **gannet** colony here is the oldest known in Britain, and was first recorded as long ago as 1516. Indeed the gannet takes its latin name *Sula bassana* from the rock. About 10,500 pairs currently nest here.

There are also good numbers of **puffins**, which nest in the crumbling walls of the old fortress and numerous **fulmars, kittiwakes, razorbills, guillemots, shags, herring gulls** and **lesser black-backed gulls**.

The rock is particularly attractive to bird photographers since the seabirds here are much more accessible than is the case at many other colonies.

Flora

FLOWERING PLANTS The flora is not particularly outstanding, but two species worthy of note are the **tree mallow** and **Babington's orache**.

Access

Local boat owners run trips around the rock every day throughout the summer months and they are well worth the cost. Landing is by prior permission only and intending visitors are advised to contact Mr Fred Marr of 24 Victoria Road, North Berwick. Staying overnight on the island is not permissible.

The Forth Islands SS 7 OS maps 66 & 67 NT 5687

There are many small islands in the Firth of Forth, but there is a group of four not far offshore from North Berwick which are of outstanding interest to naturalists. The islands are Fidra, Eyebroughty, The Lamb and Craigleith; the first three being reserves of the R.S.P.B. All are very low-lying and are of particular note for their tern colonies.

Fauna

BIRDS Between them, the islands provide a home for four species of **terns**, namely **common, arctic, Sandwich** and the rare **roseate**. The latter two have some of their biggest British colonies here, particularly on Fidra and Craigleith, although the birds tend to shift from one island to another quite frequently. Other breeding birds include **fulmars, kittiwakes, shags, cormorants** and **guillemots** although none are present in large numbers.

Another notable feature of the islands is as a moulting ground for **eiders**, and during June and July up to 2000 of them congregate here, especially on Eyebroughty.

Access

There are regular trips to all four islands from North Berwick during the summer months. It is usually possible to land on some of the islands but not others, in order to prevent too much disturbance to the rarer terns.

Aberlady Bay SS 8 OS map 66 NT 4680

Aberlady Bay is a Local Nature Reserve of the East Lothian District Council. It covers $2\frac{1}{4}$ square miles (5.8 km²), mainly of sand dunes and saltmarsh, and is of interest on account of its tern colonies and wintering wildfowl. It is situated on the south bank of the Firth of Forth, about half way between Prestonpans and North Berwick close to the A198.

Fauna

BIRDS The breeding birds include **common, arctic, Sandwich** and **little terns, shelducks, eiders** and **ringed plovers.** In winter you may see **pink-footed geese, wigeon, common** and **velvet scoters, red-breasted mergansers, long-tailed ducks, Bewick's** and **whooper swans, knot, black-tailed godwits, bar-tailed godwits** and possibly **wood sandpipers, red-necked grebes, Slavonian grebes** and various **divers.**

Flora

FLOWERING PLANTS The flora is of secondary importance but does include **sea buckthorn** and **grass of Parnassus**, both of which grow among the dunes.

Access

A footpath leads from Aberlady itself into the reserve. There are no restrictions on access although some of the more vulnerable areas may be closed off during the nesting season.

Flanders Moss SS 9 OS map 57 NS 6397

The Upper Forth basin once had some of the largest areas of raised bog in Britain. Much of this extensive mire system has now been drained and 'improved', however, but a 110 acre (44ha) remnant is of interest both on account of its birdlife and its flora. The largest part of this site is a National Nature Reserve.

Fauna

BIRDS The moss is well known as a winter roost, and during the summer months the moss holds several species of breeding birds including **curlews, grey herons, red grouse** and **black-headed gulls.**

Flora

FLOWERING PLANTS A speciality of the reserve is the rare **Labrador tea plant**. Other notable species are **bog rosemary, bog asphodel, cranberry, bog myrtle, ling, cross-leaved heath, hares-tail cottongrass, white beak-sedge** and **deer grass**.

MOSSES These include *Sphagnum tenellum, S. magellanicum, S. papillosum, S. rubellum, S. cuspidatum, S. recurvum, S. fuscum, S. molle, S. palustre, S. fimbriatum* and *Polytrichum commune*.

Access

The reserve lies just west of the B822 about 6 miles (10 km) south of Callander, but it may only be visited by permission of the Scottish Wildlife Trust – applications for permits should be addressed to the Scottish Wildlife Trust at 25 Johnston Terrace, Edinburgh EH1 2NH – and from the Nature Conservancy Council. Access to all parts of the site is across private land.

Ailsa Craig SS 10 OS map 76 NX 0299

Ailsa Craig is a small uninhabited island situated about 10 miles (16 km) west of Girvan in the Firth of Clyde. It is extremely rugged and is surrounded by cliffs, some of which rise sheer to over 400 ft (120 m). The summit is 1111 ft (338 m) above sea level. The island is privately owned and is important on account of its seabird populations, particularly its gannet colony which is probably the third largest in Britain.

Fauna

BIRDS About 20,000 pairs of **gannets** currently nest on The Craig, which also holds about half that number of **kittiwakes**, about 4000 pairs of **guillemots**, and about 2000 pairs of **razorbills**.

There are smaller colonies of **fulmars** and **eiders** and a few pairs of **black guillemots** and **shags**. **Herring gulls** and **lesser black-backed gulls** also breed in good numbers with fewer **greater black-backed gulls**.

Puffins once numbered hundreds of thousands until a shipwreck at the turn of the century brought brown rats to the island. Puffins, of course, are burrow nesters and therefore very susceptible to predation by rats and now only a handful remain.

Other nesting birds include **rock pipits, rock doves, twite, wrens**, and occasionally **oystercatchers**. The island also supports at least one pair of **ravens** and **peregrine falcons** nest in most years. Both **carrion crows** and **hooded crows** may be seen here.

MAMMALS The island is overrun by both **brown rats** and **rabbits**. **Pygmy shrews** are also present and both **common seals** and **grey seals** are frequently seen in the surrounding seas although they do not breed on the island.

Flora

FLOWERING PLANTS The flora is not particularly outstanding, but there are one or two species which are worthy of note including **tree mallow, navelwort, English stonecrop, cliff spurrey, sea radish, sea campion, wood sage, thrift** and masses of **bluebell.**

FERNS **Bracken** covers quite large areas of the island and **common buckler fern** is found in places. **Sea spleenwort** may be found in some of the caves.

Access

Permission to stay on the island should be sought from Mr I. Girvan, 'Millcraig', Henrietta St, Girvan. Local boat owners will take you across.

Once on the island, it is possible to walk completely around it, below the cliffs, but only at low tide. There is also a path ascending the cliffs.

Threave Wildfowl Refuge SS 11 OS map 84 NX 7460

The Galloway district of southern Scotland has long been well known to wildfowlers and birdwatchers alike on account of its wintering geese. The lower reaches of the Rivers Ken and Dee and their associated lochs and swamplands are particularly interesting areas, and wintering geese are endemic throughout this region.

It is an obvious place to create a wildfowl sanctuary and the National Trust for Scotland have done precisely that, at Threave. The refuge lies about $1\frac{1}{2}$ miles (2.5m) south-west of Castle Douglas near to the A75.

Fauna

BIRDS The reserve includes the feeding and roosting grounds of a large variety of wildfowl including some 1500 **greylag geese**, several hundred **Greenland white-fronted geese, pink-footed geese** and **bean geese. Barnacle, brent** and **Canada geese** are also recorded quite frequently, **whooper swans** are regular and **Bewick's swans** are occasional visitors.

The ducks include **wigeon, mallard, teal, pintails, shovelers, golden-eye, goosanders, gadwalls, smew** and **scaup. Herons, little grebes** and **cormorants** are also frequent visitors.

Access

The reserve is open to the public from the first of November until the end of March, and the Trust has provided several observation hides for use by the visiting public. Visitors are asked to keep to approach roads which are signposted locally.

Mull of Galloway SS 12 OS map 82 NX 1530

The Mull of Galloway is a small rocky headland which lies at the southern tip of the Rhinns Peninsula about 20 miles (32 km) south of Stranraer. One of the principal attractions here is the seabird colonies, and part of the area is managed as a reserve by the R.S.P.B. but the flora is also interesting.

Fauna

BIRDS The 280 ft (85 m) high cliffs have small nesting colonies of **guil-lemots, razorbills** and **kittiwakes** with lesser numbers of **cormorants** and **shags**. The best colonies are on the southern cliffs in the vicinity of the lighthouse.

Six miles (10 km) to the east, in Luce Bay, are several tiny rocky islands known as the Scare Rocks which have a small, but increasing, **gannet** colony.

Flora

FLOWERING PLANTS The extremely rare **purple mountain milk-vetch** has been recorded growing along the cliffs here and this is its only known location in southern Scotland. The site is also notable as the northernmost British limit for at least three other flowering plants, namely **golden samphire, rock samphire** and **rock sea lavender**.

Other interesting species are **roseroot, lovage, spring squill, purple milk-vetch, yellow vetch, cliff spurrey, bloody crane's bill, sea campion, English stonecrop** and **thrift**.

Access

The A716 runs all the way down the Rhinns Peninsula from Stranraer as far as Drummore. From Drummore, take the B7041 southwards for about $2\frac{1}{2}$ miles (4 km) until it joins the minor road which takes you to the lighthouse, right out on the Mull. No special permits are required.

Caerlaverock SS 13 OS maps 84 & 85 NY 0766

The huge estuary of the Solway Firth covers about 100 square miles (260 km²) of mudflats and saltmarsh and is undoubtedly one of the finest refuges for wintering wildfowl in Britain. Some of the best areas are protected by the National Nature Reserve of Caerlaverock which is about 7 miles (11 km) south-east of Dumfries and covers 21 square miles (54.6 km²) about $2\frac{1}{4}$ square miles (6 km²) of which are saltmarsh, the remainder sand and mud. The Wildfowl Trust also has a reserve at nearby Eastpark Farm and there are several other good viewpoints which overlook the estuary.

Fauna

BIRDS **Barnacle geese** are one of the main attractions, over 8000 of them having been counted here in recent years. Spitzbergen is the summer home of these geese, whereas the **pink-footed** and **greylag geese** and **whooper swans** which share the Solway with them are mainly from Iceland. Among the ducks which may be encountered are **pintail, wigeon, mergansers, scaup** and **shelduck**.

The Solway is also about the fifth largest haunt of wintering waders in Britain and can hold up to 80,000 in a good season. The principal species are **oystercatchers, knot, dunlin, curlews, golden plovers** and **redshanks**.

About 75 other bird species have been recorded passing over the estuary on migration, including **peregrine falcons** and **merlins**.

During the summer months the saltmarshes hold nesting **lapwings, redshanks, dunlin, oystercatchers, lesser black-backed gulls** and **black-headed gulls**.

Flora
FLOWERING PLANTS The flora is not of outstanding interest, but there are one or two notable species growing on the marshes such as **saltmarsh rush, chestnut sedge** and **northern marsh orchid**.

Access
Visitors may walk over most of the reserve, but are advised not to go out on to the foreshore because of the danger from fast-running tides. The Wildfowl Trust reserve at Eastpark Farm caters admirably for birdwatchers and has a number of hides and displays on wildlife, etc. It may be found at NY 052656. There is a small admission charge.

Quite good views over the estuary may also be had from Carsethorn and Southerness Point, both of which are to the east of the River Nith, and from the B725, a few miles south of Dumfries.

St Abb's Head SS 14 OS map 67 NT 9269
St Abb's Head is a nature reserve which is owned by the National Trust for Scotland and managed in co-operation with the Scottish Wildlife Trust. It consists of a series of cliffs which rise to a maximum height of about 300 ft (90 m), but there are accessible beaches.

Fauna
BIRDS There are large numbers of breeding seabirds on the cliffs including 16,000 pairs of **kittiwakes**, over 15,000 pairs of **guillemots** and smaller numbers of **razorbills, fulmars, shags** and a few **puffins** and **rock pipits**.

Flora
FLOWERING PLANTS The cliff flora includes **roseroot, purple milk-vetch, thrift, sea campion, lovage, spring sandwort, kidney vetch,** and **common rock-rose**.

Access
St Abb's Head is best reached by the track which leaves the B6438 about half a mile from St Abb's village.

Galloway Forest Park SS 15 OS maps 77 & 83 NX 4285
The Galloway Forest Park lies to the north of Newton Stewart, and covers something in the region of 180 square miles (about 466 km^2). The western part of the park is occupied by the Glentrool Forest, whilst to the east are upland pastures and mountains including Merrick which, at 2770 ft (843 m), is the highest peak in southern Scotland.

The entire park is run by the Forestry Commission.

Fauna

BIRDS The hills within the park are quite rich in birdlife and have breeding snipe, dunlin, curlews and **golden plovers**. Merlins and **red grouse** occur in heathery areas, and there are **ring ouzels** on higher ground. There are also **ravens, hooded crows, peregrines** and one or two pairs of **golden eagles**.

Hen harriers and short-eared owls occur where the hills have been planted with young conifers, and **black grouse** are also frequent. The older, more established forests have **redpolls, siskins, willow tits** and **buzzards**, and **crossbills** have bred on occasions.

MAMMALS Both **red deer** and **roe deer** inhabit the area, the former on the hills and the latter in the forests. There are also several herds of **feral goats** along with **mountain hares** and **foxes**.

REPTILES AND AMPHIBIANS **Adders** and **common lizards** are found in suitable habitats throughout the park.

Flora

FLOWERING PLANTS The Glentrool Forest, which covers about 25 square miles (65 km²) is almost wholly composed of exotic conifers although there are a few oakwoods at the south-western corner of Loch Trool (NX 400788).

The hills have a variety of vegetation. Merrick itself is largely upland sheep pasture although it supports a few alpines on higher ground. These include **purple hawkweed, starry saxifrage, mossy saxifrage, roseroot, alpine meadow-rue, alpine bistort**, a montane variety of **thrift, downy willow** and, in wet flushes, **purple mountain saxifrage**.

The hills of Craignaw (NX 4583) and Dungeon Hill (NX 4685) are more heathery with **ling, bilberry, juniper** and **great wood-rush**.

FERNS **Wilson's filmy fern** is quite common throughout the area.

MOSSES AND LIVERWORTS Several interesting bryophytes may be found growing among the hills including extensive *Rhacomitrium* heath on the summit of Merrick. Other species include *Herberta hutchinsiae, Campylopus setifolius, Dicranodontium uncinatum, Pleurozia purpurea, Anastrepta orcadensis* and *Bazzania tricrenata*.

Access

The park lies to the east of the A714 Newton Stewart to Girvan road. There are numerous footpaths over the area, and Glentrool Forest is well provided with nature trails, camp sites and picnic places. There is a superb little wildlife museum just outside the park on the shore of Clatteringshaws Loch at NX 553765.

There is also a **wild goat** reserve alongside the A712 near to Murray's Monument (NX 491721). The area around Loch Trool (NX 4180) is also one of their favourite haunts.

Leighton Moss NW 1 OS map 97 SD 4875

Leighton Moss is an R.S.P.B. reserve which is situated about 3 miles (5 km) north of Carnforth. It covers some 330 acres (133 ha) of fenland and includes three or four large meres. One of the main attractions is the colony of bitterns which nest here.

Fauna

BIRDS About 12 pairs of **bitterns** currently nest on the reserve which is one of their few northern strongholds. The reserve is also home to one of the most northerly colonies of **reed warblers** in Britain, and there is also a colony of **black-headed gulls**. Other regular breeders are **mallard, teal, pochard, shovelers, tufted ducks, bearded tits, water rails, woodcock, grasshopper warblers, sedge warblers, green woodpeckers, great spotted woodpeckers, snipe** and **little grebes. Spotted crakes** have been known to breed, and **garganey** occasionally do so.

Regular winter visitors include **mallard, teal, shovelers, pintail, tufted ducks, gadwall** and **mute swans**, and **ospreys** and **marsh harriers** are often seen on passage.

MAMMALS Leighton Moss must be one of the best places in England for watching **otters. Red deer; roe deer** and occasionally **red squirrels** visit the reserve also.

Flora

FLOWERING PLANTS There are some extensive reed beds and small areas of **willow** carr but the reserve is not noted for its plant life. Probably the most distinguished species is the **northern marsh orchid**.

Access

A public footpath runs across the reserve and on this the R.S.P.B. have constructed a hide for use by the general public (SD 482751). There are other hides on the reserve which are open only on certain days of the week throughout the year. Details can be obtained from The Warden, Myers Farmhouse, Silverdale, Carnforth, LA5 0SW.

There is also a visitors' centre at SD 477750.

Arnside Knott and Eaves Wood

NW 2 OS map 97 SD 4577 & 4676

Arnside Knott is a low limestone hill which lies about 5 miles (8 km) north-west of Carnforth. It is a local beauty spot and is well known on account of the magnificent view from the summit, 517 ft (158 m) high. Much of the hill is dominated by calcareous grassland but there are also areas of woodland and scrub.

Eaves Wood, which lies about 1 mile (1.6 km) to the south, is a mixed woodland. Both sites belong to the National Trust, and Eaves Wood is jointly managed with the Lancashire Naturalists' Trust.

Fauna

BIRDS Woodcock, **great spotted woodpeckers** and **green woodpeckers** occur at both sites, and **lesser spotted woodpeckers** have been recorded from Arnside Knott. The latter is also noted for its **nightingales**.

MAMMALS Arnside Knott is occasionally visited by **red deer**.

INVERTEBRATES The **Scotch argus butterfly** has one of its very few English haunts at Arnside.

Flora

FLOWERING PLANTS Arnside Knott is noted for its population of the celebrated **Teesdale violet** which is found at only two other British sites. Other notable species here are **dark red helleborine, burnt orchid, fly orchid, birdsnest orchid, fingered sedge, spring cinquefoil, squinancy wort, carline thistle, spiked speedwell, Solomon's seal, green helleborine, hairy violet, rock-rose, buckthorn, spindle, whitebeam** and **juniper**.

Eaves Wood was originally an **ash** wood, but it now also includes **oak, birch, yew, Scots pine, larch** and **hazel**. Among the more interesting herbs are **spurge laurel, herb Paris, stinking hellebore, birdsnest orchid, dark red helleborine, fingered sedge, bloody cranesbill** and **dropwort**.

FERNS The rare **maidenhair fern** and the **rigid buckler fern** both grow at Arnside Knott.

Access

Both sites are freely open to the public and are easily accessible. There is a nature trail in Eaves Wood.

Roudsea Wood NW 3 OS map 97 SD 3382

Roudsea Wood is a National Nature Reserve of 287 acres (116 ha) which lies $3\frac{1}{2}$ miles (5.5 km) north-east of Ulverston in Cumbria. It lies across two parallel ridges; one of limestone, the other of slate. In each case the floral diversity of the woods reflects the nature of the underlying rocks. Between the two ridges is an area of fen, whilst in the east the wood merges into a raised bog, and to the north and west it gives way to estuarine marshes and mudflats. The habitats represented are thus very diverse and the floral wealth of the area is of exceptional interest.

Fauna

BIRDS **Sparrowhawks, green** and **great spotted woodpeckers, wood-cock, redstarts, blackcaps, marsh tits, garden warblers, whitethroats** and **yellowhammers** are among the numerous birds recorded.

MAMMALS **Roe deer** are resident here, and both **red** and **fallow deer** are frequent visitors.

INVERTEBRATES The woods are noted for their **moths** and have several rarities such as the beautiful **snout**, the **red-necked footman**, **satin lutestring** and **white marked moth**.

The adjacent bogs (Fish House Moss – SD 335827; Deer Dyke Moss – SD 337822; and Stribers Moss – SD 346814) are even richer in Lepidoptera (butterflies and moths), over 300 species having been recorded including the **scarce prominent** and the **silver hook**.

Flora

FLOWERING PLANTS The western slate ridge has woods of **sessile oak** with some **birch** and **rowan**, and the field layer is largely dominated by **bracken**. The eastern limestone ridge, by contrast, has woods of **pedunculate oak**, **ash** and some **yew**, and the field layer includes **sand leek**, **columbine**, **pyramidal orchid**, **fly orchid**, **birdsnest orchid**, **lily of the valley**, **star of Bethlehem**, **giant bellflower**, **pale St John's wort**, **toothwort**, **fingered sedge**, **stone bramble**, **ploughman's spikenard**, **common gromwell** and **dog's mercury**.

Between the two ridges is an area of fen which is nourished by nutrient rich ground water draining from the limestone. **Large yellow sedge** – which is only known from one other British locality – grows here along with **purple small reed**, and there are also areas of **birch** and **alder** carrs.

In the boggy area to the east, yet other plant communities may be found which contain **bog rosemary**, **bog asphodel** and **common sundew**, whilst in the north and west, the wood grades first into **alder** woodland, then into the Leven Estuary where **seaside centaury** and **brookweed** may be found.

FERNS The limestone ridge supports both **royal fern** and **adder's-tongue**, and **marsh fern** grows in the fenland between the ridges.

Access

A public footpath crosses the reserve from Greenodd (SD 315825) to Haverthwaite (SD 345836) but away from this the woods are strictly private. Permits are, however, available from the Regional Officer, North West Regional Office, Nature Conservancy Council, Blackwell, Bowness-on-Windermere, Windermere, Cumbria LA23 3JR.

Grizedale Forest NW 4 OS map 97 SD 3394

Grizedale Forest is a Forestry Commission plantation which lies between Lake Windermere and Coniston Water in the Lake District. It covers almost 12 square miles (31 km²) and, although the main purpose is to grow timber, the Commission has made a genuine effort at Grizedale to enrich the wildlife of the forest and has provided a wide range of facilities for naturalists.

Fauna

BIRDS **Capercaillies** have been introduced, as has the exotic **Reeve's pheasant**, although neither seems to have been very successful. Britain's most northerly nest of the **golden oriole** was found here in 1958.

There are also several small tarns throughout the forest where wildfowl, including **mallard, tufted ducks** and **greylag geese**, are encouraged to nest.

Other notable birds include **buzzards, ravens, pied flycatchers, redstarts, woodcock, nightjars, green woodpeckers** and **blackcock**.

MAMMALS Deer are one of the main attractions, and both **red deer** and **roe deer** are found here. As a result of selective culling in the past, the red deer stags now have some of the finest heads anywhere in Britain. Quite a sizeable herd of red deer live in the forest but the population of roe seems to be gradually declining as the forest matures.

In addition to the deer there are **red squirrels**, and the elusive **pine marten** has been reported fairly regularly.

Flora

The flora is not outstanding, most of the forest being dominated by exotic conifers. The Forestry Commission has retained areas of natural hardwoods wherever possible, however, and these extend to about 718 acres (290 ha) and are mainly **sessile oak** with **birch** and **rowan**.

Access

There are many miles of footpaths and forest rides running through the area which the public are permitted to walk along.

Several deer hides have been constructed and are available for use by the public. Details may be obtained from the Forestry Office in Grizedale village itself (SD 336945). There is also a good, but small wildlife museum here, and several nature trails and forest walks radiate from the village.

Juniper Tarn (SD 342965) is probably the best place to see wildfowl.

Helvellyn NW 5 OS map 90 NY 3415

Helvellyn is one of the highest and best-known of England's mountains. It lies a little way east of Thirlmere in the Lake District and is 3116 ft (947m) high. The main interest is botanical, especially the arctic/alpine flora.

Fauna

BIRDS The mountain is not noted for its bird life, but you may see **wheatears, meadow pipits, ring ouzels, ravens, buzzards** and the occasional **dipper**.

INVERTEBRATES **Mountain ringlet butterflies** are found here.

Flora

FLOWERING PLANTS Large areas of the lower slopes are covered with upland pasture with **sheep's fescue, viviparous fescue, bent grasses, wavy hair-grass** and **mat-grass**, and there are localized patches of **ling** and **crowberry**. Other areas are dominated by **bilberry**, and **least willow** and **stiff sedge** are also common.

There are some calcareous exposures higher up the mountain, especially in some of the corries on the eastern side such as Nethermost Cove, at the head of Grisedale Beck, and it is in these corries that most of the arctic/alpines are to be found. These include **alpine lady's mantle, roseroot, mountain sorrel, alpine scurvy grass, lesser meadow-rue, alpine meadow-rue, northern bedstraw, globe flower, mossy saxifrage, purple mountain saxifrage, yellow mountain saxifrage, starry saxifrage, spring sandwort, moss campion, purple hawkweed,** and **three-flowered rush.** There are smaller amounts of **mountain avens, arctic saxifrage, alpine mouse-ear, alpine cinquefoil, jet sedge, twisted whitlow-grass, alpine meadow-grass,** and **bluish mountain meadow-grass. Alpine pennycress, alpine bistort** and **downy willow** have been recorded in the past and may still be extant here.

FERNS **Parsley fern** and **holly ferns** are both quite common, and **mountain bladder fern** and **oblong woodsia** have been recorded from time to time.

Access

The mountain is freely accessible and there are several footpaths leading to the higher ground. The easiest approaches are from Patterdale, via Grisedale Beck, and from Glenridding, both of which are on the A592 Penrith to Windermere road.

St Bees Head NW 6 OS map 89 NX 9515

St Bees Head is a sandstone headland jutting out into the Irish Sea a few miles south of Whitehaven in Cumbria. It is an R.S.P.B. reserve and has one of the main seabird colonies in the north of England. The flora is also quite interesting.

Fauna

BIRDS The principal seabirds which nest here are **guillemots, razorbills, fulmars, kittiwakes** and **herring gulls,** all of which breed in fair numbers. There are also a few **puffins** although the colony has been declining in recent years and only a few pairs are now left. One or two pairs of **black guillemots** are present in most years.

Rock pipits are common, and **ravens** are frequently seen.

Flora

FLOWERING PLANTS Among the more interesting members of the cliff flora are **bloody cranesbill, sheepsbit, tangled wood vetch, alexanders, rock samphire, English stonecrop** and **thrift.**

FERNS **Sea spleenwort** grows here.

Access

A public footpath follows the top of the cliffs northwards from St Bees village (NX 9711) and gives good views of the wildlife.

Before venturing on to the beach below the cliffs, it is wise to check on the time of high tide or you risk being cut off.

Drigg Dunes NW 7 OS map 96 SD 0698

Drigg Dunes is a Local Nature Reserve administered by the Cumbria County Council and which lies at the confluence of the estuaries of the rivers Irt, Mite and Esk. It covers some 800 acres (324ha) and is mainly of sand dunes but there are smaller areas of saltmarsh and shingle.

Fauna

BIRDS Drigg Dunes supports one of Britain's colonies of **black-headed gulls**. Co-existing with these are colonies of **common, arctic, Sandwich** and **little terns,** and there are also **oystercatchers, ringed plovers, shelducks** and a few **mergansers**. Both **herring** and **lesser black-backed gulls** often attempt to nest, but are prevented from doing so by the authorities in order to protect the terns.

REPTILES AND AMPHIBIANS A small colony of **natterjack toads** lives on the dunes.

Flora

FLOWERING PLANTS The dunes have several interesting species including **bloody cranesbill, carline thistle, slender centaury, sea bindweed, Portland spurge, sea spurge, shepherd's cress** and **Canadian fleabane.**

Sea lavender grows on the saltmarsh and the rare **dune cabbage** may be found on shingle here.

Access

Permits are needed to visit the reserve, and these are available from The County Land Agent and Valuer, Cumbria County Council, Arroyo Black, The Castle, Carlisle CA3 8XF.

Isle of Walney NW 8 OS map 96 SD 2162

Lying just west of Barrow-in-Furness, the Isle of Walney is a long, narrow island, the southernmost tip of which is managed as a nature reserve by the Cumbria Trust for Nature Conservation. Much of the 230 acre (93ha) reserve is sand dunes, but there are also areas of saltmarsh, both freshwater and brackish pools and vegetated shingle beaches.

Fauna

BIRDS The reserve's main claim to fame is the gull colony, which is the largest in Europe. Something in the region of 30,000 pairs of **herring gulls** and slightly fewer **lesser black-backed gulls** nest here, and there are also a few pairs of **greater black-backed gulls.**

Britain's most southerly colony of **eiders** – about 300 pairs – may also be seen here, and there are small colonies of **common, arctic, Sandwich** and, sometimes, **roseate terns.**

Other breeding birds include **shelducks, oystercatchers, ringed plovers, stonechats, linnets** and in winter the island is used as a high tide roost by up to 20,000 **oystercatchers** and smaller numbers of **knot, teal, wigeon** and **shelducks.**

Flora

FLOWERING PLANTS The dune flora includes **sea spurge, wall pepper, heart's-ease pansy, harebell, small bugloss, lesser hawkbit, wall speedwell, sea campion, viper's bugloss, henbane, burdock, houndstongue, common mullein, dovesfoot cranesbill** and **early scurvy grass.** The saltmarsh has **sea blite, sea lavender, sea spurrey, sea purslane,** and **buckshorn plantain.**

The yellow **horned-poppy** grows on the shingle.

Access

The unclassified road running southwards along the Isle of Walney takes you straight to the reserve entrance. The public are admitted for a nominal fee, but are not allowed to leave the $1\frac{1}{2}$ mile (2.5 km) long nature trail without permission of the resident warden.

Whitbarrow Scar NW 9 OS map 97 SD 4487

The limestone district of south Cumbria holds a wealth of interest for naturalists, but has few sites which are quite as interesting as Whitbarrow Scar. It is a low hill with limestone pavements, screes and a rich calcicole flora. It is flanked on both sides by some attractive woodlands.

250 acres (100 ha) of the Scar are managed as a nature reserve by the Cumbria Trust for Nature Conservation.

Fauna

BIRDS **Buzzards** nest in the surrounding woodlands, which also have **woodcock, green** and **great spotted woodpeckers.**
MAMMALS The woods are inhabited by **roe deer,** and **red deer** visit the area from time to time.

Flora

FLOWERING PLANTS The limestone scarp is exceptionally rich in calcicoles which include **blue moor-grass, angular Solomon's seal, ploughman's spikenard, bloody cranesbill, common rock-rose, lesser meadow-rue, spring sandwort, pale St John's wort, glaucous sedge, low sedge, dropwort, spring cinquefoil, carline thistle, tormentil, common dog violet, horseshoe vetch, small scabious, squinancy wort, stone bramble, burnet rose, lady's bedstraw** and **mountain melick.**

There are areas of scrub which have **whitebeam, juniper, yew, hazel, holly, birch, ash** and **buckthorn.**

The woods to the east of the Scar are mainly of **oak** and **ash** and have **dark red helleborine, common twayblade, great mullein** and **low sedge.**

FERNS The Scar holds **common** and **green spleenwort, wall rue, rustyback fern, limestone polypody** and the **rigid buckler fern.**

MOSSES AND LIVERWORTS Among the more noteworthy bryophytes are *Homomallium incurvatum, Rhytidium rugosum, Amblystegiella confervoides, Amblystegiella sprucei, Isothecium striatulum, Brachythecium glareosum, Tortella nitida* and *Funaria meuhlenbergii.*

Access

Whitbarrow Scar lies about 6½ miles (10.5km) south-west of Kendal. It is accessible either from the village of Howe (SD 457788) from where a footpath ascends through the woods and on to the Scar itself, or by footpath from near Witherslack Hall (SD 437860). No permits are required, but visitors are asked not to stray from the public rights of way unless a permit has been obtained from the Cumbria Trust for Nature Conservation, Church Street, Ambleside, Cumbria.

Ainsdale Dunes NW 10 OS map 108 SD 2810

This system of sand dunes is one of the largest and botanically richest anywhere in Britain. It occupies a zone some 6 miles (10.5km) long and nearly 1 mile (1.6km) wide between Southport and Formby. Part of the area is managed as a National Nature Reserve, part is scheduled as a Site of Special Scientific Interest and yet a third section is owned by the National Trust.

Fauna

MAMMALS Some of the older dunes have been planted with trees and support **red squirrels.**

REPTILES AND AMPHIBIANS The dunes are a major stronghold of the **natterjack toad** and the colony here is the largest in the north. **Sand lizards** are also found here, their most northerly British station.

Flora

FLOWERING PLANTS The younger dunes are quite rich in lime, and have a most interesting flora which includes **sea rocket, sea holly, yellow wort, common centaury, felwort, slender rush, field gentian, grass of Parnassus, sea spurge, Portland spurge, sand catstail, dune fescue, sea buckthorn, round-leaved wintergreen, sharp bulrush, ploughman's spikenard, blue fleabane, carline thistle, brookweed, spring sandwort, sea bindweed, rue-leaved saxifrage, spring beauty, large evening primrose, yellow birdsnest, early marsh orchid, bee orchid, pyramidal orchid, marsh helleborine** and **green-flowered helleborine.**

A speciality is **dune helleborine,** which is only known from two other

British sites. Some of the slacks contain **alder** woods and others are dominated by **creeping willow**. Some of the older dunes have been planted with **Scots, Corsican** and **Austrian pines.**

Other old dunes support heathland.

Access

The National Nature Reserve is centred at map reference SD 2809. There is a visitors' centre and a number of footpaths, but a permit is needed away from these. This can be obtained from the Regional Officer, North West Regional Office, Nature Conservancy Council, Blackwell, Bowness-on-Windermere, Cumbria LA23 3JR. The National Trust section – which is, incidentally the best place to see the squirrels – is slightly to the south at SD 2708, and is open to the public.

Elsewhere, the dunes are privately owned but there are no restrictions on access to most of the area. In fact much of the area is thronged with holiday-makers during the summer months.

Martin Mere   NW 11   OS map 108   SD 4214

Martin Mere is a sanctuary of the Wildfowl Trust which is both a haven for wild geese, ducks and waders as well as for a collection of exotic waterfowl. It lies about 8 miles (13 km) east of Southport and covers a 360 acre (145 ha) remnant of a huge fen, most of which has been drained.

Fauna

BIRDS One of the main attractions is up to 15,000 **geese,** mainly **pink-footed,** which feed here during the winter months but there are many other species of wildfowl including **whooper swans, mute swans, greylag geese, mallard, pintails, wigeon, teal, tufted duck, pochards** and **coots.** A variety of waders also occur including **snipe, curlews** and **lapwings.**

Access

Access is via the unclassified roads from Rufford. The Mere is open every day except Christmas, and there is a small admission charge which includes entry to the visitors' centre and use of the numerous hides which overlook a large area of fen.

The Dee Estuary   NW 12   OS maps 108 & 117   SJ 2085

The Dee Estuary covers approximately 40 square miles (over 100 km²) of mudflats and saltmarsh between England and Wales, and is one of the most important wintering refuges for wildfowl and waders in Great Britain. There are several nature reserves in the area; probably the best-known is Hilbre Islands, which belong to the Hoylake U.D.C. This reserve consists of three small islands which are accessible on foot across the sands at low tide and which are used as a high-tide roost by tens of thousands of waders. A second reserve on the estuary is owned by the British Steel Corporation. It includes a large area of saltmarsh and a series of freshwater lagoons and reed beds known as Shotton Pools.

Fauna

BIRDS Among the bird species which may be seen on Hilbre Islands are **knot, oystercatchers, dunlin** and **sanderlings**. There are lesser numbers of **black** and **bar-tailed godwits, redshanks, purple sandpipers, curlews, turnstones** and **grey plovers**, and occasionally **spotted redshanks, whimbrel, greenshanks, little stints, curlew sandpipers** and others. The wildfowl include **pintails, shelducks, mallard, teal, wigeon, shovelers, scaup, common scoters, eiders** and **red-breasted mergansers**. The estuary frequently holds over 125,000 birds!

The Shotton Pools reserve includes a colony of **common terns** which nest on artificial rafts there. Also breeding are **black-headed gulls, reed buntings, sedge warblers, snipe, common sandpipers** and **little grebes**. Frequent visitors include **bramblings, stonechats, whinchats, bearded tits** and a variety of ducks such as **teal, pochard, pintails, goldeneye**, etc. The saltmarsh holds nesting **redshanks, oystercatchers, lapwings, mallard, shelducks** and **water rails**, whilst in the winter several birds of prey may be found here including **kestrels, merlins, peregrines, hen harriers, sparrowhawks** and **short-eared owls**.

Access

Of the three Hilbre Islands, the main island is permanently inhabited and a permit is required from Hoylake U.D.C., Hoylake, Wirral, Cheshire, to visit it. The other two islands – Little Hilbre and Little Eye – are better high-tide roosts and no permits are needed. Visiting them can be dangerous on account of the tides. To be safe, you should set out from the promenade at West Kirby (SJ 210868) at least two hours before a high tide is due and walk straight to Little Eye, continuing to the others, if desired, from there.

To visit the British Steel Corporation areas a permit must be obtained from the Works Relations Manager, The British Steel Corporation, Shotton Works, Deeside, Clwyd, who will also provide full details of access.

Another good vantage point from which to see the estuarine birds is the Point of Ayr (SJ 1285) which is on O.S. map 116. Access here is unrestricted.

Calf of Man NW 13 OS map 95 SC 1564

The Calf of Man is a small rugged island which lies about $\frac{3}{4}$ mile (1.2 km) from the south-western tip of the Isle of Man. It covers just over 600 acres (242 ha) and is leased by the National Trust to the Manx National Trust who manage it with the Manx Museum. The island is principally a bird sanctuary and migration watchpoint, and there is a bird observatory there.

Opposite Calf Sound is another reserve of the Manx National Trust, known as Spanish Head, which covers 256 acres (103 ha) and has 400 ft (122 m) high cliffs.

Fauna

BIRDS Over 150 migratory bird species have been recorded by the observatory, and breeding birds include **choughs, hooded crows, ravens, short-eared owls, guillemots, razorbills, puffins, fulmars** and **kittiwakes**.

Access

Day visitors are welcome to land on The Calf, boats being available from both Port St Mary and Port Erin. People wishing to visit the observatory can obtain details from The Secretary, The Manx Museum, Douglas, The Isle of Man.

Spanish Head is accessible by public footpath from Cregneish, and boatmen at Port St Mary run trips beneath the cliffs.

Rostherne Mere NW 14 OS map 109 SJ 7484

Rostherne Mere is a large eutrophic lake (see page 38) lying about 10 miles (16 km) south-west of Manchester which has been declared a National Nature Reserve on account of the wildfowl populations which it holds. The reserve includes areas of woodland and farmland as well as the mere itself, the whole covering about 375 acres (150 ha).

Fauna

BIRDS The main interest of the mere is as a winter refuge for wildfowl. Up to 4000 **mallard** and 2500 **teal** have been recorded with smaller numbers of **wigeon, pintails, shovelers, pochard, tufted ducks, goldeneye, goosanders** and **ruddy ducks**. The mere is also a winter roost for up to 20,000 **gulls**, principally **black-headed** and **herring gulls**.

Among the more frequently noted passage migrants are **Bewick's swans, shelducks** and **terns**.

Breeding birds include **mallard, coots, great crested grebes, Canada geese, reed warblers** and occasionally **little grebes** and **tufted ducks**.

Access

There is no public access to the reserve other than to the A.W. Boyd memorial hide, which overlooks the mere. Permits to use the hide available from Mr D.A. Clarke, 13 Kingston Drive, Sale M33 2FS.

Borrowdale Woods NW 15 OS map 90 NY 2618

Borrowdale is situated to the south of Keswick in the Lake District, and is well known for its magnificent scenery. Its beauty derives, in part at least, from the extensive woodlands which occupy the lower hillsides of the dale, but these same woods also have a wealth of interest for naturalists. There are six main woods: Castle Head Wood (NY 2722; 20 acres/8 ha); The Ings (NY 2623; 10 acres/4 ha); Great Wood (NY 2721; 106 acres/42 ha); Lodore-Troutdale Woods (NY 2618; 914 acres/370 ha); Johnny's Wood (NY 2514;

87 acres/35 ha); and Seatoller Wood (NY 210 acres/85 ha).

All of them are owned by the National Trust.

Fauna

BIRDS **Buzzards** nest in some of the woods and are often seen flying over the nearby fells. There are also **pied flycatchers**, **wood warblers** and **grey wagtails**.

MAMMALS There are a few **red squirrels** in the woods, and the rare **pine marten** still survives in the Dale Head area (NY 2215).

Flora

FLOWERING PLANTS All six woods are essentially of **sessile oak** with areas of **ash** and **hazel**, but there are also many other tree species including **birch**, **holly**, **rowan** and **wych elm**. The shrub layer is not generally well developed because of the grazing pressure of domestic stock in the past, although Great Wood has been affected less than the others. Where the shrub layer is present it consists of **bird cherry**, **blackthorn**, **hawthorn** and **bramble**. Great Wood, The Ings and Lodore-Troutdale Woods also include areas of **alder** and **willows** where they meet Derwentwater.

The herbaceous flora includes a good many grasses such as **wavy hairgrass**, **sweet vernal grass**, **red fescue**, **wood fescue** and **slender false brome**, and there is also some **bilberry**. Other herbs are the uncommon **touch-me-not**, **herb Robert**, **small cow-wheat** and **alpine enchanter's nightshade**.

Alpine lady's mantle and **yavering bells** grow on the nearby fells.

FERNS The extremely rare **forked spleenwort** may be found growing on rocks in Johnny's Wood. Elsewhere you may find **ferns** such as **common buckler**, **male**, **lady**, **hard**, **oak**, **beech**, **lemon-scented** and **Scottish filmy**. **Bracken** is common in places.

MOSSES AND LIVERWORTS The woods are generally considered to be one of the most important sites in England for Atlantic bryophytes. The **moss** flora includes *Hylocomium umbratum*, *Hypnum callichroum*, *Bartramia halleriana*, *Ptilium crista-castrensis* and *Sematophyllum novae-caesareae*.

The **liverworts** include *Radula voluta*, *R. aquilegia*, *Jubula hutchinsiae*, *Colura calyptrifolia*, *Plagiochila tridenticulata*, *Frullania germana*, *F. microphylla*, *Marchesinia mackaii*, *Adelanthus decipens*, *Sphenolobus helleranus* and *Jamesonieloa autumnalis*.

LICHENS Great Wood and Seatoller Wood are also noted for their lichens, which include *Parmelia plumbia*, *P. laevigata*, *P. taylorensis*, *Bacidia affinis*, *B. isidiacea*, *Lecides berengeriana*, *Lopadium pezizoideum*, *Micarea violacea*, *Lobaria pulmonaria*, *L. laete-virens*, *Sticta sylvatica* and *S. limbata*.

Access

The woods are freely open to the public, and are easily accessible from Keswick via the B5289 Keswick to Borrowdale road. Numerous footpaths run through the woods and over the surrounding fells.

Gait Barrows NW 16 OS map 97 SD 4877

Gait Barrows lies in limestone country about 4 miles (6.5km) north of Carnforth and not far from Eaves Wood and Arnside Knott (NW 2). A National Nature Reserve, it consists of what is probably the finest example of limestone pavement in Britain together with some surrounding woods, but the nearby Haweswater Tarn is included here as well.

Fauna

BIRDS Haweswater Tarn holds a few pairs of nesting **bitterns** and **water rails** and is occasionally visited by **ospreys** and **marsh harriers**. The **lesser spotted woodpecker** is said to reach its northern British limits in the Gait Barrow woods.

MAMMALS **Red squirrels** and **roe deer** occupy the woods, and **red deer** sometimes visit the area.

Flora

FLOWERING PLANTS The limestone pavement itself has the **angular Solomon's seal, tutsan, bloody cranesbill, hemp agrimony, saw-wort, northern bedstraw** and **blue sesleria**. There are also patches of scrub with **ash, hazel, yew, holly, privet, dogwood, juniper, buckthorn, small-leaved lime** and **spindle**, and the rare **whitebeam** *Sorbus lancastriensis* which is endemic to Britain and confined to the limestone of northern Britain. These areas of scrub have their own herbaceous flora which contains **lily of the valley, stone bramble, fingered sedge, deadly nightshade, pale St John's wort, dark red helleborine** and **mountain melick**.

Surrounding the pavements are more mature woods which were previously managed as **hazel** coppice with **ash** and **pedunculate oak** standards. **Beech, silver birch** and **hornbeam** are also present and the lower layers of the wood are largely dominated by **bramble** with **dog's mercury, bluebell, primrose, sanicle, common enchanter's nightshade, common dog violet** and **slender false brome**.

The woodlands around Haweswater hold **common buckthorn, alder buckthorn, deadly nightshade, birdseye primrose** and several **orchids** including **early purple, fragrant** and **common twayblade**. The tarn is surrounded by **reed** beds which are dominated by the **common reed** and have **bog rush, hop sedge, bladder sedge, fen rush, common sedge, marsh helleborine, common butterwort** and **horseshoe vetch**. The aquatic plants include **shining pondweed, broad-leaved pondweed, flat-stalked pondweed, blunt-leaved pondweed, greater bladderwort, ivy duckweed** and both **white** and **yellow waterlilies**.

FERNS The moist grikes (cracks) of the limestone pavement provide an ideal environment for many species of ferns including several rare ones. Some of the notable species are **hartstongue fern, hard shield fern, rigid buckler fern** and **rusty back fern**.

(Above) Viviparous lizard, an inhabitant of dry heaths, woodland glades and mountain slopes.
(Below) Purple mountain saxifrage.

Spectacular view of the Devil's Kitchen, Cwm Idwal (see page 126).

Access

The area lies only a little way to the west of the A6, and can be reached via the unclassified roads which run between Yealand Redmayne and Arnside. Most of the land is privately owned, but there is a good network of public footpaths through the area, including one which passes Haweswater.

Morecambe Bay NW 17 OS map 97 SD 4070

Morecambe Bay is an enormous expense of tidal mud and sand lying between Lancaster and Barrow-in-Furness. At low tide, more than 60 square miles (over 155 km²) of mudflats are exposed including the estuaries of the Rivers Kent, Leven and Keer, and the bay holds the largest concentrations of wintering waders anywhere in Britain – although there are surprisingly small numbers of wildfowl. There are several areas of saltmarsh around the periphery of the bay including a large acreage near Carnforth which is owned by the R.S.P.B., and the area discussed here also includes the small limestone promontory of Humphrey Head which juts out into the bay a few miles south of Grange-over-Sands.

Fauna

BIRDS Recent counts have suggested that over a quarter of a million waders alone may use the bay in winter, and these include some 85,000 **knot**, 45,000 **oystercatchers**, 44,000 **dunlin**, 14,000 **sanderling**, 14,000 **curlews**, 12,000 **redshanks**, 8000 **bar-tailed godwits** and 7000 **ringed plovers**. Smaller numbers of **grey plovers**, **whimbrel**, **greenshanks** and **turnstones** also occur.

As regards wildfowl, there are up to 6000 **shelducks**, and fewer **mallard**, **shovelers**, **pintails**, **eiders**, **goldeneyes**, **scaup**, **tufted ducks**, **wigeon**, **common scoters**, **smew**, **long-tailed ducks**, **goosanders** and **red-breasted mergansers**. About 3000 **pink-footed geese** roost further south at Cockerham Sands by the estuary of the River Lune, although sometimes they may use the Milnthorpe Sands on the Kent Estuary. There are also a few **greylags** and **white-fronted geese** from time to time.

Herons, **cormorants**, and sometimes both **red** and **black-throated divers** can be seen on the Leven Estuary by Greenodd.

Flora

FLOWERING PLANTS Most of the numerous patches of saltmarsh are regularly used for sheep grazing which has had the effect of encouraging **grasses**, although there are other plants present also, including the localized **few-flowered spike rush**, **chestnut sedge**, **glaucous sedge**, **carnation sedge**, **sea plantain**, **sea aster**, **thrift** and **slender centaury**.

The 130 ft (40 m) high cliffs of Humphrey Head support **goldilocks**, **western spiked speedwell**, **hoary rock-rose**, **bloody cranesbill**, **rock samphire**, **spotted catsear**, **spring cinquefoil** and **wild liquorice**.

Access

There are innumerable good vantage points overlooking the bay. One of the best is the high tide roost at Hest Bank which lies just to the west of the A1505 Morecambe to Carnforth road at SD 468668. Other good places are the Kent Estuary, which can be viewed from the B5282 just north of Arnside (SD 4578), the Leven Estuary, which can be seen from the A590 near Greenodd (SD 3182), and Humphrey Head (SD 3973). There are many others besides but it is unsafe to venture on to the mudflats unless you are absolutely sure about the tides.

Lindisfarne NE 1 OS map 75 NU 1342

Much of Holy Island, the surrounding mudflats, and a system of sand dunes on the mainland nearby, are included in the huge Lindisfarne National Nature Reserve. The reserve covers a total of 12¾ square miles (32.7km²) and is one of the most important wintering refuges for wildfowl and waders in northern England, as well as being of interest to botanists on account of the dune flora.

Fauna

BIRDS Between Holy Island itself and the mainland lie the vast expanses of Holy Island Sands and Fenham Flats and these, together with Budle Bay to the south (NU 1536), are the wintering grounds of some 60,000 waders and wildfowl. 25,000 **wigeon** head the list with up to 1000 **brent geese** and the biggest English flock of **whooper swans**; about 200. **Greylag geese, pink-footed geese, Bewick's swans, eiders, scoters, goldeneye** and **long-tailed ducks** are also frequent visitors and the waders, which can number 30,000, include **bar-tailed godwits** and **dunlin**.

Some of the cliffs on Holy Island itself have nesting **fulmars**.

Flora

FLOWERING PLANTS There are two distinct areas of dunes, one on Holy Island and the other at Ross Links on the mainland (NU 1437). The Holy Island dunes contain more calcareous shell sand than the Ross Links system, and are consequently more fertile. Some of the most notable species here are **marsh helleborine, early marsh orchid, northern marsh orchid, common spotted orchid, coralroot orchid, sand catstail, rough clover, curved sedge, chestnut sedge, round-leaved wintergreen, lovage, pirri-pirri bur, sea couch grass, common butterwort** and **creeping willow**.

The flora of Ross Links includes **lyme grass, hybrid marram, purple milk-vetch, field mouse-ear, lesser meadow-rue** and **field gentian**. The older dunes here have developed into heathland with **ling** and **bell heather**.

MOSSES AND LIVERWORTS *Catoscopium nigritum* and *Amblyodon dealbatus* grow on the Holy Island dunes and *Drepanocladus lycopodioides* and *D. sendtneri wilsonii* may be found on Ross Links.

Access

The reserve lies immediately east of the A1 and about 10 miles (16 km) south of Berwick-upon-Tweed. It is generously provided with footpaths although by and large there are no restrictions on access over much of the nature reserve.

Holy Island lies about 1 mile (1.6 km) from the mainland at its nearest point and is easily reached at low tide by a causeway which runs across the sands.

Farne Islands NE 2 OS map 75 NU 2337

The Farne Islands are one of the very few archipelagos on the east coast of England. There are about 28 islands in all, although the exact number depends on the state of the tide. They lie between $1\frac{1}{2}$ and 5 miles (2.5–8 km) offshore, some 20 miles (32 km) south of Berwick-upon-Tweed. None of the islands is large; the largest, Longstone, being a little over $\frac{1}{2}$ mile (800 m) in length.

The Farnes are well known both for their breeding seabirds and as the home of England's largest grey seal rookery. They are protected as a nature reserve by the National Trust.

Fauna

BIRDS Several thousand pairs of **puffins, guillemots** and **kittiwakes** nest on the various islands of the group. There are smaller colonies of **razorbills, fulmars, shags, herring gulls** and **lesser black-backed gulls**, and two of the islands – Inner Farne and Brownsman – have colonies of **eiders** and four species of **terns**, namely, **common, arctic, Sandwich** and **roseate**.

MAMMALS About 7000 **grey seals** congregate on the islands during October to give birth to their pups. Their main haunts are North and South Wamses and Northern Hares. There are also large numbers of **rabbits**, especially on Inner Farne.

Flora

FLOWERING PLANTS The flora of the islands is not of outstanding interest save for the rare *Amsinckia intermedia*, a North American plant which was presumably introduced there by the lighthouse keepers.

Access

There are regular boat trips to the islands from Seahouses, and it is possible to land on Inner Farne and, weather permitting, Staple Island. Of these, Inner Farne is probably the best for birds. Such trips are run daily from April to September. Several boatmen run trips including Mr Billy Shiel, 4 Southfield Avenue, Seahouses, Northumberland.

Farndale NE 3 OS map 93 NZ 6102

Farndale is a local nature reserve of the North Yorkshire County Council. It covers 4 square miles (10.1 km²) of the banks of the River Dove just north of Kirbymoorside, about 20 miles (32 km) north-west of Scarborough.

Flora

FLOWERING PLANTS The reserve exists solely to protect the hundreds of thousands of **wild daffodils** which grow along a 7 mile (11 km) stretch of the river banks. During the flowering season the reserve is extremely attractive but is not particularly interesting once the daffodils have finished.

Access

The reserve is easily accessible from Hutton-le-Hole which lies just north of Kirbymoorside on the A170.

Washington Wildfowl Reserve
NE 4 OS map 88 NZ 3556

The Wildfowl Trust's Washington reserve is on the north bank of the River Wear, just west of Sunderland. There is a collection of exotic waterbirds as well as the numerous native wildfowl which visit the refuge.

Fauna

BIRDS The most frequently seen wildfowl are **whooper swans, wigeon, pochard, teal, redshanks** and **grey herons**, and the reserve includes a small area of woodland where **great spotted woodpeckers** and **sparrowhawks** breed.

Less frequent visitors include **little ringed plovers, green sandpipers, wood sandpipers, curlew sandpipers, greenshanks, spotted redshanks** and **woodcock**.

Access

The refuge is situated midway between Sunderland and the A1(M), and is signposted locally. It is open to the public daily (except Christmas) and has a nature trail through the wooded area.

Castle Eden Dene NE 5 OS map 93 NZ 4138

Castle Eden Dene is a steep-sided wooded valley about 12 miles (19 km) south of Sunderland and is a local nature reserve of the Peterlee Development Corporation. It covers 517 acres (209 ha).

Fauna

INVERTEBRATES The **northern brown argus** butterfly is restricted to this area. **Dingy skippers** and **large skippers** can also be found.

Flora

FLOWERING PLANTS **Pedunculate oak** and **ash** are the two dominant trees but there is also some **yew, hazel, rowan** and planted **beech**. The herbaceous flora includes **grass of Parnassus, meadow cranesbill, wood cranesbill, round-leaved wintergreen, lily of the valley, opposite-leaved golden saxifrage, birdsnest orchid, wood anemone, dog's mercury** and **bluebell**.

Access

The reserve is accessible from the A19, A1086, and from Peterlee itself. Visitors are asked not to leave the footpaths.

Colt Park Wood and Ling Gill
NE 6   OS map 98   SD 7777 & 8078

These two National Nature Reserves are both small ashwoods growing high in the Craven Pennines. Colt Park Wood is on an area of limestone pavement and covers 21 acres (8.4 ha) whilst Ling Gill, which is about 2 miles (3 km) away, occupies a steep-sided ravine, also of limestone. Both sites are slightly over 1000 ft (300 m) high.

Flora

FLOWERING PLANTS The dominant tree is **ash**, with smaller amounts of **wych elm** and **birch. Hazel, rowan** and **bird cherry** are also found as undershrubs, and the herbaceous flora includes **globe flower, wood cranesbill, melancholy thistle, baneberry, marsh hawksbeard, northern hawksbeard, giant bellflower, herb Paris, yellow star of Bethlehem, alpine cinquefoil, northern bedstraw, heath bedstraw, tormentil, water avens** and **wild angelica**.
FERNS These include **bracken** and **green spleenwort**.

Access

Ling Gill is adjacent to the Pennine Way long-distance footpath from which access may be gained. The path can be picked up from the end of the unclassified road which leaves Horton in Ribblesdale northwards.

Colt Park Wood is only accessible to permit holders. These should be requested from the Nature Conservancy Council at Archbold House, Archbold Terrace, Newcastle upon Tyne, NE2 1EG.

Malham Tarn   NE 7   OS map 98   SD 8966
Malham Tarn is a large upland lake which lies about 5 miles (8 km) north-east of Settle in the Craven Pennines. The lake and its immediate surroundings which are owned by the National Trust comprise a reserve of the Field Studies Council and one of its educational centres is situated on the northern bank of the tarn. However, the area covered here also includes a section of the surrounding farmland. Since the whole area is underlain

with limestone, the turf, cliffs, gorges and limestone pavements of the region have a most interesting flora. The Field Studies Council reserve includes an area of woodland and an interesting mire system in which both fen and raised bog have developed side by side.

Fauna

BIRDS The reserve and its immediate surroundings have **redstarts, wheatears, ring ouzels, dippers, common sandpipers, redshanks, curlews, golden plovers** and **red grouse.**

Flora

FLOWERING PLANTS Taking the fen and bog complex first, we may find **tea-leaved willow, bay willow, dark willow, birdseye primrose, red rattle, marsh valerian, marsh hawksbeard, least bur-reed, slender-leaved sedge** and **lesser tussock sedge.**

The area surrounding the tarn has several other interesting plants including **Yorkshire milkwort,** which is otherwise known only from Upper Teesdale. Other species are **alpine cinquefoil, spring cinquefoil, twisted whitlow-grass, wall whitlow-grass, spring sandwort, hutchinsia, lesser meadow-rue, grass of Parnassus, bloody cranesbill, orpine** and **whitebeam trees.**

FERNS **Bladder fern, green spleenwort, rigid buckler fern** and **limestone polypody** all grow in the area.

Access

Malham Tarn is easily reached by the unclassified roads from Settle. Only part of the reserve is open to the public and permission should be sought from the warden of the Malham Tarn Field Centre before wandering off the public footpaths. The surrounding farmland is, of course, privately owned. Three good areas for wild flowers are Malham Cove (SD 898640), Gordale Scar (SD 915640) and Kilnsey Crags (SD 972679).

Details of accommodation and educational courses at the Field Centre are available from the Field Studies Council, Malham Tarn Field Centre, Settle, Yorkshire BD24 9PU, or from the Field Studies Council, 9 Devereux Court, The Strand, London WC2R 3JR.

Bempton Cliffs NE 8 OS map 101 TA 1974

These 400ft (122m) high cliffs lie immediately north of Flamborough Head and about 4 miles (6km) from Bridlington. They are an R.S.P.B. reserve and have some of the largest seabird colonies in the north of England.

Fauna

BIRDS The most numerous bird on the cliffs is the **kittiwake,** of which there are some 40,000 pairs. There are also several thousand pairs of **guillemots,** with smaller numbers of **razorbills** and **fulmars, puffins** and **rock doves.** The cliffs are also well known for their **gannets** – there were

375 breeding pairs in 1982. It is distinguished by being the only colony in England and the only British mainland gannet colony.

Access

Access is available at all times along the public footpath which runs along the cliff top from the car park east of Bempton village.

Fairburn Ings NE 9 OS map 105 SE 4727

Fairburn Ings Reserve is a series of shallow lakes with marshy depressions and some woodland about 12 miles (19 km) south-east of Leeds which came into being as a result of mining subsidence. The lake is a winter haunt of numerous wildfowl and is an important resting place for many migrant birds. It covers 618 acres (250 ha) and is a reserve of the R.S.P.B.

Fauna

BIRDS During the breeding season the lake is home to **shovelers, pochard** and **gadwall**, and there are colonies of **reed warblers** and **sedge warblers** in the fringing reed beds. During the winter months a wide variety of wildfowl use the reserve including **whooper swans, Bewick's swans, gadwall, pochard, wigeon** and **shovelers.**

Another attraction of the lake is the huge flocks of **swallows** and **sand martins** which gather in September prior to their migration. Up to 250,000 have been counted in some years.

Access

The reserve is reached via Ferrybridge on the A1. The R.S.P.B. has erected hides at the eastern end which are available for use by the public at all times. An information centre and hide are open at weekends at the west end.

Hornsea Mere NE 10 OS map 107 TA 1847

This large eutrophic lake (see page 38) lies about 10 miles (16 km) north-east of Hull, next to Hornsea town, and is $\frac{1}{2}$ mile (.8 km) from the sea. It is a reserve of the R.S.P.B. and is important because of its wintering ducks and the migrants which rest there during spring and autumn. The reserve includes some extensive reed beds and is fringed by farmland and woods.

Fauna

BIRDS During the winter months the reserve is visited by over 2000 **mallard** and several hundred **pochard, wigeon** and **teal. Tufted ducks** and **goldeneye** are also usually present in good numbers and there are **shovelers, gadwall, goosanders** and **mute swans.**

A wide range of migrants have been recorded including **little gulls, black terns** and **Slavonian grebes.**

The breeding birds include **mallard, shovelers, gadwall, pochard, tufted ducks** and over 500 pairs of **reed warblers.**

Flora

FLOWERING PLANTS The surrounding reed beds have quite a varied flora, although they contain no great rarities. This includes **lesser bulrush, common reed, glaucous sedge, carnation sedge, marsh thistle, lady's smock, yellow flag, water forget-me-not, pond sedge, great pond sedge, hornwort** and **red rattle.**

Lesser pondweed, fennel pondweed and **Canadian pondweed** grow in the lake itself.

Access

The reserve is open to the public throughout the year but only on certain days of the week, and visiting arrangements may change from time to time. Intending visitors are advised to check with the warden before planning their visit. The address is: The Warden, The Bungalow, The Mere, Hornsea HU18 1AX.

Good views of the mere can be obtained from the B1244 which runs along its northern shore, and a public footpath to the south of the lake touches the shoreline at one point.

Spurn Point NE 11 OS map 113 TA 4115

Spurn Point is a long narrow promontory jutting out into the Humber Estuary about 20 miles (32 km) south-east of Hull. It is largely composed of sand and shingle and has a bird observatory from which the vast flocks of waders and wildfowl which winter on the estuary may be studied. The promontory is a reserve of the Yorkshire Wildlife Trust.

Fauna

BIRDS During the winter months an average of about 3000 wildfowl and 40,000 waders live on the mudflats to the west of the point. The principal species are **wigeon, mallard, scaup, shelducks, knot** and **redshanks** although during migration periods all kinds of birds may appear: **terns, waders, divers** and a variety of passerines.

Flora

FLOWERING PLANTS The sand and shingle of the promontory holds several interesting plants such as **sea buckthorn, sea holly, sea bindweed, dark-green mouse-ear, spring beauty, rough clover, spring vetch, bur chervil, blue fleabane, chicory** and **lyme grass.**

Access

The reserve may be reached from Kilnsea via the B1445. A track runs along the peninsula but this is submerged at high tides; an entry fee is charged for cars. Details of accommodation at the bird observatory may be obtained from The Warden, Spurn Bird Observatory, Kilnsea via Patrington, Hull, North Humberside.

Ingleborough Fell NE 12 OS map 98 SD 7474

Ingleborough Fell is a 2373 ft (723 m) high mountain which lies close to Ingleton in the Craven Pennines. It is mainly composed of limestone with some coarse sandstones, and is well known to botanists on account of the flora of its limestone cliffs, screes and pavements.

Flora

FLOWERING PLANTS Most of the area is used as sheep pasture and is dominated by grasses such as **sheep's fescue, quaking grass, blue moor grass, brown bent, sweet vernal grass, purple moor-grass, mat grass** and a certain amount of **heath rush**, although some of the deeper clints and grikes on the limestone pavements which are inaccessible to the sheep have a more varied and interesting flora.

Some areas, such as the Scar Close region (SD 750778), are ungrazed and are far more rewarding botanically, with plants such as **lily of the valley, bloody cranesbill, saw-wort, lesser meadow-rue, melancholy thistle, globe flower, wall rue, zig-zag clover** and **hairy rockcress**. The moister grikes have their own distinctive flora which includes the uncommon **alpine cinquefoil, pink stonecrop, northern bedstraw, birdseye primrose, spring sandwort, stone bramble, mountain melick** and **baneberry**.

Higher up the mountain, above the 2000 ft (600 m) mark, several arctic/alpines begin to appear, especially on the more inaccessible cliffs and crags where they are safe from grazing. They include **purple mountain saxifrage, yellow mountain saxifrage, mossy saxifrage, roseroot, alpine meadow-grass** and **purple hawkweed**.

Wild thyme and **salad burnet** may be found on lower ground along with the very rare **Scottish sandwort**, which is otherwise restricted to Scotland. This belongs to a separate sub-species – *anglica* – which is not found anywhere else in Britain.

There are also patches of heather moor, which have developed where acid drift overlies the limestone, and these areas mainly consist of **ling** and **bilberry** with **tormentil, wood sage** and **devilsbit scabious**.

FERNS Several notable ferns grow in the grikes and clints including **hartstongue fern, hard shield fern, green spleenwort, male fern, rigid buckler fern, limestone polypody** and **holly fern**.

Access

Ingleborough lies within the triangle formed by the A65, the B6479 and the B6255. It is privately owned but because it lies within the Yorkshire Dales National Park, there is no shortage of footpaths and tracks over the area which is very popular with fellwalkers. Scar Close is a National Nature Reserve to which access is by permit only. These can be obtained from the Nature Conservancy Council, Archbold House, Archbold Terrace, Newcastle upon Tyne, NE2 1EG. Moughton Fell (SD 7971) and Raven Scar (SD

7275) are also worth visiting.

Colt Park Wood (NE 6) lies on the north-eastern flank of the mountain.

Skipwith Common NE 13 OS map 105 SE 6537

Skipwith Common is an area of lowland heath which lies about 10 miles (16km) south of York. It covers about $1\frac{1}{4}$ square miles (3.2km²) and is probably the largest lowland heath in the north of England. The site also includes areas of woodland and valley mires.

Fauna

BIRDS The bird life includes **nightjars, stonechats, whinchats, wheatears, whitethroats, lesser whitethroats, grasshopper warblers, linnets, curlews,** all three British **woodpeckers, short-eared owls, long-eared owls, barn owls, tawny owls** and **little owls.** The pools and marshes have **willow tits, reed warblers, water rails** and several species of duck.

MAMMALS A herd of **fallow deer** lives on the common.

Flora

FLOWERING PLANTS Most of the common is covered with a wet heath type of vegetation dominated by **cross-leaved heath, purple moor-grass, deer grass** and **heath rush.**

Other parts are drier and have **ling** and **bell heather,** and there is some colonization by **birch** and **pine.**

Parts of the site are covered with fen which has probably been created by peat cutting in the past and now contains some interesting wild flowers including **marsh bedstraw, marsh pennywort, large birdsfoot trefoil, yellow loosestrife, meadow thistle, lesser skullcap, marsh cinquefoil, soft rush, jointed rush, star sedge, common spike-rush** and **alder buckthorn.**

FERNS **Narrow buckler fern** grows in some of the fens.

Access

Skipwith Common lies immediately south of Skipwith village and can be reached via the A19 from York. A large part of the area is now managed as a nature reserve by the Yorkshire Wildlife Trust and there is a nature trail.

Moor House and Cross Fell NE 14 OS map 91 NY 7729

Cross Fell at 2930ft (893m), is the highest point in the Pennines and lies about 12 miles (19km) east of Penrith on the border between Cumbria and Co. Durham. To the south, the Nature Conservancy has established the enormous National Nature Reserve and outdoor research station of Moor House, which covers over 15 square miles (39km²).

The area includes a variety of rock types including limestone, sandstone and the Whin Sill, composed of quartz dolerite. About half of the area is covered with blanket bog and the rest is upland pasture and heather moor. The weather conditions in this region can be extremely hazardous.

Fauna

BIRDS Several species of wader nest on the fells including **lapwings, curlews, golden plovers, dunlin** and **redshanks**. A large part of the area was formerly managed as grouse moor and **red grouse** are still fairly common in parts. Other birds include **meadow pipits, wheatears, twite, ring ouzels, short-eared owls, ravens** and **dippers**.

Flora

FLOWERING PLANTS The flora of the area is extraordinarily rich and varied. The blanket bog is mainly dominated by **common cottongrass, soft rush** and **bottle sedge** with **common sundew, bog myrtle** and **bog asphodel. Starry saxifrage, alpine willowherb, chickweed willowherb, water forget-me-not** and **alpine foxtail grass** grow on the higher ground. The mire is locally subject to the effects of nutrient-rich ground water draining from limestone outcrops and in such areas other species start to appear. These include the rare **yellow mountain saxifrage, pink stonecrop, grass of Parnassus, three-flowered rush** and several sedges including **common, yellow, tawny, flea, separate-headed** and **carnation sedges**.

The rare **spring gentian** is found on limestone outcrops on Bellbeaver Rigg and the equally rare **alpine forget-me-not** and **alpine catstail** may be found on Cross Fell, which also has **roseroot, alpine bistort, mountain pansy, mountain everlasting, northern bedstraw, twisted whitlow-grass, alpine cinquefoil, mossy saxifrage** and **spring sandwort**.

The last species is also found growing around some of the old lead workings in the area along with the **alpine penny-cress, upland scurvy grass** and **felwort**.

Other parts of the area are covered with an upland heath with **ling, bilberry, crowberry** and **cloudberry**, and wetter regions have **hare's-tail cottongrass, deer grass** and **cross-leaved heath**.

FERNS **Lesser clubmoss** and **marsh horsetail** may be found in the blanket bogs, and **green spleenwort** and **holly fern** grow on the limestone on Cross Fell.

MOSSES AND LIVERWORTS The bryophyte flora includes several uncommon calcicoles including *Pseudoleskea catenulata, Encalypta rhabdocarpa, Rhytidium rugosum, Distichum inclinatum, Mnium orthorhynchum, Entodon orthocorpus, Lophozia lycopodiodes, Drepanocladus intermedius, Campylium stellatum, Cratoneuron commutatum, Scorpidium scorpioides* and *Camptothecium nitens*.

The summit of Cross Fell is covered with a species of the **moss** *Rhacomitrium*, and *Haplodon wormskjoldii* may be found growing on animal remains.

Access

Perhaps the best way to see the area is to follow the Pennine Way long-distance footpath from near Alston (about 20 miles/32km) north-east of Penrith on the A686). This takes you over the summit of Cross Fell and through parts of the Moor House and Upper Teesdale National Nature Reserves. There are other footpaths in the area also, but the Moor House reserve is not open away from these except by permit. The address for permits is the Regional Officer, North West Regional Office, Nature Conservancy Council, Blackwell, Bowness-on-Windermere, Windermere, Cumbria LA23 3JR.

South Stack N. Wales 1 OS map 114 SH 2082

This is an R.S.P.B. reserve which lies at the western tip of Holy Island, Anglesey. The main reason for its establishment is to protect the seabird colonies, although the flora is also of great interest.

Fauna

BIRDS The South Stack cliffs have some of the largest auk colonies in North Wales with almost 2000 pairs of **guillemots** and perhaps half that number of **razorbills**. **Puffins** are less common, with no more than about a hundred pairs. There are also a few **fulmars**, **kittiwakes**, **cormorants** and **shags** and the area is frequented by several pairs of **choughs**.

MAMMALS A few **grey seals** breed in caves at the adjacent headland of North Stack.

Flora

FLOWERING PLANTS The cliffs both within and outside the nature reserve, and the nearby areas of maritime heathland, carry a most interesting flora. It includes **spotted rock-rose** and **field fleawort**, both of which are unknown outside North Wales. Other noteworthy species are **golden samphire**, **cliff spurrey**, **English stonecrop** and **spring squill**.

Access

No permits are required to visit the reserve. A long and tortuous stairway descends from the car park at the top of the cliffs to the lighthouse at the bottom, offering quite good views of the seabird colonies as it does so. Much of the adjacent area is also freely accessible, and the walk from South Stack to Penrhyn Mawr is botanically rewarding since this is where most of the interesting plants are to be found.

Newborough Warren N. Wales 2 OS map 114 SH 4165

Situated at the southernmost tip of Anglesey, adjacent to the Cefni Estuary, Newborough Warren N.N.R. includes a large system of sand dunes with areas of marsh and shingle, and includes the small rocky promontory of Llanddwyn Island. Unfortunately, much of the original area of sand dunes has been damaged by afforestation, but the reserve is still one of the largest and most important dune systems in Wales.

The reserve covers $2\frac{1}{2}$ square miles ($6.3\,km^2$).

Fauna
BIRDS The fauna of the reserve is not particularly outstanding. There are colonies of **herring gulls** and **lesser black-backed gulls** among the dunes. The adjacent estuary, however, is a haunt of wintering wildfowl and waders which may include **pintails, shelducks, goldeneye, wigeon, teal, whooper swans, redshanks, dunlin, ruff, oystercatchers, curlews, greenshanks** and both **black** and **bar-tailed godwits**. **Ospreys** are occasionally noted on passage.

Cormorants breed on some small rocks just off Llanddwyn Island.

Flora
FLOWERING PLANTS Although **marram-grass** is the dominant plant on the mobile dunes near the sea, **dune pansies, sea spurge, sand catstail, mouse-ear chickweed** and a few other species also grow there. **Early marsh orchid, northern marsh orchid, yellow birdsnest, meadow saxifrage, grass of Parnassus, round-leaved wintergreen** and **common butterwort** occur on the damper sites and some of the slacks are dominated by **creeping willow**. The older dunes are developing into heathland.

The saltmarsh flora includes **sea rush**, and **grey sallow**. **Golden samphire** grows on Llanddwyn Island.

Access
Permits are required to visit the reserve away from the public rights of way. Applications should be addressed to the Nature Conservancy Council at Penrhos Rd, Bangor, Gwynedd LL57 2LQ.

Much of the estuary is visible from the main A4080, but one of the best places for birdlife is the 'Cob', a small lagoon at map reference SH 410683 which usually holds a variety of waterbirds throughout the year.

Great Ormes Head N. Wales 3 OS map 115 SH 7683
Great Ormes Head, or Pen-y-Gogarth, is a rocky headland lying immediately north-west of Llandudno. It is best known as a playground for the thousands of holiday-makers who flock to the North Wales coast each year, most of whom are quite oblivious to the seabird colonies which thrive there as well as the fascinating calcicole flora. The Head covers 592 acres (240 ha) and is managed as a Country Park and local nature reserve.

Fauna
BIRDS There are fair-sized colonies of **guillemots** and **razorbills** on the Head, and smaller numbers of **puffins, kittiwakes, fulmars** and **shags**. **Ravens** are frequently seen, and **rock pipits** are common.
MAMMALS A herd of **feral goats** may be seen here.
INVERTEBRATES The **cistus forester moth** has its only known Welsh site here, and the **silver-studded blue butterfly** is often seen.

Flora

FLOWERING PLANTS The Orme is the only British site for the **Great Ormes berry**, our only native cotoneaster. Two close relatives also grow here, namely **Khasia berry** and **rockspray**. Other notable species include **goldilocks**, which is only known from four other British sites, both **common** and **hoary rock-roses**, **spotted catsear**, **spiked speedwell**, **spring cinquefoil**, **hutchinsia**, **dark red helleborine**, **spring squill**, **bloody cranesbill**, **mountain everlasting** and **spring sandwort**.

Access

The Head is easily accessible from Llandudno and visitors have a choice of reaching the summit either by using the minor road which runs around the promontory, by taking the tramcar or by using the new cable car. Numerous footpaths criss-cross the area. Indeed, the only problem regarding access is avoiding the crowds.

Cwm Idwal N. Wales 4 OS map 115 SH 6459

Lying about 5 miles (8 km) west of Capel Curig, Cwm Idwal was the first Welsh National Nature Reserve, and is probably the best-known British location for arctic/alpine flowers outside Scotland. It consists of a cwm or corrie on the north side of the Glyder Mountain, and is a classic location for the study of geomorphology. Glacial erosion here has also exposed part of an enormous syncline high on the corrie walls, and cutting through this is a short but spectacular gorge known as the Devil's Kitchen which has been formed by the action of a waterfall.

The reserve covers 984 acres (398 ha).

Fauna

BIRDS The reserve is not famed for its fauna, although the birds here include **ravens**, **ring ouzels**, **wheatears**, **common sandpipers** and **dippers**.

MAMMALS A herd of **feral goats** ranges the higher parts of the reserve.

Flora

FLOWERING PLANTS Cwm Idwal is one of the very few British sites where the **Snowdon lily** may be found. This attractive plant is only known in this country from the mountains of Snowdonia, its next nearest site being in Switzerland. Another interesting species is the rare **tufted saxifrage**, a delightful little flower which is found practically nowhere else in Britain outside Scotland, and which was rapidly approaching extinction here until the Nature Conservancy, in collaboration with Liverpool University, collected the seed from some of the few remaining specimens, cultivated them under artificial conditions, and reintroduced them to Cwm Idwal in some numbers. The plant now has one of its main British strongholds here.

Other notable species here include **arctic saxifrage**, **purple mountain** saxifrage, mossy saxifrage, spring sandwort, northern bedstraw, mountain avens, moss campion, alpine meadow-grass, bluish mountain meadow-grass, jet sedge, hair sedge, three-flowered rush, twisted whitlow-grass, alpine cinquefoil, globe flower, roseroot, northern rockcress, arctic mouse-ear, mountain sorrel, lesser meadow-rue, purple hawkweed, Welsh poppy and New Zealand willowherb.

Llyn Idwal, which lies in the bottom of the cwm, has some interesting aquatic alpines including **water lobelia, awlwort** and **shoreweed.** Llyn Clyd (SH 634597) and Llyn-y-Cwm (SH 637584) both hold **bogbean.**

FERNS The ferns include **parsley fern, holly fern, green** and **common spleenworts, lemon-scented fern, beech fern, oak fern, Wilson's filmy fern, alpine clubmoss, stagshorn clubmoss, fir clubmoss** and **lesser clubmoss.** The aquatic fern, **pillwort,** may be found in Llyn Idwal.

Access

The reserve lies adjacent to the A5 trunk road. There are no restrictions on access, and a footpath leads to the high tops and the Devil's Kitchen.

Snowdon N. Wales 5 OS map 115 SH 6054

Snowdon (or Y Wyddfa) is the highest point in Wales at 3560ft (1085m). It is probably not widely known, however, that $6\frac{1}{2}$ square miles (16.7km²) of the mountain have been designated as a National Nature Reserve. The main interest is botanical, although the fauna is quite rich, too, and the reserve includes areas of moorland, bog and about 150 acres (60ha) of woodland as well as having a superb alpine flora on the high tops.

Fauna

BIRDS **Buzzards, ravens, choughs, ring ouzels** and **wheatears** may be found.

MAMMALS Snowdon is one of the few places outside Scotland where **mountain hares** may be found. They were introduced here during the last century, and a few still survive on the heights above 1500ft (456m). Other mammals include **feral goats.**

INVERTEBRATES Two species of moths deserve special mention since they are confined to the Snowdon area. They are the **weaver's wave** and **Ashworth's rustic.**

Flora

FLOWERING PLANTS The most distinguished member of the flora is the rare **Snowdon lily** which is confined to Snowdon and a few neighbouring mountains, but there are also many other interesting alpines including **purple mountain saxifrage, mossy saxifrage, spring sandwort, northern bedstraw, moss campion, twisted whitlow-grass, alpine cinquefoil, common sundew, bog asphodel, northern rockcress, roseroot, lesser meadow-rue, mountain sorrel, purple hawkweed** and **Welsh poppy.**

Llyn Teyrn (SH 642547) holds **water lobelia**.

FERNS **Parsley fern, holly fern, alpine woodsia** and **oblong woodsia** are all found among the hills, and Llyn Teryn has **common quillwort**.

Access

There are several routes to the summit, but probably the easiest is the Miner's track which starts from the Llanberis Pass at map reference SH 647556. There are parking facilities here and a nature trail. A second trail starts at SH 627506.

A quicker and less tiring method is to take the mountain railway from Llanberis to the summit and walk down.

Bardsey Island N. Wales 6 OS map 123 SH 1221

Bardsey Island lies about 2 miles (3km) from the westernmost tip of the Lleyn Peninsula and covers 370 acres (150 ha). It is owned by the Bardsey Island Trust, who run a bird observatory, and there are also large colonies of breeding seabirds.

Fauna

BIRDS Bardsey has the largest colony of **Manx shearwaters** in North Wales. Over 3000 pairs currently nest there with fewer numbers of **storm petrels. Guillemots, razorbills** and **shags** also nest in small numbers, and there are a few **oystercatchers, ravens** and **choughs**.

Bardsey is also a good migration watchpoint, the lighthouse serving to attract a great many migrants to the island. Large numbers of common species are recorded each year, and there are usually a few exciting rarities. Indeed, the observatory holds a number of 'first records' both for Wales and the British Isles.

MAMMALS **Grey seals** often haul out on to the island although none breeds here.

Flora

FLOWERING PLANTS **Darnel fescue, cliff spurrey, spring squill, early scurvy grass** and **thrift** are among the most notable plants.

Access

Boats sail to Bardsey from Pwllheli every Saturday throughout the summer months. Hence daily visits to the island are not possible, but anyone wishing to stay at the observatory is invited to do so. Full details of the visiting arrangements are available from Mrs H. Bond, 21a Gestridge Rd, Kingsteignton, Newton Abbot, Devon.

Rhinog N. Wales 7 OS map 124 SH 6530

The Rhinog Mountains lie about 6 miles (10 km) north-west of Dolgellau and rise to slightly over 2300 ft (700 m). Unlike many Welsh mountains, the grazing pressure here is very light and, in consequence, the hills are covered with extensive spreads of heather. The interest of the area is further enhanced by the abundance of small pools and bogs and the occurrence of a few relict woods on the lower ground.

One of the most interesting areas has been declared a National Nature Reserve of 991 acres (401 ha) and two adjacent areas are owned by the National Trust.

Fauna

BIRDS Among the more notable birds are **buzzards, merlins, ravens, ring ouzels, wheatears, common sandpipers, golden plovers, dunlin** and **teal.** Perhaps surprisingly, **red grouse** are relatively scarce here since the heather is too old to supply them with the tender young shoots which form their main food.

MAMMALS A herd of about 100 **feral goats** roam the area, which they share with **polecats** and **badgers.**

Flora

FLOWERING PLANTS Most of the hills are covered with **ling** which, unlike that on most heather moors, is rarely burned and has been allowed to regenerate naturally. The **lesser twayblade** orchid may be found growing beneath the **heather.** There is also a little **bilberry.**

On higher ground, the terrain is more rugged. **Mossy saxifrage** grows on boulders here, and **bog myrtle** may be found in some of the bogs.

FERNS **Bracken** dominates parts of the hills, and both the **Scottish** and **Tunbridge filmy ferns** may be found in places.

MOSSES AND LIVERWORTS Several notable bryophytes grow under the heather including *Barzania tricrenata, Ptilium cristacastrensis, Herberta hutchinsiae* and *Anastrepta orcadensis.* In the woodlands, and in some of the moist ravines on the lower slopes, are *Bartramidula wilsonii, Gymnocolea acutiloba* and *Leptodontium recurvifolium.*

Access

No permits are needed to visit either the National Nature Reserve or the adjacent National Trust areas.

The easiest approach is from Harlech. Follow the A496 southwards to Llanbedr, thence along the unclassified roads eastwards along Cwm Nantcol. A footpath leaves this road at SH 634259 and takes you towards Rhinog Fach (2333ft/711m).

Morfa Harlech and Morfa Dyffryn
N. Wales 8 OS map 124 SH 5835 & 5625

These two National Nature Reserves lie just north and south of Harlech respectively and are separated from each other by about 4 miles (6.5 km).

Morfa Harlech covers 2 square miles (4.9 km²) and includes sand dunes, mudflats and saltmarsh. Morfa Dyffryn covers 500 acres (202 ha) and, although there are also saltings and saltmarsh here, the vast bulk of the reserve is sand hills.

Fauna

BIRDS Both reserves are mainly of botanical interest although Morfa Harlech is the winter home of small numbers of wildfowl which include **whooper swans, mallard, teal, wigeon** and **shovelers.** During the summer the marshes here are home to a colony of **black-headed gulls.**

Flora

FLOWERING PLANTS The rare estuarine **spike rush** grows on the saltmarsh at Morfa Harlech along with **sea meadow-grass, sea rush, cord grass, dotted sedge, chestnut sedge, saltmarsh sedge** and **distant sedge.** The last two are said to form hybrids here.

The dunes here have **pyramidal orchid, bee orchid, maiden pink, smooth catsear** and **heart's-ease pansy**, and the slacks hold **northern marsh orchid, early marsh orchid, sharp rush,** and **greater bladderwort.**

The slacks at Morfa Dyffryn have **green-flowered helleborine, sharp rush** and **creeping willow. Sea spurge** is also common here.

FERNS The curious **moonwort** grows on the dunes at Morfa Harlech and **fir clubmoss** may be found in some of the slacks there.

Access

A permit is needed to visit either site. Intending visitors should apply to The Nature Conservancy Council, Penhros Rd, Bangor, Gwynedd LL57 2LQ.

Cader Idris N. Wales 9 OS map 124 SH 7213

This 2927ft (893m) high mountain lies just south of the Mawddach Estuary and roughly half-way between Dolgellau and Machynlleth. About 1½ square miles (4km²) of it have been designated as a National Nature Reserve, principally to protect the montane flora.

Fauna

BIRDS The birdlife includes **merlins, buzzards, ring ouzels, dippers** and **common sandpipers.**

MAMMALS A small herd of **feral goats** inhabits the mountain, and **polecats** are said to be common.

Flora

FLOWERING PLANTS Large areas of the mountain are dominated by **bilberry heath**, and upland pastures with **sheeps fescue, mat grass** and various **bent grasses.** Smaller areas have **ling**, and **crowberry** and **heath rush** are also found but the main interest lies in the alpines.

Cader Idris is noted as being the southernmost British site for several alpine plants including **moss campion** and **purple hawkweed.** A notable rarity here is **hairy greenweed**, which probably has its northernmost British site here and is otherwise only known from the Lizard (SW 10) and parts of Sussex.

Other notable species include **mossy saxifrage, purple mountain saxifrage, spring sandwort, roseroot, mountain sorrel, upland scurvy grass, lesser meadow-rue, mountain melick, globe flower, Welsh poppy** and **stone bramble.**

FERNS The very rare **forked spleenwort** may be found on the mountain, along with **green spleenwort.** Some of the damp gorges which occur on the lower slopes provide a habitat for the **soft shield fern, Wilson's filmy fern** and the **Tunbridge filmy fern.**

MOSSES AND LIVERWORTS Several bryophytes reach their southern British limits here including *Leptodontium recurvifolium, Scapania ornithopodes, Herberta adunca* and *H. hutchinsiae.* The **woolly fringe moss** is found on the hill, and in the moist gorges lower down are *Jubula hutchinsiae, Radula voluta, Adelanthus decipiens, Plagiochila tridenticulata* and *Marchesinia mackaii.*

Access

By and large there are no restrictions on access except to some of the wooded areas for which permission from the Nature Conservancy is required. A good route over the mountain is the footpath which runs from near Dolgellau to the B4405 near Tal-y-Llyn via the summit and Llyn Cau.

Llyn Vyrnwy   N. Wales 10   OS map 125   SH 9821

Llyn Vyrnwy is a large man-made reservoir about 10 miles (16 km) south-west of Bala. It is surrounded by forestry plantations and hill farmland and the whole area is controlled by the Severn–Trent Water Authority. The R.S.P.B. are co-operating with the Water Authority to protect and encourage the wildlife of the area. There is an information centre, nature trails, a public hide overlooking the lake and scores of nest boxes have been erected in the woodlands. The area is also interesting from the botanical point of view.

Fauna

BIRDS Over 100 species of birds have been recorded on the reserve. Among those which regularly nest are **great-crested grebes, teal, mallard, goosanders, woodcock, curlews, common sandpipers, golden plovers, dippers, redstarts, pied flycatchers, stonechats, ring ouzels, wood warblers, green woodpeckers, great spotted woodpeckers** and **ravens.**

Crossbills also frequent the woods and may have bred, and **hen harriers** and **peregrines** are occasionally seen. During the early spring the lake is a roosting place for up to 3500 **black-headed gulls.**

MAMMALS These include **polecats, badgers, red foxes,** and **red squirrels.**

INVERTEBRATES Several interesting **butterflies** have been recorded including the **high brown fritillary, silver washed fritillary, dark green fritillary, large heath** and **purple hairstreak.**

Flora

FLOWERING PLANTS Among the woods and hills surrounding the lake are **Welsh poppy**, **opposite-leaved golden saxifrage**, **starry saxifrage**, **common sundew**, **bog asphodel**, **bog pimpernel**, **New Zealand willowherb**, **lesser twayblade**, **globe flower**, **ivy-leaved bellflower**, **lesser skullcap** and **mountain pansy**.

FERNS These include **beech fern**, **oak fern**, **rusty back** and **parsley ferns**.

Access

There are numerous footpaths and forest rides along which visitors are free to wander. The information centre is situated at the west end of the dam (SH 985215), and the two nature trails start from here. The R.S.P.B. has erected a hide on the lake shore at SH 971232 and it is freely available to the public.

Coed Camlyn N. Wales 11 OS map 124 SH 6539

Coed Camlyn is a relict sessile oak wood which lies to the south of the Vale of Ffestiniog and includes a National Nature Reserve of 157 acres (63 ha). The woods are well known to botanists, especially lichen and bryophyte enthusiasts.

Flora

FLOWERING PLANTS Although **sessile oak** is dominant, there is quite a wide variety of tree species including **birch**, **holly**, **beech**, **sweet chestnut** and some **sycamore**. Most of the ground flora is of **bilberry** with **purple moor-grass**, **bent grasses** and **wavy hair-grass**. At one time, large areas were overgrown with **rhododendron**, but this has now been controlled by the reserve managers. **Great wood-rush** and **wood sorrel** are present in the herb layer.

FERNS **Royal fern** occurs sparingly and **Tunbridge filmy fern** and **hay-scented buckler fern** are also present.

MOSSES AND LIVERWORTS The bryophyte flora is very rich and includes *Sematophyllum demissum*, *Hylocomium umbratum*, *Hypnum callichroum*, *Adelanthus decipiens*, *Colura calyptrifolia*, *Drepanolejeunea hamatifolia*, *Harpalejeunea ovata*, *Radula voluta* and *Marchesinia mackaii*.

LICHENS Notable lichens include *Rinodina isidioides*, *Pannaria sampaiana*, *Thelopsis rubella*, *Parmelia horrescens*, *Thelotrema lepadinum*, *Haematomma elatinum* and *Lecidea cinnabararinum*.

Access

The reserve lies near to the A496 Ffestiniog to Harlech road, but is only open to permit holders. The address for permits is the Nature Conservancy Council, Penrhos Road, Bangor, Gwynedd LL57 2LQ.

Coed Ganllwyd N. Wales 12 OS map 124 SH 7224

This 59 acre (24ha) woodland lies on the eastern side of the Rhinog Hills (N. Wales 7). It is crossed by the gorge of the Afon Gamlan and includes the well-known waterfall of Rhaiadr-ddu which, in addition to being very attractive, also helps to create the humid conditions enjoyed by a wide range of bryophytes. The wood is declared as a National Nature Reserve.

Flora

FLOWERING PLANTS **Sessile oak** is the principal tree species, but there is also some **pedunculate oak, birch, sycamore, wych elm, beech, rowan** and **gean**. **Hazel** is a common shrub and there is some **holly, hawthorn, blackthorn** and **alder buckthorn**.

The herbaceous flora includes **bluebells, foxglove, common cow-wheat, tormentil, heath bedstraw, dog's mercury, common enchanter's nightshade, herb Robert, herb bennet** and **selfheal**.

FERNS Both **Wilson's** and **Tunbridge filmy ferns** grow here, and there is also the **hay-scented buckler fern**.

MOSSES AND LIVERWORTS The reserve is well known for its bryophytes which include *Campylopus setifolius, Leptodontium recurvifolium, Hylocomium umbratum, Colura calyptrifolia, Jubula hutchinsiae, Drepanolejeunea hamatifolia, Harpalejeunea ovata, Radula voluta, R. aquilegia, Frullania microphylla, Plagiochila tridenticulata, Sematophyllum demissum, S. novae-caesareae, Adelanthus decipiens* and *Mylia cuneifolia*.

Access

The reserve lies close to Ganllwyd village which is on the A487 Dolgellau to Ffestiniog road. No permits are needed to visit the woodland.

Dovey Estuary (including Borth Bog and Ynys-hir) S. Wales 1 OS map 135 SN 6595

The Dovey Estuary (Aberdyfi) lies about 10 miles (16 km) south-west of Machynlleth, and is one of the most important wildfowl refuges in Wales. Much of the estuary is protected as a National Nature Reserve which includes mudflats, saltmarsh, a system of sand dunes and part of Borth Bog (Cors Fochno). This is one of the largest examples of a raised bog in Britain, and lies immediately south of the estuary. A little way to the east, the R.S.P.B. have their 630 acre (255 ha) reserve known as Ynys-hir.

Fauna

BIRDS During the winter, the estuary can hold up to 3000 ducks, numerous waders and a relic flock of up to 80 **Greenland white-fronted geese**; the latter feeding mainly on Borth Bog and roosting on the estuary. The ducks include **wigeon, goldeneye, pintails, mallard, teal, shelducks,** and **red-breasted mergansers**, the last two of which breed here. **Oystercatchers, redshanks** and **curlews** are among the commonest waders.

The R.S.P.B. reserve of Ynys-hir includes both deciduous and conifer woodland where **buzzards, redstarts** and **pied flycatchers** nest. There is also a small **heronry** on the reserve; **dippers** and **ravens** are often seen, and **nightjars** nest on the hillside.

MAMMALS The district is a stronghold of the **polecat**, and **otters** are occasionally seen.

INVERTEBRATES Borth Bog is one of the two known localities where the **rosy marsh moth** still survives. It also has the bog bush cricket, and a great variety of dragonflies.

Flora

FLOWERING PLANTS Botanically speaking, Borth Bog is the most interesting part of the area, although the sand dunes north of Ynyslas (SN 607928) have both **northern marsh orchid** and **early marsh orchid**. The latter is also found on Borth Bog along with **common sundew, great sundew, long-leaved sundew, bog myrtle, bog rosemary** and **bog asphodel**. Around the edges of the bog are areas of carr dominated by **grey sallow** and which hold several other notable species such as **tussock sedge, common reed, marsh cinquefoil, bogbean, marsh violet, white sedge, yellow flag** and **hemp agrimony. Sea rush** and **bog rush** are also present.

FERNS The attractive **royal fern** grows among the carrs.

Access

The A493, which runs along the northern shore, offers quite good views over the estuary. Access to the N.N.R., including Borth Bog, is restricted and intending visitors are advised to contact the Nature Conservancy Council's Warden at Llwyn Awel, Talybont, Aberystwyth.

Ynys-hir is open to the public but only on certain days of the week, and visiting arrangements may be subject to alterations from time to time. Particulars of current visiting days are available from The Warden, Cae'r Berllan, Eglwysfach, Machynlleth SY20 8TA.

Tregaron Bog S. Wales 2 OS map 147 SN 6964

Tregaron Bog is widely acclaimed as the finest example of a raised bog in the whole of England and Wales. It is a National Nature Reserve covering 3 square miles (7.6km²) and lies about 12 miles (19km) south-east of Aberystwyth. It is of interest to both botanists and birdwatchers.

Fauna

BIRDS The breeding birds include **curlews, snipe, redshanks, teal** and other ducks. **Red kites** are often seen in winter along with **buzzards, hen harriers** and **peregrine falcons.**

MAMMALS The bog is said to be a stronghold of the **polecat**, the specimens here being of a smaller and redder variety than those found elsewhere in Wales. **Water voles, foxes** and **otters** also frequent the area.

Flora

FLOWERING PLANTS The flora includes **ling, cross-leaved heath, purple moor-grass, deer grass, reed grass, tufted hair-grass, cottongrass, white beak sedge, crowberry, soft rush, long-leaved sundew, bog asphodel** and **bog rosemary.**

Access

Good views over the bog may be had from the B4343 which runs along its eastern side. Access is restricted to the old railway walk, however, unless a permit has been obtained from the Nature Conservancy Council, Minawel, Ffair Rhos, Ystrad Meurig, Dyfed or Plas Gogerddan, Aberystwyth, Dyfed.

Gwenffrwd and Dinas s. Wales 3 OS map 147 SN 7546

These two blocks of oak woodland lie some 9 miles ($14\frac{1}{2}$km) north of Llandovery and, together with an area of moorland, constitute a $1\frac{3}{4}$ square mile (4.8km²) reserve of the R.S.P.B.

Fauna

BIRDS One of the principal attractions here are the **red kites** which nest nearby, but there is much else, too, including **buzzards, merlins, red grouse, ring ouzels, wheatears, common sandpipers, dippers, pied flycatchers, redstarts** and **wood warblers**.

MAMMALS The mammals include **polecats, red squirrels** and **badgers**.

Flora

FLOWERING PLANTS The dominant tree is **sessile oak**, with **ash, alder, rowan, birch, wych elm, holly, hawthorn, grey sallow**, and **eared sallow**. Smaller plants include **sweet vernal grass, wavy hair-grass, bilberry, wood sorrel, bluebell, herb Robert, meadowsweet** and **golden saxifrage**.

FERNS **Male fern, common polypody, Wilson's filmy fern** and **oak fern** are to be found.

Access

The reserve is accessible from Llandovery via the village of Rhandir-Mwyn. The Dinas has a nature trail which is open all the time, but otherwise the reserve is only open on certain days of the week. Visiting arrangements may change from time to time, so intending visitors are advised to contact the warden in advance for full particulars. The address is: Troedrhiwgelynen, Rhandir-Mwyn, Llandovery, Dyfed SA20 0PN.

Ramsey Island s. Wales 4 OS map 157 SM 7023

Ramsey Island is a 650 acre (263 ha) R.S.P.B. reserve which lies a few miles west of St David's Head, Dyfed. The main interest is the seabird colonies and the grey seal rookery.

Fauna

BIRDS Regular breeders include **guillemots, razorbills, fulmars, shags, cormorants, kittiwakes, herring gulls, lesser black-backed gulls, greater black-backed gulls, choughs, oystercatchers, wheatears, stonechats, ravens, buzzards**, and **peregrine falcons**.

The island is also a noted migration watchpoint.

MAMMALS Ramsey is one of the largest **grey seal** rookeries in Wales and about 200 pups per year are born here.

Access

Boats from St Justinian (SM 723252) sail round the island daily throughout the summer, and the trips offer excellent views of the spectacular 170 ft (52 m) high cliffs and caves to the west of the island. There is a small landing fee, and hostel accommodation is available for those who wish to stay.

Grassholm S. Wales 5 OS map 157 SM 5909

Grassholm is both the smallest and the most outlying of the four Dyfed bird islands. It lies about 10 miles (16 km) offshore and covers a mere 22 acres (9 ha). The interest is centred on the huge gannet colony which is probably the fourth largest in Britain. Grassholm is an R.S.P.B. reserve.

Fauna

BIRDS **Gannets** normally nest on cliff ledges, but since Grassholm is very low-lying and has no cliffs of any size, the 20,000 or so pairs of gannets which inhabit the island are forced to nest here on almost level ground. Grassholm is unique among British colonies in this respect.

Sharing the island with the gannets are much smaller numbers of **guillemots, razorbills, puffins, kittiwakes, herring gulls, greater black-backed gulls, shags, rock pipits** and **ravens**.

Access

Access to the island is not easy, largely on account of the difficulty in landing, which can only be accomplished in the calmest of weather. Details can be obtained from the R.S.P.B. Wales Office, Frolic Street, Newtown, Powys SY16 1AP.

Skomer S. Wales 6 OS map 157 SM 7209

The island of Skomer lies about 1 mile (1.6 km) west of the Dyfed coast and is the largest and most easily accessible of the four seabird islands in the area. It extends to 759 acres (307 ha) and is a National Nature Reserve although it is managed by the West Wales Naturalists' Trust. Although the main attraction is seabirds, there are other birds besides and the flora is also quite interesting. Skomer is also well known on account of its unique sub-species of vole.

Fauna

BIRDS The most numerous bird species on the island is the **Manx shearwater**, over 100,000 pairs of which have riddled the island's turf with their burrows. **Puffins** are also numerous, and doubtless there is a good deal of competition between them, the shearwaters and the innumerable rabbits for the best burrows! There are also a few **storm petrels**.

The cliffs have their share of seabirds, too, including over 2000 pairs of **guillemots**, 1500 pairs of **razorbills** and 2000 pairs of **kittiwakes**. Other birds include **fulmars, shags, herring gulls, cormorants, lesser black-backed gulls, greater black-backed gulls, ravens, oystercatchers, rock pipits, wheatears, curlews, snipe, little owls, short-eared owls, kestrels** and **buzzards**.

The island is also quite a good watchpoint for migratory birds.

MAMMALS The most distinguished member of the mammal fauna is the **Skomer vole** (*Clethrionomys glareolus skomerensis*), a sub-species of the bank vole, which is restricted to the island. Sharing the island with this problematical rodent are **field mice, pygmy shrews, common shrews** and, as was mentioned previously, **rabbits**. There is also a small **grey seal** rookery which produces about 100 pups annually.

Flora

FLOWERING PLANTS The flora is very much of secondary importance, but does include a few noteworthy species including **spring squill, English stonecrop, heath pearlwort, cliff spurrey** and **rock samphire**.

FERNS **Sea spleenwort** is found here.

Access

Boats sail to Skomer daily throughout the summer (except Mondays) from Martins Haven, which is a few miles west of Marloes (SM 793084). No permits are needed although a landing fee is charged in addition to the cost of the trip itself.

Skokholm   S. Wales 7   OS map 157   SM 7305

Skokholm Island lies a few miles south of Skomer (S. Wales 6) and is rather smaller, covering 247 acres (100 hectares).

Fauna

BIRDS About 35,000 pairs of **Manx shearwaters** nest on Skokholm, as well as several thousand **puffins** and **storm petrels**. There are also colonies of **guillemots** and **razorbills**, although nothing like the numbers which inhabit nearby Skomer Island.

Other breeding birds include **fulmars, oystercatchers, herring gulls, lesser black-backed gulls, greater black-backed gulls** and **stock doves**. **Ravens** have also bred here, and the island is well situated to receive a wide variety of migrants including **merlins, peregrines, dotterel, whimbrel, greenshanks, green sandpipers, wood sandpipers, purple sandpipers, ruff, arctic skuas, turtle doves, red-backed shrikes, black redstarts, choughs** and **alpine swifts**.

Access

The island does not attract many day visitors, and many people prefer to go to neighbouring Skomer instead since this is much easier to visit and has a greater variety of breeding birds.

Interested readers are referred to *The Island* by Ronald Lockley, which is published as a paperback by Penguin.

Worms Head S. Wales 8 OS map 159 SS 4188

Worms Head is a rocky promontory at the south-western tip of the Gower Peninsula. It consists of a row of four small hills which rise to a maximum height of about 150 ft (46 m) and which, when seen in profile are somewhat reminiscent of an enormous sea monster. This probably explains the name of the promontory since 'wurm' is the Welsh for dragon.

Being composed of limestone the cliffs are botanically rich, and there are also some small seabird colonies. The Worm is a part of the South Gower Coast National Nature Reserve of 116 acres (47 ha).

Fauna

BIRDS The seabird colonies include several hundred pairs of **kittiwakes** and **guillemots**, with fewer **razorbills, fulmars** and **shags**. **Puffins** were once extinct here but now appear to be making a comeback. **Herring gulls** and **rock pipits** also breed in fair numbers. The headland is also a fairly good migration watchpoint and **common scoters** are frequent in winter.

Flora

FLOWERING PLANTS The following species may be found: **navelwort, spring squill, golden samphire, cliff spurrey, bloody cranesbill, rock samphire, rock sea-lavender, sea storksbill, thrift** and **common rock-rose**.

Access

A public footpath runs from the village of Rhossili to the end of the peninsula but it is only passable at low tide. The Head is completely cut off at high water, so intending visitors are advised to consult local tide tables to avoid being marooned. Visitors are asked to avoid the Worm during the bird nesting season, March to May.

Oxwich Bay S. Wales 9 OS map 159 SS 5085

Situated on the southern coast of the Gower Peninsula, Oxwich Bay National Nature Reserve covers 542 acres (220 ha) of sand dunes, saltmarsh, fresh water marsh and pools and small areas of oak and alder woodlands. The sand hills in particular are a rich hunting ground for botanists, and the area is also of interest to birdwatchers, especially during the winter months.

Fauna

BIRDS A variety of waders and ducks may be seen in the bay in winter. They include **wigeon, shovelers, sanderling, bar-tailed godwits** and **knot**. **Water rails** breed in the marshes and **green woodpeckers** and **stonechats** are also regular nesters.

Flora

FLOWERING PLANTS The sand dunes are quite rich in lime and correspondingly fertile. Among the most noteworthy members of the flora are the rare **Welsh gentian** and the **Argentine dock** which grow in dune slacks here. Other interesting species are **early marsh orchid, southern marsh orchid, marsh helleborine, yellow-wort, bloody cranesbill, evening primrose, sea spurge** and **sea holly.**

The saltmarshes have **sea-lavender, marsh mallow, parsley water dropwort** and **saltmarsh rush,** and elsewhere you may find **Babington's orache, tree lupin, everlasting pea, tubular water dropwort, fen rush, flowering rush, sea buckthorn,** and **bogbean.**

Whitebeam trees grow among the woodland.

FERNS **Rusty back ferns** grow here.

Access

The reserve is easily accessible from the unclassified road which runs between Oxwich village and the A4118. A couple of public footpaths leave this road and cross the dunes to the beach, but away from these a permit from the Nature Conservancy is needed. Applications should be made to the Nature Conservancy Council, 44 The Parade, Roath, Cardiff CF2 3AB.

Craig Cerrig Gleisiad S. Wales 10 OS map 160 SO 0121

The National Nature Reserve of Craig Cerrig Gleisiad lies about 6 miles (9.5 km) south-west of Brecon and includes two low sandstone hills both just below 2000 ft (610 m). It is primarily of interest on account of the montane flora, and is the southernmost British station of several alpines.

Fauna

BIRDS The animal life here is not of outstanding interest although **peregrines, merlins, buzzards, ravens, ring ouzels, common sandpipers** and **dippers** are among the birds of the area.

Flora

FLOWERING PLANTS **Purple mountain saxifrage, globe flower** and **least willow** all reach their southernmost limits here. Other notable species are **mossy saxifrage, lesser meadow-rue** and **heath rush.**

Large areas are dominated by **ling** and **bilberry** and there is plenty of **harestail cottongrass** near the summits.

Access

The reserve lies to the west of the A470 but a permit from the Nature Conservancy Council, Penrhos Road, Bangor, Gwynedd LL57 2LQ is needed to visit it.

Craig Y Cilau S. Wales 11 OS map 161 SO 1915

Craig y Cilau is an interesting escarpment about 7 miles (11 km) west of Abergavenny. The shallow dip slope is overlain with gritstone, whereas the craggy scarp slope is limestone and the cliffs here have a rich calcicole flora in consequence. The site also includes an extensive cave system which extends for over 20 miles (32 km) underground and possibly much further. The site has been designated a National Nature Reserve and covers 157 acres (63 ha).

Flora

FLOWERING PLANTS The gritstone plateau is largely covered with rough grassland and **bilberry**, **heather** and **crowberry**. The main floral interest, however, is on the limestone crags which have **angular Solomon's seal**, **alpine enchanter's nightshade**, **mossy saxifrage** and **mountain melick**.

There are also four rare species of **whitebeams** which grow here on the crags, one of which, *Sorbus minima*, is restricted to this, and one other neighbouring site. The other three are *S. leptophylla*, *S. anglica* and *S. porrigentiformis*.

FERNS **Green spleenwort** and **limestone polypody** grow here.

Access

The reserve is accessible from Crickhowell via the network of minor roads and public footpaths. A permit from the Nature Conservancy Council Warden at Windyridge, Pennorth, Brecon, is needed to enter the caves but otherwise there are no restrictions on access.

Cwm Clydach S. Wales 12 OS map 161 SO 2112

This 50 acre (20 ha) National Nature Reserve contains what is probably the most westerly surviving natural beechwood in Wales. It lies about 6 miles (10 km) west of Abergavenny in the Clydach Valley, and is in two blocks.

Flora

FLOWERING PLANTS Although **beech** is the dominant tree throughout, there is a wide range of other trees, too. This variety reflects the underlying rocks which range from limestone to sandstone, the former giving rise to fertile basic soils, the latter to more acidic ones. The lime-rich areas have **ash** and **wych elm** as well as the **beech**, and there is also some **yew** and **holly**. Where the soil is more acid, **sessile oak** and **birch** may be found along with some **rowan**. Three uncommon types of whitebeam are also known in the area, namely *Sorbus leptophylla*, *S. leyana* and *S. minima*.

Some of the more noteworthy herbs are **wall lettuce, dog's mercury, broad-leaved willowherb, bilberry, great wood-rush** and **ramsons**.

FERNS The ferns are well represented and include **soft shield fern, hard shield fern, golden scales male fern, hard fern, lady fern, hartstongue** and **bracken**.

Access

The woods are situated on the southern side of the Clydach Valley just east of Brynmawr near to the A465. A public footpath runs through part of the reserve and a permit is required to visit other parts of the reserve. This can be obtained from the Nature Conservancy Council, 44 The Parade, Roath, Cardiff CF2 3AB.

St David's Head S. Wales 13 OS map 157 SM 7428

St David's Head lies at the extreme western tip of Dyfed and consists of a series of 250 ft (76 m) high cliffs and an extensive area of maritime heath. The area is owned by the National Trust.

Fauna

BIRDS The area is noted for its **choughs** and there are also **ravens, buzzards** and **rock pipits**.

MAMMALS There are one or two small **grey seal** rookeries below the cliffs.

Flora

FLOWERING PLANTS The cliffs themselves hold **spring squill, cliff spurrey, wild chives, kidney vetch, wall pepper, thrift, heath pearlwort, sheepsbit**, a dwarf variety of the **ox-eye daisy** and the extremely rare **hairy greenweed**, which grows in some abundance here. There is also a type of **sea-lavender** – *Limonium paradoxum* – which has its only known site here.

The maritime heathland behind the cliffs is dominated by **ling** with **bell heather** and **western gorse**.

Access

No special permits are needed and the area is freely accessible from St David's via the B4583.

Stackpole Head S. Wales 14 OS map 158 SR 9796

Stackpole Head proper lies about 4 miles (6½ km) south of Pembroke near to Stackpole Quay but the area discussed here includes the 8 mile (13 km) stretch of coastline which runs westwards from Stackpole Head to Linney Head. The coast here consists mainly of limestone cliffs, but there are also two sandy bays (Barafundle and Broad Haven) with dunes and a series of lakes known as Bosherston Lake.

Most of the area is the property of the National Trust and is a National Nature Reserve.

Fauna

BIRDS The cliffs have several species of seabirds including **guillemots, razorbills, fulmars, kittiwakes,** and **shags,** and there are also **rock doves, ravens, wheatears, choughs** and, sometimes, **peregrines**.

Flora

FLOWERING PLANTS The flowering plants of the cliffs include **thrift, sea plantain, buckshorn plantain, dark-green mouse-ear, darnel fescue grass, rock sea-lavender, cliff spurrey, scurvy grass, sea pearlwort, wild thyme, glaucous sedge, spring squill, tormentil, squinancy wort, golden samphire, common twayblade** and the very rare **small rest-harrow** which is only found here, on the nearby Gower Peninsula, Berry Head and in the Channel Islands.

Bosherston Lake holds **fennel pondweed, curly pondweed, Canadian pondweed** and **spiked water milfoil** and species of **stonewort**.

Access

The area may be reached either from the east via Stackpole village, from the middle via Merrion or from the west via Castlemartin. Most of the area is freely accessible, but the National Trust estate here includes a certain amount of farmland and there is a tank range which is also out of bounds.

Coombes Valley M 1 OS map 119 SK 0052

Coombes Valley is a steep-sided valley with a rocky stream which lies a few miles south east of Leek. It is well wooded, chiefly with oak, and interspersed with bracken slopes and pastures. It is maintained as a nature reserve by the R.S.P.B. and covers some 260 acres (105 ha).

Fauna

BIRDS The reserve is mainly of interest to birdwatchers and the birdlife includes **tree pipits, wood warblers, sparrowhawks, redstarts, pied flycatchers**, all three British **woodpeckers, woodcock, dippers** and **kingfishers**.

Access

The reserve may be reached from the unclassified road which leaves the main A523 about 3 miles (4.8 km) south-east of Leek. It is closed from January to March and is only open on certain days of the week throughout the rest of the year. The warden will advise on the precise times of opening and his address is: Six Oaks Farm, Bradnop, Leek, Staffs ST13 7EU.

Dove Dale M 2 OS map 119 SK 1453

The picturesque River Dove rises in the southern Pennines and flows, for much of its course, through the limestone country of the southern Peak District, before joining the River Trent by Burton-upon-Trent. In this area the National Trust have set aside a $4\frac{1}{2}$ mile (7 km) stretch of the Dove Valley as a nature reserve.

The southern part of the reserve is extensively wooded with natural ash woods whilst further north, especially in the tributary valleys of Biggin Dale and Wolfscote Dale, there are fertile grasslands and limestone outcrops with a most interesting calcicole flora.

Flora

FLOWERING PLANTS   The woodlands are predominantly **ash** with some **beech, pedunculate oak, yew, rowan, field maple, holly** and **white-beams** (*Sorbus aucuparia, S. aria* and *S. rupicola*). **Blackthorn** and **hawthorn** are common shrubs, and the herbaceous flora includes **mountain currant, burnet rose, butterbur, wild strawberry, herb Bennet, dog's mercury, reed grass, brooklime** and **meadowsweet**.

Biggin Dale, to the north of the reserve, has **hutchinsia, field garlic, Nottingham catchfly, dark red helleborine, common helleborine, bloody cranesbill, black bryony, pale St John's wort, glaucous sedge, flea sedge, common rock-rose, wild thyme, kidney vetch, dog's mercury, red hemp nettle, hairy rockcress, marjoram**, and a large variety of grasses including **false oat, yellow oat, meadow oat, Yorkshire fog, quaking grass, sweet vernal grass** and **crested hair-grass**.

Wolfscotte Dale in the north-east also has **Nottingham catchfly** along with **mossy saxifrage, upright brome grass, wild angelica, common valerian** and **burnet saxifrage**.

Access

The reserve lies about 4 miles (6.5 km) north-east of Ashbourne. There are no roads along the valley but the area is freely accessible on foot. The woods may be reached either from the end of the unclassified road which leaves the Ilam–Thorpe road at SK 146505, or by footpath from Milldale (SK 139547).

Biggin Dale is reached from Biggin Village (SK 147595) and Wolfscotte Dale by footpath from SK 128586.

Chartley Moss   M 3   OS map 128   SK 0228

Chartley Moss is the largest basin mire in Britain. It lies about 7 miles (11 km) north-east of Stafford and is scheduled as a National Nature Reserve covering 104 acres (42 ha). It consists of a huge raft of *Sphagnum* moss which is actually floating on about 30 ft (9 m) of water – the so-called 'schwingmoor' type of bog which is quite uncommon in this country.

Flora

FLOWERING PLANTS   The *Sphagnum* raft has a number of interesting bog species growing on it such as **cranberry, crowberry, bog rosemary, common sundew, common cottongrass, harestail cottongrass, ling** and **cross-leaved heath**. Some **birch** and **pine** seedlings also grow among the moss.

There are one or two breaks in the raft which are fringed by **graceful sedge, tufted sedge** and **soft rush**, and one area is quite base rich and has **purple small reed, marsh valerian, common sedge, tussock sedge** and **common skullcap**.

FERNS   **Marsh fern** grows here.

M

MOSSES AND LIVERWORTS *Sphagnum recurvum* is the dominant species of moss here, but there are several others as well including *S. papillosum*, *S. capillaceum*, *S. magellanicum* and *Aulacomnium palustre*.

Access

Schwingmoor bogs are both delicate and potentially dangerous and the reserve should not be visited without permission from the Nature Conservancy Council. Applications for permits should be sent to the Nature Conservancy Council, Attingham Park, Shrewsbury, Salop SY4 4TW. No visits are allowed without supervision.

Cannock Chase   M 4   OS maps 127 & 128   SJ 9818

Cannock Chase is a huge tapestry of heathland, woodland, bogs, fens and streams which lies about 8 miles (13km) south-east of Stafford. It is designated as an Area of Outstanding Natural Beauty and is thus protected, to some degree, from adverse developments and it forms a most valuable wildlife sanctuary. The Chase covers about 26 square miles (68km²), about 10 square miles (26km²) of which are occupied by the Cannock Chase Forest. Much of the remainder is common land and other parts are privately owned.

Fauna

BIRDS The Chase is one of the most important sanctuaries for wild birds in the Midlands. The birds include the elusive **nightjar** along with **redstarts, wood warblers, grasshopper warblers, whinchats** and **long-eared owls.**

INVERTEBRATES The uncommon **angle-striped sallow moth** is found on Cannock Chase. Other moths include the **anomalous.**

Flora

FLOWERING PLANTS Much of the area is dominated by heathland which holds the unusual **hybrid crowberry.**

A variety of woodland types are present including **sessile oak** and **birch** with **alder** coppices and **willow scrub,** but perhaps the main botanical interest is in the numerous valley mires which hold **cranberry, few-flowered spike rush, separate-headed sedge, grass of Parnassus, bog asphodel, bog pimpernel, marsh valerian, common sundew, great sundew, common butterwort, tawny sedge, flea sedge, marsh pennywort** and **common spotted orchid.**

Access

The Chase lies roughly within a triangle bounded by the A34, the A513 and the A460. It is adequately provided with footpaths and also incorporates an information centre and wildlife museum which is situated at SK 018172.

Earl's Hill M 5 OS map 126 SJ 4004

Earl's Hill is a reserve of the Shropshire Trust for Nature Conservation which lies a little way south-west of Shrewsbury. The lower slopes of the hill are clothed with some interesting woodlands which peter out on the higher ground and give way to cliffs and scree.

The reserve covers 105 acres (42 ha).

Fauna

BIRDS The woods hold a variety of the commoner woodland birds including **pied flycatchers, redstarts, wood warblers** and all three British **woodpeckers**. Outside the woods **buzzards, kestrels** and **ravens** may be seen, and **dippers** frequent some of the streams.

INVERTEBRATES Butterfly enthusiasts should look out for the **grayling** and the **dark green fritillary**.

Flora

FLOWERING PLANTS The most interesting plants grow on the cliffs and among the screes. The uncommon **large-leaved lime** may be found here along with **alternate-leaved golden saxifrage, navelwort, rock stonecrop, bloody cranesbill** and **shining cranesbill**.

Access

The Hill is easily reached from Pontesbury which lies on the A488 about 7 miles (11 km) south-west of Shrewsbury. There is a visitors' centre which is open every weekend during the summer, and a fine nature trail which will take you to the summit 1047 ft (322 m) high, and with superb views over the surrounding countryside.

Wyre Forest M 6 OS map 138 SO 7576

The Wyre Forest lies about 5 miles (8 km) west of Kidderminster and covers an area of about 6 square miles (15.5 km²). Although basically an oak woodland, its character and structure have been shaped by many influences in the past, and it includes areas of old coppice and modern conifer plantations as well as relics of the natural oak forest. Much of it is managed as a National Nature Reserve, and is one of the most important wildlife sanctuaries in the Midlands.

Fauna

BIRDS **Redstarts** and **pied flycatchers** have one of their few Midland haunts here, and **kingfishers** nest along the banks of Dowles Brook and some of its tributaries.

MAMMALS A herd of introduced **fallow deer** still occupies the woods which also shelter **otters, dormice** and several species of **bats**.

REPTILES include **adders, grass snakes** and **slow worms**.

INVERTEBRATES Two moths worthy of special mention are the **Kentish glory** and the **alder kitten**.

M

Flora

FLOWERING PLANTS The forest is largely dominated by **sessile oak** but there are many other tree species besides including **ash, elm, small-leaved lime, wild service** and **alder**. Some of the more interesting herbs are **narrow helleborine, columbine, heath sedge, lily of the valley, mountain melick, wood cranesbill, bloody cranesbill, bilberry, ling, bell heather, common cow-wheat, broad-leaved cottongrass, dog's mercury** and **primroses**.

Access

The major part of the forest lies between the A456 and the B4149, and may be reached from either. It is criss-crossed by numerous footpaths and forest hides which are available for public use.

Chaddesley Woods M 7 OS map 139 SO 9273

Chaddesley Woods is a National Nature Reserve which lies about 7 miles (11km) east of Kidderminster.

Flora

FLOWERING PLANTS The woods are dominated by a mixture of **sessile** and **pedunculate oaks** with some **ash** and **birch**. Parts of the wood have been managed as a **hazel coppice** in the past and there are areas of **alder** along some of the streams. Among the most noteworthy herbs are **violet helleborine, thin-spiked wood sedge, saw-wort** and **pepper saxifrage**.

Access

The woods lie just north of the A448 and may be reached by a public footpath which leaves this road at SO 906725 and runs through the reserve. In order to leave the footpath, however, a permit from the Nature Conservancy Council, Attingham Park, Shrewsbury, Salop SY4 4TW is needed.

Brockhampton Wood M 8 OS map 149 SO 6855

Brockhampton Wood lies about halfway between Worcester and Hereford on the main A44. It is a nature reserve of the National Trust and is basically an old oakwood, although it now also supports an interesting variety of exotic trees. There is also a small, but interesting, pool.

Fauna

BIRDS The birdlife includes **buzzards, ravens, woodcock, redstarts, pied flycatchers** and **wood warblers. Little grebes** breed on the pool.

Flora

FLOWERING PLANTS The woods are dominated by a mixture of both **sessile** and **pedunculate oak** but there are many other trees besides including **beech, larch, giant redwood** and **giant sequoia**.

Access
The reserve lies immediately north of the A44 about 2 miles (3.2 km) east of Bromyard. No permits are necessary and the National Trust has built a nature trail.

Chee Dale M 9 OS map 119 SK 1172
This picturesque dale is actually part of the Wye Valley and lies about 4 miles (6.5 km) east of Buxton in the Peak District National Park. It lies in limestone country and includes ashwood and calcareous grassland, the whole extending to 60 acres (24 ha). The area is managed as a nature reserve by the Derbyshire Naturalists' Trust.

Fauna
BIRDS **Dippers** and **kingfishers** may be found along the river, and the woods have several common woodland species including **wood warblers** and **blackcaps. Kestrels** and **house martins** nest on some of the crags which cut across the reserve.

Flora
FLOWERING PLANTS The woods are principally of **ash** with some **rowan, birch, yew, wych elm** and **whitebeam.** Shrubs include **buckthorn, guelder rose, bird cherry** and **dogwood,** and the herbaceous flora has **lily of the valley** and **globeflower.**
    The grassland holds **cowslips, grass of Parnassus** and **Jacob's ladder.**
FERNS **Moonwort** grows on the grasslands.

Access
The reserve is accessible by footpath either from Blackwell (SK 125720) or from the A6 at SK 115722. Visitors are asked not to leave the paths.

Blacktoft Sands EA 1 OS map 112 SE 8423
Blacktoft Sands lies at the confluence of the Rivers Ouse and Trent, where they join to form the Humber. It is an R.S.P.B. reserve and includes artificial lagoons and a very large tidal reedbed. The reserve is important for its wintering wildfowl, passage waders and reedbed breeding species.

Fauna
BIRDS There are large numbers of **mallard, teal, wigeon, shelducks, dunlin** and **oystercatchers. Short-eared owls** and **bearded tits** may also be seen in winter, and the latter also breed among the reed beds here together with **water rails, reed warblers, sedge warblers** and **grasshopper warblers.**

Access
No special permits are needed to visit the reserve which is open at all times. A car park is situated $\frac{1}{2}$ mile (.8 km) from Ousefleet from which several hides are readily accessible. There is a small charge for entry.

Saltfleetby–Theddlethorpe EA 2 OS map 113 TF 4890

The Saltfleetby–Theddlethorpe National Nature Reserve lies about halfway between Grimsby and Skegness on the Lincolnshire coast. It consists of a 4 mile (6.5 km) strip of coastline with mudflats, sand dunes and both salt and freshwater marshes and extends, in all, to $1\frac{3}{4}$ square miles (4.4km²).

Fauna

BIRDS Hen harriers and short-eared owls are regularly seen here in winter, and a variety of waders such as ringed plovers, oystercatchers, bar-tailed godwits, knot, whimbrel, green sandpipers, wood sandpipers, spotted redshanks, curlew sandpipers and ruff appear here during their migrations, as also do shore larks and twite.

MAMMALS Badgers and foxes inhabit the reserve.

REPTILES AND AMPHIBIANS A small population of natterjack toads lives among the dunes.

Flora

FLOWERING PLANTS The system of dunes is rich in calcium and displays a superb succession from young, mobile dunes to 600-year-old ones. There are several interesting plant species here including pyramidal orchid, bee orchid, sea buckthorn, sea couch grass, lyme grass, lesser meadow-rue, carline thistle and dewberry.

Both the southern marsh orchid and early marsh orchid may be found growing in the dune slacks, and areas of freshwater marsh have lesser water plantain, bog pimpernel, marsh pea, great pond sedge, great water dock, common skullcap, sea rush, brookweed and common reed.

The saltmarshes have sea meadow-grass, sea plantain, thrift, sea purslane, sea rush and sea club-rush.

Access

The reserve runs parallel to the main A1031 coast road. Access is easily gained by leaving this main road eastwards along any one of several minor roads or, alternatively, by the public footpath which leaves Saltfleet village at TF 456934 and runs more or less all the way along the length of the reserve to Theddlethorpe St Helen.

No special permits are needed.

North Norfolk Coast EA 3 OS maps 132 & 133 TF 7145

The northern coast of Norfolk has an almost unbroken string of nature reserves which stretch a distance of about 20 miles (32 km) from Holme in the west to Cley in the east. The reserves are administered by several authorities including the National Trust, the Nature Conservancy Council, the R.S.P.B. and the Norfolk Naturalists' Trust, and the habitats they represent include mudflats, saltmarshes, sand dunes and areas of shingle.

The westernmost of this string of reserves is Holme Dunes, property of the Norfolk Naturalists' Trust which includes sand dunes, a reed-fringed pool known as Broad Water and a small area of scrub. Next comes the R.S.P.B. reserve of Titchwell which has been developed as shallow lagoons, reedswamp, saltmarsh and sand dunes for a variety of birds. The adjacent Scolt Head Island is a National Nature Reserve (N.N.R.) which is largely made up of shingle, whilst nearby Holkham N.N.R. consists mainly of mudflats backed by dunes. The shingle promontory of Blakeney Point comes next and is a reserve of the National Trust, and finally there are the famous Cley Marshes which belong to the Norfolk Naturalists' Trust.

Fauna

BIRDS The birdlife of the area is really quite outstanding, and several interesting species nest on the various reserves. These include **bearded tits, oystercatchers** and **ringed plovers** at Holme, whilst between them Scolt Head Island and Blakeney Point have the largest colony of **Sandwich terns** in the country (700 pairs) and **common terns**, too. Cley Marshes hold breeding **bitterns, bearded tits, garganey** and **water rails**, and **marsh harriers, black-tailed godwits** and **ruff** are quite frequently seen here during the summer.

During the winter months the mudflats of Holkham attract vast numbers of wildfowl including 1200 or so **brent geese, mallard, teal, wigeon, gadwall, shovelers, goldeneye, eiders, shelducks** and various waders such as **dunlin, knot** and **turnstones**. Holme Dunes are also good for waders and over 25,000 **knot** have been counted here along with **sanderling, bar-tailed godwits, grey plovers, whimbrel, little stints, wood sandpipers, green sandpipers** and **spotted redshanks**. **Hen harriers** and **short-eared owls** are also regular winter visitors here. Cley Marshes are equally exciting, and in winter can hold **curlew sandpipers, little gulls**, and **marsh harriers** and all kinds of rarities such as **waxwings, bluethroats, Mediterranean gulls** and **barred warblers**. Indeed, there is no guessing just what might turn up next!

Shore larks, snow buntings, Lapland buntings and **twite** are regular winter visitors all along the coast.

REPTILES AND AMPHIBIANS A small colony of **natterjack toads** lives on Holkham N.N.R.

Flora

FLOWERING PLANTS The saltmarshes at Titchwell, Holme, Blakeney, and Cley are among the richest areas of the Norfolk coastline as far as plant life is concerned. The rare **matted sea-lavender**, which is confined to the Norfolk coast, grows here along with **lax sea-lavender, common sea-lavender, sea heath, lesser cord grass, fragile glasswort, bushy glasswort** and **perennial glasswort**.

Holme Dunes are also very interesting botanically, and matted sea-lavender has another of its few sites here. Other notables include sea heath, sea bindweed, grey hair-grass and several orchids such as pyramidal, bee, early marsh, southern marsh and marsh helleborine.

Holkham Dunes also have bee and pyramidal orchids, marsh helleborine and sea buckthorn. The geese which winter on Holkham flats feed on both common eel-grass and dwarf eel-grass.

The shingle of Blakeney Point and Scolt Head Island has shrubby seablite, sea bindweed, slender sea knotgrass, sea pea, sharp rush, suffocated clover, burrowing clover, rock sea-lavender and yellow horned-poppy.

Access

Holme Dunes
The reserve lies a little way north of the main A149 near the village of Holme-next-the-Sea from where access may be gained. A special permit from the Norfolk Naturalists' Trust is required, however, and this should be requested from the Warden, The Firs, Broadwater Road, Holme-next-the-Sea, Hunstanton, Norfolk PE36 6LQ.

Titchwell
Access is allowed along the two sea walls which form the boundary of the reserve. The two paths start from the A149, one at TF 750436 and the other at TF 764437. The R.S.P.B. has a visitors' centre with car park west of Titchwell village.

Scolt Head Island
The only way to reach this National Nature Reserve is by boat from Brancaster Staithe (TF 7944). No permits are needed but access to the tern colonies is restricted during the nesting season.

Holkham
The reserve here includes some areas of farmland which are strictly out of bounds, but elsewhere access is unrestricted. The best access is along the foreshore from TF 915456.

Blakeney Point
Apart from the tern colonies, which are closed off during the nesting period, Blakeney Point is freely accessible to the public. It may be reached either from the Cley Coastguard Station (TG 048455) by foot – a 3 mile (5 km) walk – or by boat from Morston (TG 0043).

Cley Marshes
Good views of the marshes may be had from the public footpath which runs along the sea wall to the east of the reserve starting from TG 060442. Permits to use the hides on the reserve may be obtained from the Warden at Watcher's Cottage, Cley, Holt, Norfolk, or from the visitors' centre which is a little way east of Cley village on the main A149.

Hickling Broad and Horsey Mere

EA 4 OS map 134 TG 4121

These two nature reserves are both part of the Norfolk Broads, and are connected to each other by a short channel. Hickling Broad is scheduled as a National Nature Reserve and managed by the Norfolk Naturalists' Trust and it includes large reed beds and areas of fen and woodland. Horsey Mere belongs to the National Trust and is likewise surrounded by extensive reed beds.

Fauna

BIRDS The birdlife of both sites is of particular note. **Bearded tits** and **bitterns** have one of their main strongholds here, and **marsh harriers** occasionally nest among the reeds. **Garganey** and **gadwall** nest quite regularly, and the wintering birds usually include some 1300 **teal**, 700 **shovelers** and smaller numbers of **mallard, wigeon, pochard, tufted ducks, goldeneye** and **mute swans**.

Because of their close proximity to the sea, they also attract an interesting variety of migrants. **Ospreys, black terns** and **spoonbills** are not infrequent visitors.

INVERTEBRATES The **swallowtail butterfly** has one of its few strongholds here.

Flora

FLOWERING PLANTS Hickling Broad is one of the very few British sites where **holly-leaved naiad** may be found. This rare aquatic plant is only known in this country from three or four of the Norfolk Broads. A second speciality here is **marsh sow-thistle** which, likewise, is restricted to the Broads area. Other notable species include **cowbane, milk parsley, water violet, greater bladderwort** and **whorled water milfoil**. The latter species also occurs in Horsey Mere, which has **marestail**, too.

FERNS **Royal fern** grows in the reed beds of Hickling Broad, and mat-forming **water fern** may be found in Horsey Mere.

Access

Hickling Broad

Probably the best way to see the reserve is on one of the escorted water trails which are run during the week from May to September, by the Norfolk Naturalists' Trust. Details of these trips and prior bookings may be obtained by phoning Hickling 276.

Nature trails and observation hides are also available on the reserve, and details and permits are available from the warden's office (closed Tuesdays). (Map reference TG 428222).

Horsey Mere

A public footpath skirts the edge of the reed beds to the north of the mere starting from the B1159 just south of Horsey village (TG 457223).

Access to the mere is now restricted.

Bure Marshes EA 5 OS map 134 TG 3316

The Bure Marshes National Nature Reserve is part of the Norfolk Broads system which lies in the Upper Bure Valley and includes Hoveton Great Broad, Hoveton Little Broad, Ranworth Broad, Cockshoot Broad and the Woodbastwick wetlands. The fens and carrs of the reserve are of considerable botanical interest, and the area is very attractive to birdlife. The reserve extends to slightly over 1000 acres (404ha).

Fauna

BIRDS The Bure Marshes are an important breeding site for **bearded tits**. **Water rails, grey herons** and both **reed warblers** and **sedge warblers** also nest, and **common terns** breed on artificial rafts on Ranworth Broad. Overwintering birds include **mallard, shovelers, teal, wigeon, pochard** and **greylag geese**.

MAMMALS The mammals are represented by **otters** and the introduced **coypu**.

INVERTEBRATES The **swallowtail butterfly** has one of its few strongholds here.

Flora

FLOWERING PLANTS The edges of the broads show a most interesting succession from fen, through **alder** carr and eventually to woodland. The fen flora includes **cowbane, marsh pea, lesser tussock sedge, common sedge, common reed, fen rush, bog myrtle, frog-bit** and **milk parsley**.

The carrs are predominantly **alder** with **bird cherry, black currant, red currant, gooseberry, alder buckthorn, buckthorn, guelder rose, bittersweet, great bindweed, yellow flag** and **tussock sedge**.

FERNS **Royal fern** and **marsh fern** grow in the carrs.

Access

There is a nature trail near Hoveton Great Broad (at map reference TG 158322 – about $2\frac{1}{2}$ miles (4km) downstream from Hoveton) which can only be reached from the River Bure.

The Norfolk Naturalists' Trust has an information centre by Ranworth Broad which is open from April to October, except Mondays, and is accessible from Ranworth village (TG 3514).

Elsewhere, a written permit from the Nature Conservancy is needed to visit the area which, in any case, is largely inaccessible owing to the nature of the terrain. Applications for permits should be addressed to the Nature Conservancy Council, 60 Bracondale, Norwich, Norfolk NOR 58B.

Breydon Water EA 6 OS map 134 TG 4907

Breydon Water is the name given to the wide estuarine basin of the River Yare just before it meets the sea at Great Yarmouth. The extensive mudflats of the estuary are a reserve of Great Yarmouth Borough Council, and are a splendid wintering ground for waders and wildfowl.

Fauna

BIRDS The principal birds which winter here are **pink-footed geese, brent, white-fronted** and **bean geese, Bewick's swans, shelducks, shovelers, wigeon, pintails, goldeneye, scaup, cormorants, bar-tailed godwits, short-eared owls, hen harriers** and occasionally **spoonbills** and **avocets. Merlins** and **peregrine falcons** are less frequent visitors, but **black terns** are fairly regular on passage. Quite a variety of rare waders have been recorded here over the years.

Access

Public footpaths run along both the north and south banks of Breydon Water and are easily accessible from Great Yarmouth. Another useful vantage point from which to see many species is by pleasure cruiser.

Rex Graham Reserve EA 7 OS map 155 TL 7576

This small reserve of the Suffolk Conservation Trust exists solely to protect one of the only two known British colonies of the rare soldier orchid. The reserve is situated a few miles east of Mildenhall and is open to the public for only one day each year!

Flora

FLOWERING PLANTS In addition to the rare and extremely attractive **soldier orchid** there are **twayblades** and **ploughman's spikenard.**

Access

Details of access and visiting arrangements for the year are available from the Suffolk Naturalists' Trust, Park Cottage, Saxmundham, Suffolk IP17 1DQ.

Weeting Heath EA 8 OS map 144 TL 7588

Weeting Heath is a National Nature Reserve of 338 acres (127ha) which lies in the Breckland area of East Anglia not far from Thetford. The Thetford Heath and Cavenham Heath (EA 9) nature reserves are close by. Weeting Heath is largely dominated by chalk grassland and has several Breckland specialities.

Fauna

BIRDS **Stone curlews** and **wheatears** are both fairly common here, and **crossbills** occasionally nest in old pine trees at the northern end of the reserve.

MAMMALS **Rabbits** are a very important factor in maintaining the Breckland heathland, and the Nature Conservancy has carried out a great deal of research on their grazing effects here. **Moles** are also common.

INVERTEBRATES The area has two notable **spiders**, namely *Walckenaera* *stylifrons*, which is only known in Britain from this site, and the only slightly commoner *W. incisa.*

Flora
FLOWERING PLANTS Three of the more noteworthy Breckland specialities are **smooth rupture-wort**, **Breckland wild thyme** and **Breckland spring sedge**, but there are many other interesting species including **spiked speedwell**, **maiden pink**, **wall bedstraw**, **lesser meadow-rue**, **purple fescue**, **tor grass** and **sand sedge**.
FERNS Quite large areas are dominated by **bracken**.
MOSSES AND LIVERWORTS The **moss** *Rhytidium rugosum* is very common here.

Access
There are two observation hides on the reserve which are open from April to August during which time there is a seasonal warden on site. Elsewhere, the reserve is only accessible to permit holders. The address for permits is the Nature Conservancy Council, 60 Bracondale, Norwich, Norfolk NOR 58B.

Cavenham Heath EA 9 OS map 155 TL 7573
Cavenham Heath is one of several National Nature Reserves which lie in the Breckland area of East Anglia. It is mainly heathland with smaller areas of woodland and lime-rich grassland.
See also Weeting Heath (EA 8).

Fauna
BIRDS The birdlife includes **nightjars**, **stone curlews**, **red-backed shrikes** and **woodlarks**, but unfortunately all four of these uncommon species are declining in numbers here. Other birds include all three British **woodpeckers**, **woodcocks**, **whinchats**, **tree pipits**, **linnets**, **grasshopper warblers**, **willow warblers**, **redpolls**, **reed buntings** and **yellowhammers**.
MAMMALS Small numbers of **roe deer** are resident on the reserve.
INVERTEBRATES Three notable **spiders** are *Clubiona rosserae*, which is only known from one other British site, *Marpissa pomatia* and *Hygrolycosa rubrofasciata*. There are also **grayling** and **small heath butterflies**, and **emperor** and **beautiful yellow underwing moths**.

Flora
FLOWERING PLANTS Much of the area is dominated by **ling** and **cross-leaved heath** with **sand sedge**, **sheeps sorrel**, **common centaury**, **sand spurrey**, **mossy stonecrop**, **common dodder**, **petty whin** and **bush grass**. To the north of the reserve is an area of lime-rich grassland which has **maiden pink** and **dwarf thistle**, and to the south and east are areas of previously disturbed ground which have **pale toadflax**, **Scotch thistle**, **purple fescue grass**, **wall pepper**, **common cudweed**, **black medick**,

thyme-leaved sandwort, field mouse-ear, viper's bugloss, weld, wild mignonette, musk thistle, dark mullein, common mullein, common melilot, white melilot and Canadian fleabane.

FERNS Some of the reserve has been invaded by birch scrub where narrow buckler fern may be found. Bracken is locally dominant in places.

MOSSES AND LIVERWORTS The moss *Ptilium crista-castrensis* grows among the heather and several other species may be found in the birch scrub including *Pleurozium schreberi, Hypnum cupressiforme, Polytrichum commune, Dicranum scoparium* and *Leucobryum glaucum*.

LICHENS *Cladonia impexa* and *Cetraria aculeata* grow here.

Access

Parts of the reserve, particularly along the banks of the River Lark, are freely accessible and may be reached from the Temple Bridge about 1 mile (1.6 km) west of Icklingham (TL 7773). Other areas are only open to permit holders. Applications for permits should be sent to the Nature Conservancy Council, 60 Bracondale, Norwich, Norfolk NOR 58B.

Mickfield Meadow EA 10 OS map 156 TM 1362

Mickfield Meadow is a small wet meadow which is owned by the Suffolk Conservation Trust. Its main attraction is the population of snakes head fritillaries, and it is one of the best sites in Britain to see this rare and attractive flower. The reserve covers about $4\frac{1}{2}$ acres (2 ha).

Flora

FLOWERING PLANTS The snakeshead fritillary and pepper saxifrage grow here.

Access

The reserve lies just north of Mickfield village which is just off the A140 about 10 miles (16 km) north of Ipswich. No special permits are needed, but visitors are asked to notify the Suffolk Naturalists' Trust first, at Park Cottage, Saxmundham, Suffolk IP17 1DQ.

Walberswick EA 11 OS map 156 TM 4774

Walberswick is a National Nature Reserve of 2 square miles (5.1 km²) which lies just south of Southwold, not far from the R.S.P.B. reserve at Minsmere (EA 12). It has much the same range of habitats as Minsmere including both salt and freshwater pools and marshes, carr, birch scrub and heathland.

Fauna

BIRDS The breeding birds include reed warblers, sedge warblers, water rails, bearded tits, shovelers, gadwall, teal, mallard, shelducks and garganey. Marsh harriers and bitterns have also bred.

Passage migrants and overwintering species include hen harriers, marsh harriers, short-eared owls, snow buntings, shore larks, twite, ruff, little stints, both mute and Bewick's swans, and many ducks.

INVERTEBRATES Several uncommon species of **moths** have been taken on the reserve including **white mantled wainscot, flame wainscot** and **Fenn's wainscot.**

Flora

FLOWERING PLANTS The rare **marsh sow-thistle** grows among the fresh-water reed beds, and the saltmarshes have **sea purslane, common sea-lavender, sea aster, sea rush, sea meadow-grass, common orache** and **sea milkwort.** The shingle beach which runs between Walberswick and Sizewell has **yellow horned-poppy, sea pea, sea campion** and **sea kale.**

Access

The reserve is accessible by footpath from Walberswick village (TM 492746). Several paths cross the area, and although a permit from the Nature Conservancy is needed to leave them, much of the birdlife may be seen without doing so.

Minsmere EA 12 OS map 156 TM 4667

The R.S.P.B. reserve at Minsmere is one of the best-known bird reserves in the country. This 2 square mile (5.4km²) reserve lies about 2 miles (3 km) south of Dunwich, and is primarily a freshwater marsh with open pools and reed beds, although there are also areas of heath and woodlands.

Fauna

BIRDS The birdlife of Minsmere is outstanding throughout the year. The reserve is probably best known for its **avocets,** and is a stronghold of the **bearded tit,** but there are also many other breeding birds including **bitterns, marsh harriers, water rails, common** and **Sandwich terns, gadwall, garganey, mallard, teal, shovelers** and **shelducks.**

Regular winter visitors include both **mute** and **Bewick's swans,** most of the above-mentioned species of duck and **wigeon.** Autumn brings all kinds of rarities; **spoonbills, great grey shrikes** and **black terns** being among the most regular.

Flora

FLOWERING PLANTS The reserve does not hold a great deal of interest for botanists, but the rare **marsh sow-thistle** grows in some of the reed beds.

Access

There is a large public hide on the reserve which is reached from the Dunwich Cliffs car park (TM 475680) and is open at all times.

The reserve proper is only open on certain days of the week, and visiting arrangements may change from time to time. Details can be obtained from The Warden, Minsmere Reserve, Westleton, Saxmundham, Suffolk IP17 2BY.

Havergate Island EA 13 OS map 169 TM 4248

The 280 acre (113 ha) Havergate Island lies in the estuary of the River Ore about 15 miles (24km) east of Ipswich and is a reserve of the R.S.P.B. It is well known to birdwatchers as the main stronghold of avocets in this country, and several other notable bird species frequent the island, too.

Havergate is part of a National Nature Reserve which includes the shingle beaches of Orford Beach and Shingle Street.

Fauna

BIRDS About 100 pairs of **avocets** regularly nest on the marshes of the island which they share with **common** and **Sandwich terns** and occasionally **short-eared owls**. After the breeding season, some **avocets** leave and many spend the winter on the Tamar Estuary in Devon, but an increasing number are remaining over winter. Wintering wildfowl include **teal, pintails, shovelers, mallard, wigeon, shelducks** and **Bewick's swans. Knot, grey plovers, hen harriers** and **short-eared owls** also occur.

INVERTEBRATES The rare **spider** *Praestigia duffeyi* was discovered on Havergate as recently as 1953, and four other notable spiders are also known from the area, namely *Lycosa arenicola, Sitticus rupicola, Trichoncus offinis* and *Euophrys browninge*.

Flora

FLOWERING PLANTS The saltmarshes bordering the estuary have **sea-lavender, sea purslane, sea couch grass, sea meadow-grass, sea aster, grass-leaved orache, thrift, sea plantain** and **perennial glasswort.**

The shingle beaches have **sea pea, yellow vetch, sea kale** and **yellow horned-poppy.**

Access

The reserve is open to the general public, but because of the limited number of people which can be accommodated at any one time, prior booking must be made. Enquiries should be sent to The Warden, 30 Mundays Lane, Orford, Woodbridge, Suffolk IP12 2LX. Having obtained a permit, access is gained by boat from Orford.

Roydon Common EA 14 OS map 132 TF 6822

Roydon Common is an area of heathland which lies a short distance east of King's Lynn in Norfolk and covers about 450 acres (182 ha). The site includes several bogs which are most interesting from the botanical point of view.

Flora

FLOWERING PLANTS Most of the heathland is covered with **ling**, together with **petty whin** and **parasitic dodder**. There are some areas of bare sandy ground where **sand sedge, pill sedge** and **small hair-grass** grow. Elsewhere you may find **lady's bedstraw, barren strawberry, birdseye speedwell, common dog violet** and **wood sage. Birch** trees are starting to invade the heath in places.

Wetter parts of the heath have **cross-leaved heath, purple moor-grass, deer grass, common cottongrass** and **heath rush,** and the bogs proper contain **bog asphodel, cranberry, common reed, bog rush, fen rush, bog myrtle, bog pimpernel, heath spotted orchid, bog orchid, southern marsh orchid, red rattle, few-flowered spike-rush, slender spike-rush, many-stalked spike-rush, bristle club-rush** and **meadow thistle.** The bogs are also of particular note for their insectivorous plants which include all three British **sundews (common, great** and **long-leaved), Irish bladderwort, small bladderwort** and **common bladderwort.**

Alder and **willow** carrs have developed in places, with **marsh marigold, tussock sedge, water forget-me-not** and **grass of Parnassus.** FERNS **Royal fern** and **marsh fern** grow in some of the carrs.

MOSSES AND LIVERWORTS Mosses include *Campylipus introflexus, Polytrichum piliferum* and *P. juniperinium* growing on the heathland; and several species of *Sphagnum* as well as *Polytrichum commune, Drepanocladus revolvens, D. lycopodioides, D. aduncus, Ctenidium molluscum, Riccardia pinguis, Pellia epiphylla, Camptothecium nitens, Philonotis calcarea* and *Dicranum spurium* in the bogs.

Access

The common is freely accessible, and lies near to Roydon village which is about 6 miles (10 km) east of King's Lynn just off the A148.

Gibraltar Point and The Wash

EA 15 OS map 122 TF 5558

The Wash, that enormous expanse of tidal mud and silt which indents the coasts of Lincolnshire and Norfolk, is the second most important haunt of wintering waders in Britain, and one of the most important sites for wintering wildfowl. Altogether, the mudflats cover over 100 square miles (260 km²) and include the estuaries of the rivers Welland, Nene and Ouse. There are several good vantage points and high-tide roosts, perhaps the best-known of which is Gibraltar Point, which is on the Lincolnshire coast about 3 miles (5 km) south of Skegness.

Gibraltar Point is a Local Nature Reserve – the first one to be designated in Britain in fact – and is run jointly by the local authority and the Lincolnshire and South Humberside Trust for Nature Conservation. The reserve covers 1057 acres (428 ha) and includes sand dunes and saltmarshes which are of interest to botanists, besides providing a high-tide roost for wintering birds. There is also a bird observatory here.

Fauna

BIRDS The wintering waders, which can total about 200,000 birds include 85,000 knot, 45,000 dunlin, 12,000 curlews, 10,000 oystercatchers and smaller numbers of bar-tailed godwits, grey plovers, redshanks, sanderling, ringed plovers, whimbrel, curlew sandpipers, green sandpipers, wood sandpipers, spotted redshanks, turnstones and ruff.

The wildfowl include some 3000 brent geese, 2000 pink-footed geese, 10,000 wigeon, 2000 common scoters, 1500 shelducks and numerous mallard, teal, velvet scoters, scaup and eiders, as well as divers.

Hen harriers and short-eared owls winter on some of the saltmarshes bordering The Wash, and the bird observatory at Gibraltar Point has recorded snow buntings, shore larks, Lapland buntings, great grey shrikes and a variety of skuas, chats, warblers, flycatchers and terns. Little terns and ringed plovers breed on the reserve.

MAMMALS Both common and grey seals may be seen in The Wash where they often haul out on sandbanks. The common seals have their main British breeding grounds here, and there are perhaps 5000 in the area. Their most favoured haunts are the sandbanks by the estuaries. The grey seals are much scarcer, but they may be seen on the Dog's Head Sandbanks.

Flora

FLOWERING PLANTS Numerous saltmarshes may be found bordering The Wash, and some of the commonest flowering plants which grow in them are cord grass, sea meadow-grass, sea purslane, common seablite, sea arrow-grass, sea aster and sea-lavender.

The Gibraltar Point reserve itself has sea holly, sea bindweed, shrubby seablite, sea heath and sea buckthorn scrub.

Access

Gibraltar Point is easily reached from Skegness. There is a nature trail and information centre which is open daily from May to October, and at weekends throughout the rest of the year. Details of accommodation at the bird observatory may be obtained from the Warden, Gibraltar Point Bird Observatory, Skegness, Lincolnshire.

Other good areas for birdwatching on the Wash include the R.S.P.B. reserve at Snettisham, Norfolk (TF 6433), which is open to the public and is provided with hides; and Hunstanton (TF 6741). (Both these sites are shown on OS sheet 132.)

Other high-tide roosts are the Ouse mouth (TF 5925), the Nene outfall (TF 4926), and Boston Point (TF 3939).

Ouse Washes SE 1 OS map 143 TL 3975

During the 17th Century the vast expanse of low-lying fenland which existed just south of The Wash was drained. Hundreds of miles of ditches and drainage cuts were built, rivers were canalized and a number of huge overflows were created where excess water could be stored during periods of heavy winter rainfall when the new drainage channels could not be expected to cope. One of these enormous overflows is the Ouse Washes, and it is now one of the most important wildfowl haunts in the country.

Basically it consists of two parallel dykes about 1 mile (1.6 km) apart and 20 miles (32 km) long which are designed to contain the overflow from the River Ouse. The Ouse itself has been partly canalized and diverted to run along the top of the two dykes. These canalized sections are now known as the New and Old Bedford Rivers. The Washes run more or less parallel to the A10 Cambridge to King's Lynn road and are now protected by three conservation authorities. Between them the R.S.P.B., the Wildfowl Trust and the local naturalists' trust own almost half of the entire length of the Washes.

The birdlife is outstanding and the flora is also extremely interesting.

Fauna

BIRDS During the winter the Ouse Washes hold one of the most exciting assemblages of wildfowl to be seen anywhere in the country. In an average year there may be between 30–40,000 **wigeon**; 42,000 were counted in one year! One out of every three British **pintails** spends at least some of the winter here, and the Washes also have Britain's biggest wintering flock of **Bewick's swans**; some 1200 at present. Other wildfowl include **mallard, shovelers, teal, gadwall, pochard, tufted ducks** and **mute** and **whooper swans**, and there are also flocks of **golden plovers** and a few **short-eared owls**.

During the summer Britain's only breeding **ruffs** may be found here, and there are nesting **black-tailed godwits, garganey, gadwall, mallard, shelducks, shovelers, teal, tufted ducks, pintails, redshanks, snipe** and both **reed warblers** and **sedge warblers**. **Black terns** have started to nest here in recent years.

Flora

FLOWERING PLANTS The winter floods bring down a good deal of nutrient-rich silt and mud, which acts as a natural fertilizer, and the seeds of a great many plants, many of which have taken root in the numerous ditches which criss-cross the Washes. These include **fringed water lily, yellow water lily, sweet flag, tasteless water pepper, least water pepper, frog-bit, great water parsnip, ivy duckweed, fat duckweed, common duckweed, great duckweed, flowering rush, wild celery, sea aster** and **sea club-rush**.

The Old Bedford River has **thread-leaved water crowfoot, arrowhead, long-stalked pondweed, perfoliate pondweed, water violet, river water dropwort, marestail** and **Canadian pondweed**.

Access

A public footpath runs along the dykes on each side of The Wash, but when walking here it is best to keep a low profile so as to avoid disturbing the birds. The R.S.P.B. has a series of hides which are freely available to the public and are reached from Purls Bridge (TL 478871). There is also an R.S.P.B. information centre here.

The Wildfowl Trust refuge, which is centred around Welney (TL 526942) also has a series of hides and a modern observatory.

Chippenham Fen SE 2 OS map 154 TL 6469

Chippenham Fen is a National Nature Reserve which lies about 3 miles (5km) north of Newmarket and includes areas of relict fen, carr and woodland. It covers 258 acres (103ha).

Fauna

BIRDS This is one of the few nature reserves in Britain where the elusive **stone curlew** may be seen. **Water rails** also breed here.

INVERTEBRATES The fen is well known for its population of the **silver barred moth**, an extremely localized species which has one of its main strongholds here.

Flora

FLOWERING PLANTS The reserve includes areas of carr with **alder** and **willows**, and other woodlands with **ash, birch** and **sycamore**. The flora also includes the rare **Cambridge parsley**, which is only known from one other British site, **common sedge, tawny sedge, glaucous sedge, bog rush, fen rush, common reed, purple moor-grass, tufted hair-grass, quaking grass, saw-wort, meadow thistle, fragrant orchid, southern marsh orchid, marsh helleborine, hemp agrimony, common butterwort** and **meadowsweet**.

Access

The reserve lies a little way north of Chippenham village, but a permit from the Nature Conservancy is needed in order to visit it. Applications for permits should be sent to the Nature Conservancy Council, Godwin House, George St, Huntingdon PE18 6BU.

Wicken Fen SE 3 OS map 154 TL 5570

Wicken Fen is a nature reserve of the National Trust. It lies about 10 miles (16km) north-east of Cambridge and is one of the few surviving remnants of the huge wetland which once occupied this part of the country. The reserve is only maintained in its present condition by artificial management of the water table. It covers 730 acres (295ha).

Fauna

BIRDS Breeding birds include **marsh** and **Montagu's harriers, long-eared owls, great crested grebes** and **grasshopper warblers**. **Bitterns, bearded tits, black terns, shovelers** and **wigeon** often turn up during the winter months, and **mallard, teal, pochard** and **tufted ducks** are found here more or less throughout the year.

INVERTEBRATES Wicken Fen is one of the few British sites where the swallowtail butterfly may be seen, if re-introduction attempts succeed.

Flora

FLOWERING PLANTS The uncommon milk parsley, which is the food plant of the swallowtail butterfly, grows here along with meadowsweet, marestail, fen bedstraw, water forget-me-not, purple loosestrife, yellow loosestrife, wild angelica, marsh pea, greater spearwort, lesser water plantain, fine-leaved water dropwort and creeping willow as well as the omnipresent common sedge.

Some parts of the fen have developed into a carr with alder, sallow, alder buckthorn and blackthorn, and there is also some woodland of pedunculate oak and ash.

Access

Wicken Fen lies close to the B1085 by Wicken village. It is open throughout the year, but visitors are not encouraged to leave the footpaths. There is a hide overlooking the 100 acre (40 ha) mere.

Tring Reservoirs SE 4 OS map 165 SP 9013

The four Tring Reservoirs: Wilstone, Marsworth, Startops End and Tringford, were built during the early part of the 19th Century to serve the Grand Union Canal. They were evidently constructed on marshland, and relics of the marsh flora may still be found today around the edges of the reservoirs. The area is also important to naturalists on account of the wintering wildfowl and other birdlife.

Tring Reservoirs lie about 2 miles (3 km) north of Tring, Hertfordshire, and are scheduled as a National Nature Reserve which covers 49 acres (20 ha).

Fauna

BIRDS The reservoirs are attractive to wintering wildfowl, and regular species include mallard, teal, wigeon, shovelers, pochard, tufted ducks, goosanders and mute swans. Several species of waders and terns, including black terns, frequently pass through the area in autumn.

The reservoirs are also of interest to birdwatchers because the first little ringed plovers ever to nest in Britain chose to do so here. That was in 1938, since when they have successfully spread to several other parts of the country.

Flora

FLOWERING PLANTS The flora of the reservoir margins includes southern marsh orchid, early marsh orchid, fen rush, orange foxtail, quaking grass, Yorkshire fog, bog pimpernel, marsh valerian, brown sedge, distant sedge, long-stalked yellow sedge, carnation sedge, meadow cranesbill and meadow thistle. Aquatic plants include hornwort, spiked water milfoil and Canadian pondweed.

Access

Tring is on the A41 about midway between Hemel Hempstead and Aylesbury. The reservoirs are a little way to the north, and may be reached from either the B489 or the B488. There is a nature trail on the reserve which starts from Startopsend village (SP 923143).

Ashridge Estate SE 5 OS map 165 SP 9812

This 6 square mile (16.2 km²) estate, which is about 5 miles (8 km) north-west of Hemel Hempstead in the Chilterns, is a reserve of the National Trust. Much of the estate is still actively farmed, and about 1000 acres (404 ha) is made up of botanically rich downland whilst another 1000 acres (404 ha) is wooded.

Fauna

BIRDS **Nightingales, redstarts, redpolls** and **wood warblers** may all be seen in the woodlands.

MAMMALS The woods have **fallow deer, Chinese water deer** and **muntjac,** and both **greater horseshoe bats** and **long-eared bats** are said to be common.

Flora

FLOWERING PLANTS The woodlands are predominantly of **beech** and **oak,** and hold **fly orchid** and **birdsnest orchid,** but it is the downland areas where most of the botanical interest is to be found. Species here include **pyramidal orchid, bee orchid, frog orchid, clustered bellflower, dropwort** and **horseshoe vetch.**

Access

The estate is reached from the B4506 Dunstable to Berkhamsted road and is open to the public throughout the year.

Leigh Marsh SE 6 OS map 178 TQ 8384

Situated on the north bank of the Thames Estuary immediately west of Southend-on-Sea, Leigh Marsh is a National Nature Reserve which extends to 634 acres (257 ha). It includes mudflats, saltmarsh and small areas of sand and shingle.

Fauna

BIRDS The mudflats are regularly used as a wintering ground by about 6000 **brent geese.**

INVERTEBRATES The marshes here hold a number of interesting **moths** including the **ground lackey, dotted fan foot, water ermine** and **Mathew's wainscot.** There are also **marbled white butterflies** and **Essex skipper butterflies.**

Flora

FLOWERING PLANTS Dwarf eel-grass and narrow-leaved eel-grass both grow on the mudflats and are a favourite food of the geese. The saltmarshes have spineless hornwort, common hornwort, tassel pondweed, hairy buttercup, saltmarsh rush, sea-lavender, sea arrow-grass, horned pondweed and thrift. There are also at least five different species of glassworts.

Access

Access to all parts of the reserve is unrestricted.

High Halstow SE 7 OS map 178 TQ 7778

High Halstow marshes lie on the south bank of the Thames just east of Gravesend. The saltmarsh is unfortunately rapidly deteriorating as a result of the recent construction of a sea wall, but the adjacent mudflats extend for almost 50 square miles (130km²) and are of considerable interest to birdwatchers. Near High Halstow village is Northward Hill, a famous heronry and National Nature Reserve managed by the R.S.P.B.

Fauna

BIRDS Over 2500 shelducks, 2000 mallard and 1500 wigeon regularly winter on the mudflats here, along with smaller numbers of shovelers and pintails and about 800 white-fronted geese. An average of 10–12,000 waders also use the estuary and at times the numbers involved can be much greater than this. 10,000 lapwings alone have been counted here, and 6000 curlews, 5000 dunlin and 3000 redshanks have been seen at times. Knot, grey plovers and golden plovers are also frequent.

Breeding wildfowl of the marsh include mallard, pochard, pintails, garganey, gadwall, shovelers, shelducks, teal and mute swans. Grey herons are often seen feeding here.

Flora

FLOWERING PLANTS The botanical interest of the marsh is rapidly decreasing as a consequence of the new dyke, but two of the more interesting plants which still survive here are golden dock and small red goosefoot.

Access

The area is accessible by the public footpath which starts from near St Mary's Hoo at TQ 804766. A permit is needed to visit Northward Hill. This may be obtained from the Royal Society for the Protection of Birds, The Lodge, Sandy, Beds.

The Isle of Sheppey and the Swale

SE 8 OS map 178 TQ 9966

The Isle of Sheppey is on the southern side of the mouth of the Thames, and is separated from the mainland by a narrow channel known as the Swale.

Kent County Council have a local nature reserve on the southern bank of the Swale and the Kent Trust for Nature Conservation have one on the bank also, but the whole area has so much biological interest as to be worthy of inclusion. There is a National Nature Reserve on the south-east tip of Sheppey and the R.S.P.B. has a reserve at Elmley.

Fauna

BIRDS The mudflats and saltmarshes of the Swale have some of the biggest flocks of wintering wildfowl in the south of England. **Knot, dunlin, oystercatchers, curlews** and **golden plover** are all numbered in thousands whilst **grey plovers, redshanks** and **bar-tailed godwits** are found in lesser numbers. Several hundred **brent geese** and only slightly fewer **white-fronted geese** are also regular winter visitors, and the ducks include **wigeon, mallard, shelducks, red-breasted mergansers, eiders, pochard, common scoters, teal, shovelers and pintails.**

Merlins, short-eared owls and hen harriers are also frequently seen in winter, and occasional passage migrants include **ringed plovers, black-tailed godwits, ruff, avocets, spotted redshanks, little stints, wood sandpipers, curlew sandpipers, whimbrel, green sandpipers** and **marsh harriers.**

During the summer, several species nest in the area including **tufted ducks, garganey, gadwall, mallard, teal, shovelers, pochard, shelducks, mute swans, black-headed gulls** and both **common** and **little terns.**

Flora

FLOWERING PLANTS Some interesting plants grow in the saltmarshes on the Swale's northern side, such as **procumbent meadow-grass, Borrer's saltmarsh grass, golden samphire** and **knotted bur parsley.**

The marshes at the southern tip of the Isle of Harty (TR 0165) are also interesting and have **grass vetchling, spiny rest harrow, sea clover** and **slender hare's-ear,** and at Shell Ness (TR 0567) there is a spit which has **dragon's teeth, slender sea knotgrass, yellow horned-poppy, sea holly** and **sea spurge.**

The uncommon **small red goosefoot** may be found in the waters of Capel Fleet (TR 0068).

Access

A public footpath follows much of the Swale's southern bank and is easily reached via the unclassified roads north of Faversham. The most interesting areas on the Isle of Sheppey, including Shell Ness, the Isle of Harty and Capel Fleet, may be reached from Leysdown-on-Sea. The network of public footpaths which serve this area may be conveniently picked up just south of Leysdown at TR 046693.

Chobham Common SE 9 OS map 175 SU 9764

Chobham Common is a local nature reserve of Surrey County Council. It lies about 5 miles (8 km) north-west of Woking, and is mostly heathland with areas of bog. It extends to 380 acres (154 ha).

Fauna

BIRDS The birdlife includes **nightjars, whinchats, stonechats, whitethroats, woodlarks, redstarts, sparrowhawks** and the occasional **hobby**.
MAMMALS **Badgers** are resident on the reserve.
INVERTEBRATES The common is noted for its **spiders**, which include the rare *Oxyopes heterophthalmus* which is found nowhere else in Britain. *Cheiracanthium pennyi, Uloborus walckenaerius, Micaria subopaca, Araneus alsine* and *Thomisus onustus* are also found here.

The **ant** *Formica rufibarbis* has its only known site on the British mainland here, although it is also found on the Isles of Scilly.

Flora

FLOWERING PLANTS These include **marsh gentian, common sundew, lesser gorse** and **bristle bent grass**.
FERNS **Marsh clubmoss** grows here.

Access

The reserve can easily be reached from either the B386 or the B383. No special permits are required and several footpaths run through the area.

Blean Woods SE 10 OS map 179 TR 1060

Blean Wood is an extensive area of natural deciduous woodland and old coppice which lies a few miles north-west of Canterbury. The whole wood covers about 750 acres (304 ha) and it incorporates a National Nature Reserve of 164 acres (67 ha). The R.S.P.B. has a reserve adjacent to the National Nature Reserve.

Fauna

BIRDS **Nightingales, blackcaps, lesser spotted woodpeckers, great spotted woodpeckers, nuthatchers, marsh tits, redstarts, whitethroats** and **grasshopper warblers**.
INVERTEBRATES The main faunal interest here lies in the insect life. Several woodland species with a continental distribution have managed to establish themselves at Blean Woods, and are rare or absent elsewhere in Britain. These include two **beetles** – *Gyrophaena joyioides* and *Borboropora kraatzi* – which have their only British sites here. Two other rare beetles are *Staphylinus fulvipes* and *Acritus homoepathicus*. There are also **wood ants** and **heath fritillary butterflies**.

Flora

FLOWERING PLANTS Large areas of the wood are of old coppiced **hornbeam, sweet chestnut** and **ash** with standards of **sessile oak**, but there is also a variety of other trees including **beech, rowan, wild service, aspen, alder** and **pedunculate oak**. Shrubs include **guelder rose, hazel** and **woodland hawthorn**. Other woodland plants are **broom, elegant St John's wort, bitter vetch, honeysuckle, bluebell, wood melick, heath grass, sanicle, bugle, ling, great wood-rush, hairy wood-rush, common cow-wheat, moor sedge, common yellow sedge, oval sedge, wood sage** and **heath spotted orchid**.

Access

The woods are situated about 3 miles (5 km) north-west of Canterbury just south of the A290. Several footpaths run through the woods, but the nature reserve itself is only open to permit holders. Applications for permits should be addressed to the Nature Conservancy Council, Zealds, Church Street, Wye, Ashford, Kent TN25 5BW.

Stodmarsh SE 11 OS map 179 TR 2261

Stodmarsh is an area of fen, open water and flood meadows which lies alongside the River Stour about 4 miles (6.5 km) north-east of Canterbury. The area was probably always low-lying, but has become even more so as a result of mining subsidence and is now so rich in both botanical and ornithological interest that it has been designated as a National Nature Reserve. The reserve covers 402 acres (163 ha).

Fauna

BIRDS Several rare and interesting species of birds nest at Stodmarsh (see below), but probably the most exciting is **Savi's warbler** which has its only British colony here. Savi's warblers previously nested in East Anglia until the latter part of the 19th Century when they became extinct here, although they are still quite common on the Continent. The species started nesting at Stodmarsh in about 1960.

Other regular nesters here are **garganey, shovelers, pochard, water rails**, and **reed, sedge** and **grasshopper warblers. Gadwall, bearded tits** and **bitterns** are also frequent summer visitors and may breed, and **marsh harriers** are also occasionally noted.

Wintering birds include nearly 2000 **mallard** and smaller numbers of **teal, wigeon, shovelers, pochard, pintails, gadwall** and a variety of waders. **Hen harriers** are also frequent in winter.

Flora

FLOWERING PLANTS Among the more interesting members of the flora are **spineless hornwort, marsh stitchwort, dittander, least duckweed, greyish bulrush, tubular water dropwort, hairy buttercup, greater spearwort, greater bladderwort, common meadow-rue, bogbean, fen rush, frog-bit, marsh cinquefoil, great water dock, great water grass, pink water speedwell, marsh arrow-grass** and **common reed**.

Access

Most of the birdlife can be seen from the Lampen Wall, a public footpath which runs from Stodmarsh village (TR 218605) to Grove Ferry (TR 235632) and which passes through the reserve and along the banks of the River Stour. Other parts of the reserve are not open to the public.

Wye Downs SE 12 OS map 189 TR 0745

The Wye National Nature Reserve lies a few miles to the north-east of Ashford in Kent. About 250 acres (102 ha) of the downs have been set aside as a reserve which includes areas of grassland, woodland and scrub. The area is known particularly for its orchids.

Fauna

MAMMALS **Badgers**, and sometimes **fallow deer**, may be seen here.

INVERTEBRATES The **feathered ear moth** appears to be more or less restricted to the vicinity of the Wye and Crundale Downs, although occasional specimens have been taken elsewhere. The **black-veined moth** is another uncommon species which is found on the reserve.

Flora

FLOWERING PLANTS No fewer than 17 species of orchids have been recorded from the reserve including **spider orchid**, **late spider orchid**, **burnt orchid**, **lady orchid**, **man orchid**, **pyramidal orchid** and **fly orchid**. The rare **Kentish milkwort** is also found here.

There are also some woodlands which are mainly of old coppiced **hazel** with **ash** standards.

Access

The reserve can easily be reached by the unclassified roads from Ashford. Part of the northern end of the reserve is freely accessible and has an information centre and nature trail, but elsewhere visitors are not allowed to leave the footpaths without a special permit.

Dungeness SE 13 OS map 189 TR 0619

Dungeness is a huge shingle promontory situated midway between Hastings and Folkestone. Over 3 square miles (8 km²) have been set aside as a reserve of the R.S.P.B. In addition to the shingle itself, the reserve includes artificial flooded pits and patches of scrub. There is also a bird observatory here although the interest is by no means restricted to birdlife, for several rare and interesting insects and plants have been recorded, too.

Fauna

BIRDS Although there are nesting colonies of **common terns** with a few **little terns** and **common gulls**, the main ornithological interest lies in the passage migrants and winter visitors. Over 3000 **mallard** and several other

(Above) Great Ormes Head: a nature reserve as well as a holiday playground (see page 125).
(Below) A range of aquatic vegetation growing in a Welsh lake.

(Above) Ashwoods growing at Dove Dale (see page 142).

(Below left) Cowslips and early purple orchids. (Below right) Round-leaved sundew.

species of duck such as **wigeon, teal, goldeneye, tufted duck, pochard, grebes** and **divers** congregate on some of the freshwater lagoons here in winter, and **hen harriers, merlins** and **short-eared owls** are also frequently seen.

Black terns are quite regular in autumn, and some of the rarer species which have been recorded at Dungeness include **bluethroats, melodious warblers, Pallas's warblers** and **rufous warblers**. Sea watching is also good.

INVERTEBRATES The insects include the very rare **Sussex emerald** and **toadflax brocade moths**, the localized **pygmy footman** and **scarce black arches**. Other notable moth species are **Kent black arches, feathered brindle, Webb's wainscot, water ermine, yarrow pug** and a pale race of the **grass eggar** which is apparently restricted to the Dungeness area.

Flora
FLOWERING PLANTS The rare **southern hawksbeard** and **Nottingham catchfly** are among the numerous species which have been recorded.

Access
The R.S.P.B. reserve is open throughout the year but only on certain days of the week, and intending visitors are advised to check with the warden before planning their visit. The address is: The Warden, Boulderwall Farm, Dungeness Rd, Lydd, Kent TN29 9PN. There is a small admission charge to the reserve.

Details of the bird observatory may be obtained from The Warden, Dungeness Bird Observatory, Romney Marsh, Kent.

Sandwich Dunes and Pegwell Bay
SE 14 OS map 179 TR 3659

Sandwich Dunes lie a little way south of the Stour Estuary and just east of Sandwich town in Kent. The dune system covers about $2\frac{3}{4}$ square miles (5.7km²) and has a very interesting flora despite being greatly disturbed by the golf links.

The Stour Estuary, which is known as Pegwell Bay, is very attractive to wildfowl and waders and the whole area is on a major migration route. The Sandwich Bay bird observatory lies nearby.

Fauna
BIRDS Regular birds of the Pegwell Bay mudflats are **whooper** and **Bewick's swans, white-fronted geese, brent geese, teal, curlews, knot, redshanks, greenshanks, golden plovers, bar-tailed godwits, ruff, whimbrel, wood sandpipers** and **green sandpipers**, although none occurs in very large numbers. **Divers** and **grebes** are also frequent visitors and **hen harriers** turn up from time to time.

The observatory has also recorded a wide variety of continental migrants.

SE

INVERTEBRATES The dunes are well known for their insects. The Lepidoptera (butterflies and moths) include **pygmy footman, rest harrow** and **bright wave moths,** and **beetle** species include several **carabid** beetles, **staphylinids** and **weevils,** some of which are very rare or localized.

Flora

FLOWERING PLANTS Sandwich Dunes are perhaps best known as one of the few haunts of the rare **lizard orchid** but there are many other exciting species, too, including the equally rare **clove-scented broomrape,** which parasitizes **hedge bedstraw** and is restricted to south-east Kent, and the closely related **sea broomrape,** which is parasitic on **sea holly.**

Other notable plants are **suffocated clover, clustered clover, burrowing clover, birdsfoot fenugreek, sand catchfly, yellow bartsia, asparagus, sea spurge, sharp rush, common storksbill** and several grasses including the rare **rush-leaved fescue, dune fescue, purple fescue** and **bulbous meadow-grass.**

Access

The dunes may be reached via the unclassified road which leaves Sandwich eastwards towards the golf course and thence by following a track across the links. Pegwell Bay can be reached by following the Stour banks.

Details of accommodation at the bird observatory may be obtained from The Secretary, The Sandwich Bay Bird Observatory, Guildford Road, Sandwich Bay, Sandwich, Kent.

Box Hill SE 15 OS map 187 TQ 1851

Box Hill is a well-known beauty spot which lies in the North Downs about midway between Leatherhead and Dorking. Owned by the National Trust, it is 965 ft (294m) high and composed of chalk. The hill derives its name from the boxwoods which occupy the steep escarpment above the River Mole, but the botanical interest extends to the chalk grasslands here, too.

Flora

FLOWERING PLANTS The **boxwoods** also include a little **yew** and **ash,** and the woodland herbs are **dog's mercury, felwort, wall pepper, stinking hellebore, ploughman's spikenard** and the rare **cut-leaved germander.** There is also some **beechwood** with **oak** and **birch, holly, gean, large-leaved lime** and more box.

Elsewhere you may find **broad helleborine, man orchid, bee orchid, columbine** and the uncommon **ground-pine.**

Access

The hill lies immediately to the east of the main A24 Leatherhead to Dorking road by Burford Bridge over the River Mole. The area is freely accessible and very popular.

Frensham, Thursley and Hankley Commons
SE 16 OS map 186 SU 9040

About 6 miles (10 km) south-east of Farnham in the Surrey hills are several areas of heath and common land including Thursley Common, Hankley Common and Frensham Common itself. They include some of the finest and most interesting heathland still surviving in Surrey, and have pools and bogs which are important sites in their own right. Parts of the area have been afforested with conifer plantations and other parts have birch and pinewoods. Most of Thursley Common is a National Nature Reserve.

Fauna

BIRDS The heathland birdlife includes **nightjars, stonechats, whinchats, snipe, redshanks** and **hobbies,** and the scrub and naturally regenerating woods hold **willow warblers, lesser whitethroats, redstarts, nightingales, sparrowhawks** and the occasional nesting **buzzard.**

Great grey shrikes often winter on Thursley Common.

On Frensham Heath is a small pool known as Frensham Little Pond which is the haunt of several water birds such as **great crested grebes, little grebes, teal** and **tufted ducks,** whilst **reed warblers** and **sedge warblers** nest in the surrounding reed beds.

MAMMALS Small numbers of **roe deer** occur on the heathland.

INVERTEBRATES The pools and mires are the breeding sites of a number of rare **dragonflies** including *Leucorrhinia dubia, Somatochlora metallica* and *Ceriagrion tenellum.*

Flora

FLOWERING PLANTS The heathland is dominated by **ling** and **cross-leaved heath,** and **lesser gorse** is also common. **Pine** and **birch** woods are also present, but the main botanical interest is in the bogs which have **bog asphodel, many-stalked spike-rush, common cotton-grass, cranberry, long-leaved sundew, bottle sedge, bogbean, small bladderwort, marsh St John's wort** and the rare **bog hair-grass.**

FERNS **Marsh clubmoss** occurs in some of the bogs.

Access

Although some of the area is privately owned, the public are allowed free access over large parts, and there are footpaths elsewhere. Perhaps the best way to see the commons is to start from Frensham Great Pond, which is near to the A287 Farnham to Hindhead road, and then to walk eastwards towards Hankley and Thursley Commons. Some of the area is used for military training and access is restricted.

Kingley Vale SE 17 OS map 197 SU 8211

Kingley Vale is a National Nature Reserve of 351 acres (142 ha) which lies a little way north-west of Chichester. Its main importance is that it contains one of the very few yew woods in Britain although there are also some deciduous woods as well as areas of chalk grassland.

Fauna

BIRDS Several common woodland species occur here such as **grasshopper warblers, blackcaps, marsh tits, chiffchaffs** and **nightingales**.

MAMMALS Both **fallow** and **roe deer** inhabit the reserve, and there are also **badger** setts.

Flora

FLOWERING PLANTS **Yew** woods have probably the densest canopy of any woodland, so it is hardly surprising that there is little other vegetation in them. Parts of the wood, however, have some **ash** with **holly, blackthorn** and **whitebeam**. There is also an area of **pedunculate oak wood** with **ash** and **hawthorn**.

The chalk downland areas are far more rewarding to botanists and have a varied calcicole flora. It is mainly dominated by **sheeps fescue** and **downy oat grass** with **salad burnet, bee orchid, early purple orchid, eyebright, wild thyme, common rock-rose, red bartsia, lady's bed- straw, hedge bedstraw, wild parsnip, squinancy wort, hoary plantain** and **hairy violet**.

Access

The reserve lies near to the village of West Stoke about 3 miles (5 km) north-west of Chichester. There is an information centre and nature trail, but away from the footpaths the reserve is only open by special permission.

Forest of Dean S 1 OS map 162 SO 6008

The enormous Forest of Dean lies on the north bank of the River Severn about 20 miles (32 km) due north of Bristol. It was originally a Royal Forest but is now in the hands of the Forestry Commission who manage it as a National Forest Park. It covers about 47 square miles (122 km²), most of which consists of old hardwood forests which have a variety of interesting wildlife.

Fauna

BIRDS The breeding birds include **buzzards, sparrowhawks, ravens, red-backed shrikes, nightjars, dippers, wood warblers, grasshopper warblers, siskins, hawfinches** and **woodlarks**. One section of the forest – the Nagshead Inclosure – has been the site of a long-term study of **redstarts, pied flycatchers, blue tits** and **great tits**, all of which nest here in hundreds of nest boxes.

MAMMALS The mammals are represented by both **red** and **roe deer, badgers, foxes, polecats** and **weasels**.

INVERTEBRATES Important **butterfly** species are the **brown argus**, the **wood white** and the **white admiral**.

Flora

FLOWERING PLANTS The forest lies partly over coal measures, partly on sandstone and partly on limestone, and the different rock types are reflected in the flora of the woods.

The central part of the forest, which lies on the coal measures, is dominated by **pedunculate oak** with some **beech** and **holly**, with **bramble, bilberry** and **fine bent grass** below. **Soft rush** grows in wetter spots.

The sandstone areas are again dominated by **pedunculate oak** accompanied by **sweet chestnut, birch, beech, holly, gean** and **rowan**. The herbaceous flora here includes **creeping soft-grass, wavy hair-grass,** and **bluebell.**

The limestone regions are mainly of **beech** and **wych elm** with smaller amounts of **pedunculate oak, sweet chestnut, ash, birch, field maple** and **rowan**. The shrubs include **holly, yew, dogwood, hazel, hawthorn, willows, elder,** and **guelder rose**. The herbs include **herb Paris, common enchanter's nightshade, common wintergreen, meadow saffron, birdsnest orchid, sanicle** and **primrose.**

Access

The forest lies between the A48 and the A4136, and is intersected by a network of minor roads. Most of the area is freely accessible to the public and there are several nature trails. Details of these and other facilities in the forest may be obtained from the Forestry Commission Warden, Crown Office, Bank St, Coleford, Gloucestershire GL16 8BA. The O.S. map references of the nature trails are: SO 540153, 608105, 569179, 620121, 562160 and 621081. A path also runs through the Nagshead Inclosure and this begins from SO 608090.

Slimbridge S 2 OS map 162 SO 7205

Slimbridge will need no introduction to wildfowl enthusiasts. It is, of course, the headquarters of the Wildfowl Trust, and has what is probably the finest collection of captive waterfowl in the world as well as being a major refuge for a large variety of ducks, geese and swans. The wild bird refuge includes about 1000 acres (404ha) of mudflats and marsh on the south-eastern bank of the Severn Estuary about 10 miles (16km) south-west of Gloucester.

Fauna

BIRDS Among the wild birds which can be relied upon to visit Slimbridge each year are 7000 **white-fronted geese**, about 400 **Bewick's swans**, several hundred **mallard** and **wigeon**, and smaller numbers of **pintails, shovelers, gadwall, teal,** and **shelducks**. A few **lesser white-fronted geese** and one or two **peregrines** also visit Slimbridge in most years, as do a large variety of waders such as **grey plovers, whimbrel, godwits,** sandpipers, greenshanks, ruff, turnstones and dunlin. Less frequent visitors include brent geese, bean geese, pink-footed geese, barnacle geese, short-eared owls, hen harriers and ospreys.

Access

Slimbridge is just west of the main A38 Gloucester to Bristol road and is well signposted locally. It is open to the public throughout the year except Christmas.

North Meadow S 3 OS map 163 SU 0994

North Meadow is an ancient area of grassland which lies about 8 miles (13 km) south-east of Cirencester. The same management has been continued here for at least the last 800 years, and consequently the area has an extremely interesting flora. It is a National Nature Reserve and covers 110 acres (45 ha).

Flora

FLOWERING PLANTS North Meadow contains what is probably the finest colony of the rare and attractive snakeshead fritillary anywhere in Britain – about 80 per cent of our total population grows here.

Other notable species are great burnet, meadow-rue, southern marsh orchid, cowslip, ox-eye daisy, betony, red and white clovers, red fescue, sweet vernal grass and rough meadow-grass. Wetter areas have marsh marigold, water dock and water plantain.

FERNS The meadow is also a noted site for adder's tongue fern.

Access

The reserve is situated about $\frac{1}{4}$ mile (400 m) north of Cricklade, which is just off the A419, south-east of Cirencester. A public footpath runs across the reserve and the fritillaries may be seen from this. A permit from the Nature Conservancy Council is needed to leave it.

Pewsey Down S 4 OS map 173 SU 1163

Pewsey Down lies on a long chalk escarpment just south of the Vale of Pewsey about 8 miles (13 km) south of Marlborough. The calcareous grassland here holds a variety of interesting plants which are protected within a 188 acre (75 ha) National Nature Reserve.

Flora

FLOWERING PLANTS The grassland is largely dominated by sheeps fescue, red fescue and upright brome grass with a great deal of glaucous sedge and salad burnet. Other species include green-winged orchid, burnt orchid, chalk milkwort, bastard toadflax, saw-wort, horseshoe vetch, kidney vetch and dwarf sedge. The rare tuberous thistle is also found here where it hybridizes with dwarf thistle.

Access

Pewsey Down may be reached by the A345 south of Marlborough. No permits are needed, but visitors are requested not to stray from the footpaths. There is a tenancy agreement over much of the reserve. No dogs are allowed, as sheep and stock are grazed on the site.

Old Winchester Hill S 5 OS map 185 SU 6420

Old Winchester Hill lies about 15 miles (24km) east of Winchester. It is composed of chalk and limestone, and covered with calcareous turf and areas of scrub and woodland. 140 acres (57ha) of the hill have been designated as a National Nature Reserve which protects some interesting iron-age remains as well as the flora and fauna.

Fauna

MAMMALS There is a well-established **badger** sett on the reserve.
INVERTEBRATES Notable **butterfly** species are the **chalk hill blue**, **green hairstreak, Duke of Burgundy fritillary**, and very occasionally, **clouded yellow**.

Flora

FLOWERING PLANTS A number of uncommon and attractive calcicoles may be found on the reserve including a total of 14 species of orchids. The grassland on the south-facing side is the most interesting area, and the flora here includes **butterfly orchid, frog orchid, fragrant orchid, autumn lady's tresses, round-headed rampion, devilsbit scabious, carline thistle, horseshoe vetch** and **kidney vetch**.

The reserve also includes a certain amount of scrub with **yew** and **juniper** and some planted **beech/ash** woods. Peake Wood, which lies on the western side of the hill is an old **hazel** coppice with **oak, beech, ash, yew, Scots pine, field maple, wayfaring tree**, and **whitebeam**. The herbaceous flora includes **bee orchid, fly orchid, common twayblade, common star of Bethlehem, common enchanter's nightshade, dog's mercury, bluebell, wood anemone, herb Robert, sanicle, arum lily** and **woodruff**.

Access

The hill is immediately east of the A32 a few miles south of Alton. No special permits are necessary for the reserve, and there is a nature trail and exhibition centre. All dogs must be kept on a lead.

Peake Wood is privately owned and there is no access to it without permission.

Chesil Beach, The Fleet and Abbotsbury Swannery S 6 OS map 194 SY 6280 and SY 5885

Chesil Beach is a vegetated shingle beach which stretches for 18 miles (29km) from Weymouth to Abbotsbury, and is one of the largest and ecologically most important of such beaches in Britain. Immediately behind this shingle bar is a large tidal lagoon known as The Fleet which is an important wintering ground for wildfowl and which also holds the largest flock of resident mute swans in the country. These are centred around the north-western end of The Fleet at Abbotsbury.

Fauna
BIRDS In winter, The Fleet holds over 4000 **wigeon**, together with **mallard**, **teal**, **tufted ducks**, **pintails**, **pochard**, **goldeneye** and **shovelers**. A small number of **brent geese** and a few **gadwall**, **scaup** and **smew** are also occasionally noted.

A colony of about 200 pairs of **little terns** and a few **ringed plovers** nest on the shingle of Chesil Beach.

The **mute swans** here, which number about 650, are the only colonial nesting mute swans in Britain.

INVERTEBRATES Chesil Beach is noted for the wingless **cricket** *Mogoplistes squamiger*, a species which is found nowhere else in Britain.

Flora
FLOWERING PLANTS Chesil Beach holds **sea kale, yellow horned-poppy, sea pea, shrubby seablite** and **rough clover**.

The vegetation of The Fleet includes **tassel pondweed, common eel-grass, narrow-leaved eel-grass** and **dwarf eel-grass**.

Access
Abbotsbury Swannery is open to the public and there is a small admission charge which also includes access to the botanic gardens there. Chesil Beach can be reached from Abbotsbury village, but the tern colonies are closed off during the nesting season.

Portland Bill S 7 OS map 194 SY 6868
Lying immediately south of Weymouth, Portland Bill is a 6 mile $(9\frac{1}{2}km)$ long peninsula jutting out into the English Channel. Its position is such that it receives an interesting variety of migratory birds, and there is a bird observatory at its southern tip from which they may be studied. The cliffs of the peninsula are also interesting from the botanical point of view.

Fauna
BIRDS The list of migrant birds which have been seen here is far too long to repeat in full, but includes all kinds of wildfowl, waders and a large variety of passerines. Some notable rarities are **Dartford, Bonelli's, melodious** and **icterine warblers,** various **chats** and **Balearic shearwaters.** The Bill is particularly good for sea watching and **shearwaters, petrels** and **auks** are regularly seen.

INVERTEBRATES A number of interesting **moths** are known to frequent the area including the **Portland ribbon wave**, the **feathered ranunculus, feathered brindle** and the **wormwood moth**.

Flora

FLOWERING PLANTS **Portland sea-lavender** flowers at its only known British site here along with **Portland spurge, golden samphire, cliff spurrey** and **rock samphire.**

Access

Details of accommodation at the bird observatory are available from: M. Rogers, The Portland Bill Bird Observatory, Old Lower Light, Portland, Dorset.

Elsewhere, most of the coastline is freely and easily accessible.

Radipole Lake s 8 OS map 194 SY 6779

Radipole Lake is an R.S.P.B. reserve which lies immediately north of Weymouth. It was formerly a backwater of the Wey Estuary which has been dammed up to form a reedy lagoon. The lake is a haunt of wintering wildfowl and a good migration watchpoint.

Fauna

BIRDS Among the most regular winter visitors here are **pochard, tufted ducks, teal, shovelers** and **mallard. Red-breasted mergansers, scaup** and **smew** are less frequent visitors.

Dunlin, greenshanks, little stints and **spotted redshanks** are recorded quite regularly; **little gulls** turn up in most years and **black terns** are frequent in autumn. **Bitterns** and **bearded tits** are also noted regularly.

Access

The reserve is open to the public at all times. Access is gained from the Swannery car park, Weymouth. There is a visitors' centre and facilities for the disabled.

Arne s 9 OS map 195 SY 9787

Arne Nature Reserve is on the Isle of Purbeck not far east of Wareham. It is a reserve of the R.S.P.B. and consists mainly of heathland with some saltmarsh and woodlands. One hide overlooks a brackish marsh with reeds, and the other is off the Shipstal public nature trail overlooking the Poole Harbour saltings.

Fauna

BIRDS This reserve is probably the best place in Britain to see the rare **Dartford warbler,** several pairs of which nest on the heathland here.

REPTILES AND AMPHIBIANS **Sand lizards** and **smooth snakes** are both found on the reserve.

INVERTEBRATES The rare **dragonfly** *Ceriagrion tenellum* has been recorded.

Flora

FLOWERING PLANTS The heathland flora includes the uncommon **Dorset heath** and **mossy stonecrop.**

Access

The reserve is easily reached by the unclassified roads from Wareham. The Shipstal part of the reserve is open to the public throughout the year. The remainder of the reserve is only accessible by permit which can be obtained from The Warden at Syldata, Arne, Wareham, Dorset BH20 5BJ.

Studland Heath S 10 OS map 195 SZ 0284

The National Nature Reserve of Studland Heath lies at the eastern tip of the Isle of Purbeck a few miles south-west of Bournemouth. Despite its name it includes many other habitats besides just heathland, such as sand dunes, woodlands, a fresh-water lake known as the Little Sea, bogs and foreshore. The whole area covers 1552 acres (631ha).

Fauna

BIRDS The Little Sea, which is overlooked by a public hide, usually holds a variety of waterfowl during the winter months. These may include both **whooper** and **Bewick's swans, pochard, tufted ducks, goldeneye, shovelers, scaup, mallard, wigeon** and **long-tailed ducks.**
  Dartford warblers nest on the heathland.

MAMMALS The mammals are represented by **roe deer** and a colony of **harvest mice.**

REPTILES AND AMPHIBIANS All six British reptiles may be found on the reserve, namely the **adder, grass snake, smooth snake, slow worm, common lizard** and **sand lizard.**

INVERTEBRATES The rare **Diver's ant** may be found here and has only one other British site, namely the New Forest. There are also **1-album wainscot moths,** and 22 species of **dragonflies** have been recorded including the rare *Ceriagrion tenellum* and *Sympetrum sanguineum.*

Flora

FLOWERING PLANTS The heathland of the reserve has a certain amount of rare **Dorset heath** and **marsh gentian. Great sundew** is found in some of the bogs and there is **sea rocket** on the foreshore, but probably the richest hunting ground for botanists is the **reed** beds which surround the Little Sea and which have **waterwort, shore weed, blunt-leaved pondweed,** and **floating spike-rush.**
Alternate water milfoil grows in the lake itself.

FERNS The small **quillwort** grows in the Little Sea, and **royal ferns** grow in the surrounding reed beds.

Access

The reserve is accessible from Poole via the Sandbanks ferry, and is adjacent to the unclassified road which runs between the ferry terminus and Studland. There are two nature trails through the area, an information centre, and a public hide on the Little Sea.

The New Forest S 11 OS maps 184, 195 & 196 SU 2806

The 100 or so square miles (260 km²) of the New Forest is a veritable paradise for naturalists. Despite its name, it is neither new, having been created in the 11th Century, nor entirely forested and it includes the largest tract of lowland heath in Britain together with areas of grassland, streams, pools and mires as well as a variety of woodland types. The Forest lies between Bournemouth and Southampton and is mostly controlled by the Forestry Commission. The public has the right of access over about two-thirds of the total.

Fauna

BIRDS The New Forest is famous for its birdlife and has such rarities as the **hobby, Dartford warblers, red-backed shrikes, nightingales, nightjars, firecrests, crossbills, hawfinches** and, in many years, **honey buzzards.** Other species include **snipe, woodlark, wood warbler, redstart, woodcock, redpolls, buzzards, sparrowhawks, stonechats** and **curlews**.

MAMMALS **New Forest ponies** are probably the best-known members of the mammal fauna, but they are only one of several larger mammals which may be found here. **Red, roe** and **fallow deer** are all found in the forest, as well as the introduced **muntjac** and **sika deer** – the latter being restricted to the southern boundaries of the forest. In addition, there are **badgers, foxes, shrews** and **grey squirrels.**

REPTILES AND AMPHIBIANS **Sand lizards, common lizards, smooth snakes** and **adders** are all found here, and there is a firmly established colony of **European tree frogs** in the south of the area.

INVERTEBRATES The insect life is also outstanding, and the Forest has long been well known to lepidopterists. The wooded areas have **butterflies** such as the **high brown fritillary, white admiral, Duke of Burgundy fritillary, purple hairstreak,** and **moths** such as **scarce Merveille du Jour, light crimson underwing, dark crimson underwing, great oak beauty** and **pale oak beauty.** The woods also have the **New Forest cicada,** which is found nowhere else in Britain.

Heathland insects include the **cinnabar moth, silver studded blue, sloe carpet moth, sharp-angled peacock** and two rare ants; the **Diver's ant** which only lives here and on Studland Heath (S 10), and the even rarer *Anergates atratulus,* which parasitizes other ants and is totally restricted to the New Forest.

The **silver hook moth** and **purple-bordered gold moth** inhabit some of the numerous mires of the forest.

Flora

FLOWERING PLANTS A wide variety of trees are found in the New Forest. **Beech** is probably the commonest native tree here, with the two **oaks** (**sessile** and **pedunculate**) next, but there are also **pine, birch, yew,** holly, **whitebeam** and many others, including several introduced exotics. Much of the woodland is very old and unenclosed; that is open to the ponies and other browsing animals which have greatly reduced the number of young saplings and hampered the natural regeneration of the woods. Many wooded areas are enclosed so as to exclude such animals.

Among the more notable wild flowers of the woods are **common cow-wheat,** the rare **coral necklace** and **common lungwort.**

The heaths support a richer and more interesting flora which includes **wild gladiolus,** a species which is only found in the New Forest. Other heathland plants are **slender marsh bedstraw, slender cicendia, marsh gentian** and **autumn lady's tresses.**

The numerous bogs which are scattered throughout the forest hold **common cottongrass, marsh pennywort, bog orchid, Irish bladderwort, small bladderwort, common sundew, long-leaved sundew, bog asphodel, bog myrtle, bog bean, bog rush, bog pimpernel, white beak sedge, marsh St John's wort, lesser skullcap** and **marsh thistle.**

In some of these bogs, **alder** carrs have developed and it is here that the rare **Hampshire purslane** may be found. This is another species which is unknown outside the New Forest, and the western part of Beaulieu Heath is a good place to search for it. Some areas also have the rare **touch-me-not.**

The streams of the area support plants such as **reddish pondweed, greater spearwort, marshwort, tubular water dropwort** and **brook-weed** whilst in the pools you may find **yellow bartsia, waterwort, lesser bulrush, frog-bit, floating spike-rush** and **lesser water plantain.**

FERNS The woodlands themselves have **beech ferns** and **marsh ferns** and **fir clubmoss** grows on some of the heaths. **Royal fern** and **marsh clubmoss** may be found in the bogs, and **pillwort** in some of the pools.

Access

The New Forest is easily reached from either the A31, A35 or A337 and the public are permitted to roam at will throughout much of the area. The whole forest is recognised by the Forestry Commission as of National Nature Reserve status.

Beaulieu Heath (SU 3500) is probably the finest area of heathland, and Hatchet Pond (SU 3601) and Sowley Pond (SZ 3796) are two of the most interesting pools. As regards the bogs, Cranesmoor (SU 1903) and Hincheslea Bottom (SU 2602) are among the best. Beaulieu Road Station (SU 349063) is a classic location for seeing hobbies.

Accommodation in the area is not difficult to find and there are several campsites, details of which may be obtained from the forestry offices scattered throughout the area.

Newtown Marsh S 12 OS map 196 SZ 4291

Newtown Marsh is an 800 acre (324ha) Local Nature Reserve of Isle of Wight County Council. Much of the area was formerly rough grazing land which was created in the 17th Century by the building of a sea wall across part of the Newtown River estuary. In 1954, however, the sea wall was breached and the area has now reverted to saltmarsh which is a favoured haunt of wildfowl and waders, and a fertile hunting ground for botanists. The reserve also includes an area of woodland.

Fauna
BIRDS During the summer the marshes hold several species of breeding birds including **shelducks, oystercatchers, redshanks, common** and **little terns** and **black-headed gulls.**

In winter up to 500 **wigeon** may be found here along with **mallard, shelducks, pintails, teal, red-breasted mergansers, brent geese, dunlin, curlews, black-tailed godwits, redshanks** and several other less regular visitors.

Nightingales breed in the woodland.

MAMMALS **Red squirrels** are found here.

INVERTEBRATES Two notable **butterflies** here are the **white admiral** and the **purple hairstreak.**

Flora
FLOWERING PLANTS The marsh itself has **marsh mallow, sea-lavender, long-leaved scurvy grass** and **grass vetchling.**

Golden samphire, sea heath, and **yellow horned-poppy** grow on the shingle spits, and the woods have **wood spurge, roast beef plant, butcher's broom, tutsan** and **saw-wort.**

Access
The reserve is accessible from Newtown, which is just north of the A3054 about half way between Yarmouth and Newport. There is a nature trail on the reserve but away from this a permit is required from Isle of Wight County Council.

Farlington Marshes S 13 OS map 197 SU 6804
Farlington Marshes are one of the most important wetlands on the south coast. They are immediately east of Portsmouth at the head of Langstone Harbour and are a nature reserve of the Hampshire and Isle of Wight Naturalist's Trust. The marshes themselves are of interest to botanists, and vast numbers of wildfowl and waders winter on the flats of Langstone Harbour, an R.S.P.B. reserve.

Fauna
BIRDS Five to seven thousand **brent geese** regularly winter in the harbour along with some 1500 **shelducks,** numerous **teal, wigeon** and **mallard,** and lesser numbers of **pintails, goldeneye** and **red-breasted mergansers.** Over 20,000 waders also frequent the area including **redshanks, dunlin, curlews, bar-tailed godwits, black-tailed godwits, grey plovers, turnstones, snipe** and **golden plovers.**

Short-eared owls are also regular winter visitors and various species of tern are often seen on passage.

MAMMALS A population of harvest mice lives on the marshes.

Flora

FLOWERING PLANTS Among the plants of the area are common eel-grass, narrow-leaved eel-grass, dwarf eel-grass, golden samphire, sea-lavender, fat duckweed, sea clover, slender birdsfoot trefoil, grass vetchling, parsley water dropwort and perennial beard-grass.

Access

The public can walk round the perimeter wall from which good views can be obtained of the marshes and the harbour mudflats. Visitors should adhere to conditions of entry stated at the entrance.

The Channel Islands S 14

The Channel Islands lie between 60 and 80 miles (96–128 km) south of the Dorset coast, and are considerably closer to France than to England. Because of the exceptionally mild climate, the flora and fauna have more in common with parts of continental Europe than with Britain and there are several species of plants and animals which are restricted, in the U.K., to the Channel Islands.

The four main islands are Jersey, Guernsey, Alderney and Sark.

Fauna

BIRDS The birdlife includes breeding Dartford warblers, Kentish plovers and cirl buntings. Alderney is particularly attractive to birds, especially seabirds, and the two rocky stacks of Les Etacs and Ortac, which lie to the west of Alderney, have almost 3000 pairs of gannets between them. Alderney also holds small numbers of breeding wrynecks, and the tiny island sanctuary of Burhou has puffins, razorbills, guillemots, storm petrels, shags, rock pipits and oystercatchers.

The nature reserve of St Ouen's Pond on Jersey includes the largest area of fresh water in the whole archepelago and has a large swamp where garganey may be seen.

MAMMALS The Channel Islands have several species of small mammals which are found on continental Europe but not elsewhere in the British Isles. These include the continental white-toothed shrew (or Alderney shrew) which is common on Guernsey, Alderney and Herm; the lesser white-toothed shrew which is found on Jersey and Sark (and the Isles of Scilly); and the Guernsey field vole which is restricted to Guernsey. There is also a distinct race of the bank vole (*Clethrionomys glareolus caesarius*) which is found only on Jersey. Red squirrels, long-eared bats and greater horseshoe bats are frequent in suitable localities.

REPTILES AND AMPHIBIANS Both green lizards and wall lizards have their only British haunts on the Channel Islands and there are also populations of the continental frog *Rana dalmatina*.

INVERTEBRATES The islands are often visited by migrant **butterflies** which come from the continent, and which are rarely seen elsewhere in the U.K. These include the **glanville fritillary, clouded yellow, Queen of Spain fritillary** and **Camberwell beauty.** Among the more notable moths are the **death's head hawk moth, convolvulus hawk moth** and **hummingbird hawk moth.**

Flora

FLOWERING PLANTS The flora of the islands runs into well over a thousand species, many of which are either absent or extremely scarce in mainland Britain, and there is only room here to list a few of the more interesting specialities. Perhaps the most celebrated Channel Island species is the **Jersey buttercup** which is only found on that island. **Purple spurge** is restricted to Alderney. Other notable members of the flora include **loose-flowered orchid, purple viper's bugloss, four-leaved all-seed, blue romulea, twin-flowered clover, upright clover, broad-leaved thrift, Alderney sea-lavender, Mexican fleabane, rough star thistle, three-cornered leek, early sand-grass, harestail grass, sharp bulrush, galingale, Jersey toadflax, sea bindweed, great sea stock, balm-leaved figwort, sea kale, golden samphire, rock samphire, common dodder, autumn lady's tresses, autumn squill, yellow horned-poppy** and **sea holly.** There is also a smaller, bushier form of **crimson clover** which is only found on Jersey and the Lizard peninsula (SW 10).

FERNS Among the more noteworthy ferns of the islands are **Jersey fern, sand quillwort, early adder's-tongue, lanceolate spleenwort, sea spleenwort, rustyback fern** and **royal fern.**

Access

The Channel Islands may be reached from most major British airports or by sea from Weymouth. Your local travel agency will be able to advise you. Interested readers are referred to the following two books which are full of information for visitors to the islands: *The Traveller's Guide to The Channel Islands*, by R.M. Lockley, published by Jonathan Cape; and *The Red Guide to The Channel Islands*, edited by Reginald J.W. Hammond, published by Ward Lock.

Lundy Island SW 1 OS map 180 SS 1345

The Isle of Lundy lies in the Bristol Channel about 11 miles (17.5 km) north of Hartland Point, Devon, and about 30 miles (48 km) south of St Gowan's Head, Dyfed. It is a little over 3 miles (5 km) in length and about $\frac{1}{4}$ mile (400 m) wide, and is largely surrounded by 400 ft (122 m) high cliffs.

It is administered by the Landmark Trust and has a bird observatory as well as a good population of breeding seabirds.

Fauna

BIRDS Lundy is well known for its **puffins** although the colonies there have declined considerably over the last few years. Other nesting seabirds include **guillemots** and **razorbills, Manx shearwaters, kittiwakes** and **fulmars**, and there are also **ravens, buzzards** and **peregrines**.

The island is also a good migration watching point, and several rare vagrants have been recorded over the years by the bird observatory.

MAMMALS The mammal fauna includes a distinct race of the **pygmy shrew** which is endemic to the island, **rabbits** and a small herd of **sika deer**. There is also a small **grey seal** rookery.

Flora

FLOWERING PLANTS The flora is not particularly outstanding except that there is one crucifer – **Lundy cabbage** – which is found nowhere else in Britain.

Access

Boats regularly sail to Lundy from Ilfracombe and Bideford. There is accommodation on the island, details of which are available from the National Trust.

Details of the bird observatory may be obtained from The National Trust also.

Bridgwater Bay SW 2 OS map 182 ST 2947

The National Nature Reserve of Bridgwater Bay covers $9\frac{3}{4}$ square miles (25.5 km^2) of mudflats and marshes and includes the Parrett Estuary, Stert Flats and Stert Island. The reserve is a few miles south-west of Burnham-on-Sea and is mainly of interest on account of the huge flocks of wildfowl and waders which gather there, although the marshes have some botanical interest, too.

Fauna

BIRDS In July, about 3000 **shelducks** congregate on the flats on the reserve where they undergo their annual moult. Most British shelducks go to north-western Germany for this purpose, and Bridgwater Bay is the only such moulting ground in Britain.

During the winter, even more birds are attracted to the bay including over 1000 **white-fronted geese**, several hundred **wigeon** and **mallard** and fewer numbers of **teal, pintails**, and **shovelers**. The wintering waders can number up to 5000, and are dominated by **black-tailed godwits, knot** and **turnstones. Merlins** and **short-eared owls** also winter in Bridgwater Bay.

Flora

FLOWERING PLANTS The saltmarshes bordering the Parrett Estuary hold **bulbous fox-tail, slender hare's-ear** and **sea barley**. The rare **honewort**, and **sea clover**, grow on some of the low cliffs.

FERNS **Water fern** may be found on the saltmarsh.

Access

Except for Stert Island, the entire reserve is open to the public without permit. The best areas for birdwatching are near Stert Point (ST 289471), where the Nature Conservancy Council has established hides and scrapes, and the footpath which runs from 'The Island' – which is actually part of the foreshore at ST 293458 – to the Brue Estuary (ST 304475).

The Avon Gorge and Leigh Woods
SW 3 OS map 172 ST 5675

Immediately west of Bristol, the River Avon flows through a deep limestone gorge which is bridged by the famous Clifton suspension bridge. On its south-western side the gorge is covered by Leigh Woods, a nature reserve owned by the National Trust and managed by the Nature Conservancy Council. The main interest is botanical, but is by no means restricted to the woodland, for the surrounding limestone cliffs also have an exciting collection of calcicoles even though they are not included in the reserve.

Flora

FLOWERING PLANTS Leigh Woods consists mainly of **ash** and both **sessile** and **pedunculate oak** with some **wych elm, yew, small-leaved lime** and several species of **whitebeam**, such as *Sorbus eminens, S. porrigentiformis, S. anglica, S. wilmottiana* and *S. bristoliensis*; the latest two species being endemic to this area. Within the woods, several interesting herbs may be found including **wood spurge, columbine, fingered sedge, birdsnest orchid, wild madder, ivy broomrape, toothwort, green hellebore, wood anemone, wild strawberry, dog's mercury** and **bluebell**.

Many other notable species may be found on the limestone cliffs and screes nearby. These include **Bristol rockcress**, which probably has its last remaining British haunt here, and **round-headed leek** which, likewise, seems to be confined to the gorge. This last species, incidentally, is liable to be confused with **rosy garlic** and **keeled garlic**, both of which may also be found on the cliffs. Other interesting species are **honewort, spring cinquefoil, Curtis's mouse-ear, spiked speedwell, autumn squill, hutchinsia, dwarf sedge** and **bloody cranesbill**. There is also a certain amount of scrub with **hornbeam** and **western gorse**.

FERNS Beech fern and **soft shield fern** both grow in the woods.

Access

Leigh Woods are easily reached from the B3124. No special permits are needed and there is a nature trail which starts from near Abbots Leigh (ST 5574).

Braunton Burrows SW 4 OS map 180 SS 4635

Braunton Burrows is one of the largest areas of sand dunes in Britain. Some of the dunes here are nearly 100 ft (30 m) high and the whole system covers

2400 acres (970 ha), 1500 acres (603 ha) of which have been designated as a National Nature Reserve. The reserve lies on the northern banks of the Taw and Torridge Estuary about 6 miles (10 km) west of Barnstaple. There is another smaller area of dunes on the southern side of the estuary.

Flora

FLOWERING PLANTS The sand is very lime-rich and, in consequence, has a most interesting flora including several rarities. These include **clustered club-rush** which has its main British stronghold on the dunes, **water germander**, which is otherwise only found in parts of East Anglia and Ireland, **Argentine dock** and **shore dock**. **Sea knotgrass** has been recorded, but is now probably extinct in Britain. Other notables include **French toadflax, great sea stock, sharp rush, sea storksbill, slender centaury, sea pearlwort, marsh helleborine, seaside pansy, sea rocket, Portland spurge, dwarf yellow sedge** and **shore weed**.

MOSSES AND LIVERWORTS The rare **moss** *Tortula ruraliformis* grows here.

Access

No special permits are needed to visit the nature reserve although visitors are not encouraged to leave the footpaths. Much of the remainder of the dune system is used as a military firing range, so access is restricted for obvious reasons. Red flags are flown during the military operations and the area is closed to visitors during these periods.

Cheddar Gorge SW 5 OS map 182 ST 4754

Cheddar Gorge is a deep limestone canyon which lies about 10 miles (16 km) south-west of Bristol in the Mendips. It is well known to botanists on account of the uncommon calcicoles which grow on the screes and cliffs, and among the ashwoods and scrub.

The north-western side of the gorge is National Trust property, and two other nearby areas are protected by the local naturalists' trust.

Flora

FLOWERING PLANTS The most distinguished member of the flora is **Cheddar pink** which is only found at one or two other sites, where it has been introduced. Sharing the gorge with Cheddar pink are **cut-leaved self-heal, little Robin, herb Robert, shining cranesbill, bloody cranesbill, Welsh poppy, lesser meadow-rue** and **Curtis's mouse-ear**.

Mossy saxifrage is said to reach its southern limit here, and **spring sandwort** and **alpine pennycress** may be found growing near some of the old lead workings in the area.

The woodland, which is dominated by **ash**, has **yew, holly, wayfaring tree** and several species of **whitebeams** including *Sorbus aria, S. anglica* and *S. porigentiformis*. The woodland herbs include **wild madder, orpine, roast beef plant, arum lily** and **common valerian**.

There are also some areas of scrub where **ling** and **western gorse** may be found along with **quaking grass, heath grass, lady's bedstraw, common rock-rose, wild thyme** and **Good Friday grass.**

Access

The B3135 road runs through the gorge itself, which is just north east of the village of Cheddar. The reserves belonging to the local naturalists' trust are the Black Rock Reserve at ST 485545 and Long Wood at ST 487555. Both of these reserves have a nature trail.

Stoke Wood SW 6 OS map 182 ST 4950

Stoke Wood is a National Nature Reserve of 86 acres (35 ha) which lies about 3 miles (5 km) south-east of Cheddar, Somerset.

Flora

FLOWERING PLANTS **Ash** is the dominant tree although there is a good deal of variety in the canopy which also has **pedunculate oak, wych elm, field maple, small-leaved lime, spindle, wild service** and the uncommon **cut-leaved whitebeam.** The shrubs include **dogwood** and **traveller's joy.** The herbaceous layer includes **purple gromwell, meadow saffron, nettle-leaved bellflower, wood spurge, spurge laurel, herb Robert, yellow archangel, dog's mercury, lesser celandine, wood anemone, primrose** and **bluebell.**
FERNS **Hartstongue fern** grows here.

Access

The wood lies near to the village of Rodney Stoke which is on the A371. A permit from the Nature Conservancy Council, Roughmoor, Bishops Hull, Taunton, Somerset TA1 5AA is needed in order to visit the reserve.

Bovey Valley Woodlands SW 7 OS map 191 SX 7878

The River Bovey rises in the eastern part of Dartmoor and flows south-east before joining the River Teign and eventually meeting the sea at Teignmouth. The upper reaches of the Bovey Valley are extensively wooded with natural deciduous woods, two areas of which have been declared as National Nature Reserves.

The first reserve, Yarner Wood, lies about 8 miles (13 km) north-west of Newton Abbot and covers 360 acres (146 ha); and the second consists of three adjacent areas, namely Woodash, Houndstor and Rudge Woods. These are 3 or 4 miles (approx. 5 km) further to the north-west and have a total area of 179 acres (73 ha).

Fauna

BIRDS **Redstarts, pied flycatchers, dippers** and **wood warblers** are to be seen.

Flora

FLOWERING PLANTS All the woods are dominated by **sessile oak**, although the soils are very variable and several other tree species are found including **pedunculate oak, ash, birch, Scots pine, alder, rowan** and **holly**.

One of the most notable herbs is the rare **heath lobelia** which grows along with **opposite-leaved golden saxifrage, wood sorrel, sanicle, primrose**, and **common cow-wheat**. There is also some **heather** and **bilberry**.

FERNS **Bracken** is quite common and **royal fern** grows in places.

MOSSES AND LIVERWORTS The **moss** *Hookeria lucens* grows here.

Access

The woods are accessible from the B3344. There are two nature trails in Yarner Wood which start from SX 787789 but to leave them, permits are required. Away from public footpaths, permits are also required for the other woods. Applications should be addressed to the Nature Conservancy Council, Roughmoor, Bishops Hull, Taunton, Somerset TA1 5AA.

Exe Estuary SW 8 OS map 192 SX 9884

Just before the River Exe meets the open sea about 8 miles (13 km) south of Exeter, it is obstructed by a sandy spit known as Dawlish Warren. The mudflats which have developed behind this spit are a National Wildfowl Refuge covering slightly over 1000 acres (404 ha) whilst the spit itself, and the banks of the estuary, are a fertile hunting ground for botanists.

Fauna

BIRDS During the winter months, vast numbers of wildfowl and waders converge on the estuary. Probably the most numerous is the **wigeon**, which often exceeds 5000 in number but there are others including all three British **swans, brent geese, teal, pintails, goldeneye, mergansers, shelducks, scoters, shovelers** and **eiders**. The waders are also well represented and number over 20,000 in most years. **Oystercatchers** are probably the commonest, whilst other species include both **black** and **bar-tailed godwits, turnstones, grey plovers** and **ruff**.

Flora

FLOWERING PLANTS Dawlish Warren is probably Britain's last remaining mainland haunt of **blue romulea**.

The saltmarshes which fringe the estuary hold **sweet flag, long-leaved scurvy grass, saltmarsh rush, rock samphire** and **sea-lavender**.

Access

The estuarine flats can be viewed from several points. On its western side they are accessible from near Powderham (SX 974843) and Starcross (SX 976820), and on the eastern shore from near Lympstone (SX 988840).

There are no restrictions on visiting Dawlish Warren.

The Isles of Scilly sw 9 os map 203 SV 9013

The Isles of Scilly lie about 28 miles (45 km) south of Land's End. Although there are over 100 islands, only five are inhabited. The wildlife of the islands is of outstanding interest. They have some fine seabird colonies, the unique Scilly shrew and a rich native flora. Furthermore, the geographical position of the group is such that they receive all kinds of displaced migrant birds, and there is an interesting assortment of exotic plants which have been accidentally introduced as a result of the extensive cultivation of bulbs; this provides one of the island's principal incomes.

Fauna

BIRDS The seabirds of the islands include England's only colonies of **storm petrels**, as well as **Manx shearwaters, puffins, common, arctic** and **roseate terns. Guillemots** and **razorbills** both nest in tunnels and among boulders as there is a lack of suitable cliffs. There are also colonies of both **lesser** and **greater black-backed gulls**, and nesting **kittiwakes, cormorants** and **shags**.

Other breeding birds include **teal, gadwalls, shovelers, shelducks, mute swans, ringed plovers, oystercatchers,** water rails, rock pipits and **stonechats**.

The list of displaced migrants which have been recorded here is very impressive, and includes American **pectoral sandpipers, yellow-headed blackbirds, Pallas's warblers, Baltimore orioles, alpine swifts, ortolan buntings** and many others.

In former years there was a bird observatory on the island of St Agnes, but this is now closed.

MAMMALS Probably the most distinguished member of the Scilly Islands' fauna is the **Scilly shrew** (*Crocidura suaveolens cassiteridum*), otherwise known as the **white-toothed shrew**, and which is found nowhere else. Its main stronghold seems to be around the Abbey gardens on the island of Tresco.

A few **grey seals** also breed.

INVERTEBRATES Two **butterflies** are endemic to the Scillies. One is a subspecies of the **meadow brown** – *Maniola jurtina cassiteridum* – and the other is a distinct race of the **common blue** which is apparently restricted to the island of Tean. Ordinary **common blues** are found throughout the islands.

Flora

FLOWERING PLANTS The Scilly Isles are well known to botanists on account of the large number of exotic plants which have been inadvertently introduced and which grow as 'weeds' in the bulb fields. These include **corn marigold, rosy garlic, musk storksbill, hairy medick, orange birdsfoot, four-leaved all-seed, western fumitory, Scilly buttercup, lesser quaking-grass, green nightshade, wormwood, pot purslane, kaffir fig, Bermuda buttercup** and **spring beauty**.

Most of the uninhabited islands are either bare rock or are covered with maritime heath where **English stonecrop** and **buckshorn plantain** may be found. There are a few areas of dunes which have **three-cornered leek, sea rocket, shore dock, yellow horned-poppy** and *Viola kitaibeliana* – a **violet** which is restricted in this country to the Scillies and Channel Islands. Brackish pools near to the sea hold **tassel pondweed, sea club-rush, sea rush, grey sallow** and **common reed**. Other notable species are **annual mercury, large cuckoo-pint, tree mallow, Cornish mallow, Babington's leek** and **saltmarsh rush**.

FERNS The **early adder's-tongue** grows on the maritime heaths.

Access

The Isles of Scilly can easily be reached either by ferry or helicopter from Penzance. The five inhabited islands – St Mary's, St Agnes, St Martin's, Tresco and Bryher – are well served by inter-island ferries, and accommodation is readily available in Hugh Town, the principal town on St Mary's island. The remaining islands should only be visited with permission from the 'governor' of the Scillies.

Good places for birdwatching are Bar Point (SV 916130) and Peninnis Point (914095) on St Mary's, Rushy Pool (874149) on Bryher, and the Great Pool and Abbey Pool (8914) on Tresco. The bulb fields should not be entered without permission, in order to prevent the spread of diseases.

The Lizard SW 10 OS map 203 SW 7018

The Lizard Peninsula is the southernmost part of the British mainland. It covers over 50 square miles (130 km²), and holds a vast wealth of interest for biologists, and particularly botanists. The most exciting area is on the south-western coast between Mullion and Lizard village. The interest here derives from the underlying serpentine, a rare type of rock that weathers into a soil which, although lacking in lime, is nevertheless alkaline on account of its high magnesium level. There are many other rock types, and so a complex pattern of soils has developed, and the floral communities of the area are unique.

The National Trust own several sections of this south-western coast including Predannack (much of which is leased to the Cornwall Naturalists' Trust) and a section of the Lizard Downs, and other areas are managed by the Nature Conservancy Council, but the whole of the coastline is of sufficient interest to justify its inclusion.

Flora

FLOWERING PLANTS An almost unbroken strip of maritime heathland follows the craggy coastline for much of the way, and has some of the most interesting plants including several which are restricted, in mainland Britain, to the Lizard although they also occur in the Channel Islands. They include **upright clover, twin-flowered clover** and **rupture wort**. Other notable species are **crimson clover, Cornish heath, sea asparagus, dwarf rush, hairy greenweed, Dyer's greenweed, spring sandwort, lesser birdsfoot trefoil, autumn squill, spotted catsear, thyme broomrape** and **saw-wort.**

Some of the streams in the Kynance Cove area (SW 685134) support **bog rush, common sedge, common reed, sea rush, hemlock water dropwort** and **pale butterwort.**

Several other interesting plants grow further inland on the Lizard Downs (SW 6913) including **pygmy rush,** on its only British site, and the **three-lobed water crowfoot, slender cicendia** and **chaffweed.**

FERNS **Sand quillwort** grows on the heathland, and is found nowhere else in mainland Britain. The **royal fern** may be found near streams in the Kynance Cove area and **pillwort** grows in pools on the Lizard Downs.

MOSSES AND LIVERWORTS The Lizard is also very rich in bryophytes and includes several rarer species including *Nitella opaca, Chara fragifera, Gongylanthus ericetorum, Colura calyptrifolia, Harpalejeunea ovata, Lejeunea mandonii, Marchesinia mackaii, Riccia bifurca, R. nigrella, R. crozalsii, R. sorocarpa, R. beyrichiana, Fossombronia husnotii, F. angulosa, F. wondraczeki, Pleurachaete squarrosa* and *Saccogyna viticulosa.*

Access

A public footpath follows the coast from Porth Mellin (SW 667197) to the Lizard Point (SW 695115), and is a very rewarding walk for botanists. It passes through the Nature Conservancy Council's reserve of Mullien Cliffs and the National Trust reserves of Predannack (SW 665159) and the Lizard Downs (SW 689131).

Other good localities on the Lizard Peninsula are Goonhilly Downs (SW 7219), Crousa Downs (SW 7618) – both areas are National Nature Reserves – and the cliffs around Coverack (SW 7818). These three sites are on O.S. map 204.

Slapton Ley SW 11 OS map 202 SX 8244

Slapton Ley is a large freshwater lagoon which is separated from the sea by a narrow shingle bar. It lies about 5 miles (8 km) south-west of Dartmouth and is rather more than 2 miles (3 km) long and about $\frac{1}{4}$ mile (400 m) wide. Although it is never more than about 10 ft (3 m) deep, it is one of the most extensive areas of freshwater in the south-west. The Ley has some large reed beds at its northern end which, together with the lagoon itself and an area of nearby woodland, comprise a 450 acre (182 ha) nature reserve of the Field Studies Council. The Council runs an education centre at Slapton Ley.

Fauna

BIRDS The lake is a favourite winter haunt of wildfowl and an important 'landing point' for many incoming spring migrants. Every common duck species has been recorded here including **pintails, pochard, eiders, tufted ducks, teal, scaup, shovelers, smew, garganey, goosanders, common** scoters, **red-breasted mergansers** and **wigeon**. The **mallard** is the only species of duck which regularly nests, however, although **garganey** have been known to do so.

There are also breeding colonies of **reed warblers** and **sedge warblers**, and breeding **linnets**, **whitethroats** and **stonechats**. **Buzzards**, **ravens** and **black terns** are not infrequent visitors, and in the winter the lake is a roosting ground for thousands of **greater black-backed gulls**.

MAMMALS **Badgers** and **foxes** are resident in the area.

Flora

FLOWERING PLANTS The shingle bar which separates the Ley from the sea is a good hunting ground for botanists and holds the rare **shore dock**, **slender sea knotgrass**, **sea radish** and **yellow horned-poppy**. **White water lily**, **curly pondweed** and **spiked water milfoil** grow in the lake itself, and the surrounding reed beds have **lesser bulrush**, **common bulrush**, **greyish bulrush**, **branched bur-reed**, **reed grass** and **amphibious bistort**. **Shore weed** grows around the lake edges but the great speciality of Slapton Ley is **strapwort**, which may be found growing around the sandy margins and is found nowhere else in Britain.

Access

The reserve is easily reached from Dartmouth via the A379. It is open to the public, but permission should first be requested from the warden of the Field Studies Centre. The address is: Slapton Ley Field Studies Centre, Slapton, Kingsbridge, Devon TQ7 2QP.

Berry Head SW 12 OS map 202 SX 9456

Berry Head is a small limestone headland just east of Brixham and about 6 miles (9.5 km) south of Torbay. It is managed as a local nature reserve by Torbay Borough Council on account of its breeding seabirds and interesting calcicole flora. The reserve covers 107 acres (43 ha).

Fauna

BIRDS The seabird populations are not large, but are of interest because they include **guillemots** and **razorbills** in one of their few south coast colonies. In addition to the auks there are **fulmars** and **kittiwakes**.

Flora

FLOWERING PLANTS The Head is noted for its assemblage of rare calcicoles. The attractive **white rock-rose**, which is otherwise only known from one British locality, is found in some quantity, as also is **narrow hare's-ear** which, likewise, has only one other known haunt on the British mainland (although it is also found in the Channel Islands).

Other notable species include **goldilocks**, which has five British stations, **white stonecrop**, **wall pepper**, **rock stonecrop**, **autumn squill**, **honewort**, **ivy broomrape**, **wild madder** and **sea spurge**. There is also a little maritime heath with **ling**, **bell heather** and **gorse**.

(Above) The Swale mudflats exposed at low tide: an important area for winter wildfowl (see page 164).
(Below) One of the 3500 ponies which roam The New Forest (see page 179).

The curious hexagonal basalt columns of The Giant's Causeway (see page 194).

Access

Berry Head is easily reached from Brixham and no special permits are needed.

St Agnes Head SW 13 OS map 200 SW 7051

St Agnes Head is on the north coast of Cornwall about 10 miles (16 km) south-west of Newquay. The coastline has some very interesting maritime heathland which is owned by the National Trust, and there are some fine cliffs which run along the coast to Godrevy Point about 10 miles (16 km) to the south. These have quite a rich flora in their own right as well as small colonies of breeding seabirds.

Fauna

BIRDS The cliff-nesting seabirds include **guillemots, razorbills** and **kittiwakes** and there are also **rock pipits, wrens** and **rock doves. Ravens** are also common and **buzzards** nest in the woodlands near Portneath.
MAMMALS Small colonies of **grey seals** breed along the coastline.
REPTILES AND AMPHIBIANS **Adders** are occasionally seen on the heathland at St Agnes.

Flora

FLOWERING PLANTS The heathland is mainly composed of **ling** and **bell heather** with a great deal of **western gorse** and some **common gorse**. The rare **Dorset heath** is present, too, but not in any quantity. Other notable species include **sheepsbit, Portland spurge, spring squill, sea plantain, buckshorn plantain, burnet rose, wild madder, wild honeysuckle, wild carrot, betony, salad burnet, saw-wort, fairy flax, early gentian, bloody cranesbill, kidney vetch, spotted catsear, pale heath violet, heath dog violet** and **bog rush**.

The cliffs to the south have the very rare **hairy greenweed**, in one of its British strongholds, along with **shore dock, common broomrape, thrift** and **least birdsfoot trefoil**.
FERNS **Sea spleenwort** grows in places along the cliffs.

Access

St Agnes Head is freely accessible and may be reached from St Agnes itself. The Cornwall Coast Path runs southwards from the Head to Godrevy Point, and beyond.

Rathlin Island NI 1 OS sheet 2 D 120530

Rathlin Island lies off the north-eastern tip of Ireland about 5 miles (8 km) north of Ballycastle. It is perhaps best known as the place where Robert the Bruce was inspired by that indefatigable spider whilst hiding in a cave there, but bird enthusiasts will also know that part of the island is an R.S.P.B. reserve and is famous for its seabirds.

The island is about 9 miles (14.5km) long and has a village and several farms, although away from these it is unspoiled and covered with grasslands and heath with many small reedy loughs. The western side has some fine cliffs.

Fauna

BIRDS About 200 species of birds have been recorded from the island including a large colony of **Manx shearwaters**. Other seabirds include **fulmars, guillemots, razorbills, black guillemots, puffins, cormorants, shags** and all six species of British **gulls: greater black-backed, lesser black-backed, herring, common, black-headed** and **kittiwake**.

Rathlin Island is one of the few Irish strongholds of the **buzzard**, and there are also **ravens, choughs** and **hooded crows**. Other breeding birds include **eiders, corncrakes, oystercatchers, ringed plovers, snipe, twite, rock pipits** and **peregrine falcons**.

Flora

FLOWERING PLANTS The flora is very much of secondary importance. One of its more notable members, however, is **tree mallow**.

Access

Rathlin Island is reached by boat from Ballycastle. There are regular trips during the summer months, but out of season it may be necessary to charter a boat specially. There is a camp site on the island but little other accommodation. No permits are required.

The Giant's Causeway NI 2 OS sheet 2 C 950445

The Giant's Causeway is best known on account of the thousands of hexagonal columns of basalt which may be seen here. These were formed when a lava floe slowly cooled and the gradually solidifying rock split into hexagonal blocks in much the same way as does a dried-out muddy pool. Obviously the area is fascinating to geologists, but the flora and fauna are also interesting.

The Giant's Causeway lies on the western side of Benbane Head and is owned by the National Trust.

Fauna

BIRDS The whole of Benbane Head has a rich avifauna which includes breeding **fulmars, black guillemots, greater black-backed gulls, herring gulls, kittiwakes, cormorants** and **shags**, although none are present in vast numbers. **Eiders, oystercatchers, ringed plovers** and **redshanks** also nest, as do **rock doves** and **rock pipits**. **Ravens, choughs, hooded crows, buzzards** and, if you are lucky, the occasional **peregrine** may also be seen from time to time.

Flora

FLOWERING PLANTS These include **spring squill** and **frog orchid**.

FERNS Sea spleenwort grows here.

Access

The Causeway is easily reached from Bushmills, about 2 miles (3 km) away.

Copeland Island NI 3 OS sheet 4 J 5984

Tiny Copeland Island lies slightly over 1 mile (1.6 km) offshore on the southern side of the entrance to Belfast Lough. Its main interest is as a migration watchpoint, and there is a bird observatory here; there is also a good variety of breeding seabirds.

Fauna

BIRDS Because Ireland is slightly off the major migration routes, the variety of bird species recorded on Copeland Island does not compare with those seen on other, more favourably placed observatories elsewhere in Britain, although many species of migrant passerines have been recorded here and the sea watching is good.

The breeding species of the island include a colony of **Manx shearwaters; common, arctic, roseate** and, sometimes, **Sandwich terns; black guillemots, eiders, hooded crows, rock doves** and **rock pipits.**

Access

The observatory includes a small hostel which accommodates 12 people and is open from March to October. Full details may be obtained from: N.D. McKee, 19 Deerpark Gardens, Belfast 14.

Strangford Lough NI 4 OS sheet 4 J 5050

Strangford Lough is a 15 mile (24 km) long sea lough which lies a few miles south-east of Belfast. Twice a day the tide drains the lough and exposes huge expanses of sand and mud which are a great attraction to geese and other wildfowl.

Fauna

BIRDS Strangford Lough is perhaps best known for its geese. About 3000 **pale-bellied brent geese** regularly winter here with smaller numbers of **greylags** and **white-fronted geese. Whooper swans** are also usually present in small numbers. **Wigeon** is the dominant duck and over 10,000 have been recorded with smaller numbers of **goldeneye, scaup, common scoters** and **red-breasted mergansers.** The wintering waders include **redshanks, oystercatchers, curlews, knot, dunlin** and **bar-tailed godwits.**

The lough also has many species of breeding birds, many of which favour the numerous islands on the western side. Nesting species include **greylag** and **Canada geese, shelducks, tufted ducks, red-breasted mergansers, great crested grebes** and **little grebes.** There are also four species of **terns,** namely **common, arctic, Sandwich** and **roseate**, although they are gradually being elbowed out of existence by the steadily increasing **black-headed gulls. Greater black-backed, lesser black-backed, herring** and **common gulls** also nest.

The breeding waders include **oystercatchers, ringed plovers** and **redshanks**, and other species are **black guillemots, rock doves, hooded crows, rock pipits, buzzards, sparrowhawks** and **short-eared owls**.

The south-western corner around Downpatrick is the best area for **geese**, whilst the **whooper swans** seem to prefer the north-east.

MAMMALS **Common seals** and **otters** are occasionally seen in the area.

Access

The area is best viewed from the A20 which runs along the eastern shore of the lough from Newtownards to Portaferry.

Lough Erne NI 5 OS sheet 3 H 007603

The River Erne rises in the Republic of Ireland and flows northwards, through Ulster, before turning west, crossing the border back into the Republic again, and eventually meeting the sea in Donegal Bay. The 35 mile (56 km) stretch of the Erne Valley which lies in Northern Ireland is largely occupied by two large loughs known as Upper and Lower Lough Erne. Both are superb bird watching spots, especially Lower Lough Erne, and the R.S.P.B. has a number of reserves there. These include Duck Island and Horse Island and the wooded lough shore around Castlecaldwell where the R.S.P.B. and the Forestry Commission have co-operated to form a bird sanctuary. However, the entire lough is so rich in ornithological interest as to justify inclusion.

Fauna

BIRDS Lower Lough is the only Irish breeding site of the **common scoter**, and the colony here now consists of about a hundred pairs. A small colony of **greylag geese**, rare nesters in Ireland, also lives here, and the woods around Castlecaldwell are one of the few Irish haunts of **garden warblers**.

Other regular nesting species are **tufted ducks, red-breasted mergansers, mute swans, oystercatchers, common sandpipers, redshanks** and **little grebes. Nightjars** may be found in the Castlecaldwell area, and Upper Lough Erne has the largest **heronry** in Ireland.

Access

The Castlecaldwell reserve is open at all times and has nature trails and public hides overlooking the lough. From time to time the R.S.P.B. organizes boat trips on the lough, details of which may be obtained from The Warden, Castlecaldwell, Leggs P.O., Co. Fermanagh.

Away from the reserves, the network of minor roads which covers the area offers several splendid viewpoints over both loughs.

Lough Neagh NI 6 OS sheet 4 J 111880

Lough Neagh lies about 12 miles (19 km) due west of Belfast and is easily the largest freshwater lake in the whole of Ireland. Indeed, it is almost an inland sea and covers 153 square miles (396 km²). It is also one of the best localities in Ireland for watching water birds, and its banks have an interesting variety of wild flowers.

The R.S.P.B. has established a reserve on its northern shore but the whole lough is sufficiently interesting to merit inclusion. Also included here is Lough Beg, a much smaller lough about 1 mile (1.6 km) to the north on the River Bann.

Fauna

BIRDS During the winter the two loughs hold immense numbers of wildfowl. About 22,000 **tufted ducks** have been recorded together with 8000 **pochard**, 4000 **goldeneye**, 1000 **scaup** and large numbers of both **whooper** and **Bewick's swans**. These numbers include some 2000 tufted ducks and 2000 pochard which regularly winter on Lough Beg, along with about 2000 **wigeon** and several hundred **pintails**.

Among the wildfowl which regularly nest on Lough Neagh are **gadwall, tufted ducks, shovelers, shelducks, red-breasted mergansers** and **mute swans. Garganey** have bred from time to time. **Great crested grebes** breed here in larger numbers than anywhere else in Ireland, and there are also plenty of nesting **little grebes**. Other breeding species include **water rails, oystercatchers, ringed plovers, common sandpipers, redshanks, common terns, greater black-backed gulls, lesser black-backed gulls, herring gulls** and **black-headed gulls**.

Lough Beg has seen some notable migrants over the years including **dowitchers, yellowlegs, buff-breasted sandpipers, white-rumped sandpipers** and **broad-billed sandpipers**.

Flora

FLOWERING PLANTS The flora is notable for several species of maritime plants which grow around the banks of the lough. These include **cliff spurrey, saltmarsh sedge** and **seaside pansy**.

The **narrow small reed** has its only Irish site at the lough's northern end, and the uncommon **holly grass** grows on the eastern banks. The very rare **American lady's tresses** also grows along the banks.

Access

The R.S.P.B. reserve is at Shanes Castle, about 2 miles (3 km) north-west of Antrim. It is open from April to August only, and there is a small entrance fee.

Elsewhere there is a good network of minor roads surrounding the lough which provide access at numerous points.

Appendices

The country code   APPENDIX 1

1 Guard against all risk of fire.
2 Keep all gates closed.
3 Keep dogs under proper control.
4 Keep to the footpaths.
5 Be careful not to damage hedges, fences or walls.
6 Take your litter home.
7 Safeguard water supplies.
8 Protect all wildlife.
9 Go carefully on country roads.
10 Respect the life of the countryside.
11 Make no unnecessary noise.
12 Leave livestock, crops and machinery alone.

Wildlife and the law   APPENDIX 2

The law concerning wildlife in our country is very complex and involves
several Acts of Parliament, so it would be impossible to give anything other
than a brief summary here. However, this should enable you to 'know the
law' in most general situations. Further information may be obtained from
the Nature Conservancy, and several organizations including the R.S.P.B.
and the R.S.N.C. publish free leaflets dealing with various aspects of
wildlife and the law.

Mammals

It is illegal to intentionally kill, attempt to kill, injure, capture, possess, sell
or disturb any of the mammals listed below. It is also illegal to damage,
destroy or restrict access to their homes or shelters, and a special licence
from the Nature Conservancy is needed in order to photograph them in
their homes: **red squirrel**, **otter**, **bats** (all species), **common dolphin**,
bottle-nosed dolphin, **common porpoise**.

It is also against the law to intentionally kill, attempt to kill, injure,
capture, possess or sell **badgers** or any parts thereof.

Deer and **seals** may only be killed in certain seasons, and there are
restrictions as to the type of weapons which may be used to do so.

In addition, the use of certain cruel or indiscriminate traps or snares, explosives, bows (including crossbows) or live decoys is forbidden, and certain other mammals (including **pine martens, dormice, hedgehogs** and **shrews**) may not be trapped, snared or killed by poisons, gas, automatic or semi-automatic weapons or by any methods involving the use of artificial light or sound recordings.

Birds

Basically, *all* wild birds are protected by law. It is illegal to intentionally kill, attempt to kill, injure, capture, possess or sell any wild bird; to damage or destroy any nest (which is in use), or to take or sell eggs. This does not apply, however, to certain 'pest' species which are listed below, and to other game and sporting birds which may be shot or taken from your land or with the landowner's consent.

The 'pest' species are: **collared dove, feral pigeon, woodpigeon, house sparrow, starling, crow, rook, jackdaw, jay, magpie, herring gull, lesser black-backed gull, greater black-backed gull.**

In addition, there is a list of specially protected species which it is illegal to disturb whilst nesting, and this includes taking photographs at or near the nest without a Nature Conservancy Council licence. These specially protected species are: **avocet, barn owl, bearded tit, bee-eater, Bewick's swan, bittern, black-necked grebe, black redstart, black-tailed godwit, black tern, black-winged stilt, bluethroat, brambling, Cetti's warbler, chough, cirl bunting, common quail, common scoter, corncrake, crested tit, crossbills (all species), Dartford warbler, divers (all species), dotterel, fieldfare, firecrest, garganey, golden eagle, golden oriole, goshawk, green sandpiper, greenshank, gyr falcon, harriers (all species), hobby, honey buzzard, hoopoe, Kentish plover, kingfisher, Lapland bunting, Leach's petrel, little bittern, little gull, little ringed plover, little tern, long-tailed duck, marsh warbler, Mediterranean gull, merlin, osprey, peregrine falcon, purple heron, purple sandpiper, red-backed shrike, red kite, red-necked phalarope, redwing, roseate tern, ruff, Savi's warbler, scarlet rosefinch, scaup, serin, shorelark, short-toed treecreeper, Slavonian grebe, snow bunting, snowy owl, spoonbill, spotted crake, stone curlew, Temminck's stint, velvet scoter, whimbrel, white-tailed sea eagle, whooper swan, woodlark, wood sandpiper, wryneck.**

Goldeneye, pintail and, in parts of Scotland, the **greylag goose**, are specially protected outside the close season.

It is also against the law to use certain cruel snares or traps. Note that handling wild birds for ringing also requires a Nature Conservancy permit. Wild birds which have been injured may be taken into captivity for treatment, but must be released once they are able to fend for themselves. They may also be killed in order to end their suffering.

Reptiles, amphibians and fish

You may not intentionally kill, attempt to kill, injure, possess or sell any of the following species: **sand lizard, smooth snake, great crested newt, natterjack toad, burbot;** nor may you damage, destroy or restrict access to any shelter which they may use whilst breeding. Note that even handling them in the field is liable to be classed as having possession and is consequently illegal.

It is also against the law to sell any of the following: **palmate newt, common newt, common frog, common toad, common lizard, slowworm, grass snake** or **adder**.

Invertebrates

You may not intentionally kill, attempt to kill, injure, capture, possess or sell; or damage, destroy or restrict access to a shelter of any of the following: **chequered skipper butterfly, heath fritillary butterfly, large blue butterfly, swallowtail butterfly, barberry carpet moth, black-veined moth, Essex emerald moth, New Forest burnet moth, reddish buff moth, field cricket, mole cricket, Norfolk aeshna dragonfly, rainbow leaf beetle, wart-biter grasshopper, fen raft spider, ladybird spider, Carthusian snail, glutinous snail** or **sandbowl snail**.

Plants

It is now illegal to uproot *any* wild plants except on your own land or with the landowner's permission.

It is also illegal to pick, uproot, damage, destroy, collect seeds from or sell any of the following:
Adder's-tongue spearwort *(Ranunculus ophioglossifolius);* **Alpine catchfly** *(Lychnis alpina);* **Alpine gentian** *(Gentiana nivalis);* **Alpine sowthistle** *(Cicerbita alpina);* **Alpine woodsia** *(Woodsia alpina);* **Bedstraw broomrape** *(Orobanche caryophyllacea);* **Blue heath***(Phyllodoce caerulea);* **Brown galingale** *(Cyperus fuscus);* **Cheddar pink** *(Dianthus gratianopolitanus);* **Childling pink** *(Petrorhagia nanteuilii);* **Diapensia** *(Diapensia lapponica);* **Dickie's bladder-fern** *(Cystopteris dickieana);* **Downy woundwort** *(Stachys germanica);* **Drooping saxifrage** *(Saxifraga cernua);* **Early spider orchid** *(Ophrys sphegodes);* **Fen orchid** *(Liparis loeselii);* **Fen violet** *(Viola persicifolia);* **Field cow-wheat** *(Melampyrum arvense);* **Field eryngo** *(Eryngium campestre);* **Field wormwood** *(Artemisia campestris);* **Ghost orchid** *(Epipogium aphyllum);* **Great Ormes berry** *(Cotoneaster integerrimus);* **Greater yellow rattle** *(Rhinanthus serotinus);* **Jersey cudweed** *(Gnaphalium luteoalbum);* **Killarney fern** *(Trichomanes speciosum);* **Lady's slipper orchid** *(Cypripedium calceolus);* **Late spider orchid** *(Ophrys fuciflora);* **Least lettuce** *(Lactuca saligna);* **Limestone woundwort** *(Stachys alpina);* **Lizard orchid** *(Himantoglossum hircinum);* **Military orchid** *(Orchis militaris);* **Monkey orchid** *(Orchis simia);* **Oblong wood-**

sia *(Woodsia ilvensis);* Ox-tongue broomrape *(Orobanche loricata);* Perennial knawel *(Scleranthus perennis);* Plymouth pear *(Pyrus cordata);* Portland sea-lavender *(Limonium recurvum);* Purple spurge *(Euphorbia peplis);* Red helleborine *(Cephalanthera rubra);* Ribbon-leaved water-plantain *(Alisma gramineum);* Rock cinquefoil *(Potentilla rupestris);* Rock sea-lavender *(Limonium paradoxum);* Rough marsh mallow *(Althaea hirsuta);* Round-headed leek *(Allium sphaerocephalon);* Scottish sandwort *(Arenaria norvegica);* Sea knotgrass *(Polygonum maritimum);* Sickle-leaved hare's-ear *(Bupleurum falcatum);* Small Alison *(Alyssum alyssoides);* Small hare's-ear *(Bupleurum baldense);* Snowdon lily *(Lloydia serotina);* Spiked speedwell *(Veronica spicata);* Spring gentian *(Gentiana verna);* Starfruit *(Damasonium alisma);* Starved wood-sedge *(Carex depauperata);* Teesdale sandwort *(Minuartia stricta);* Thistle broomrape *(Orobanche reticulata);* Triangular club-rush *(Scirpus triquetrus);* Tufted saxifrage *(Saxifraga cespitosa);* Water germander *(Teucrium scordium);* Whorled Solomon's seal *(Polygonatum verticillatum);* Wild gladiolus *(Gladiolus illyricus);* Wood calamint *(Calamintha sylvatica).*

National nature reserves APPENDIX 3

(An asterisk indicates that the reserve is described in this book.)

Scotland

Achanarras Quarry, Highland
Allt-nan-Carnan, Highland*
Ben Eighe, Highland*
Ben Lawers, Tayside and Central*
Ben Lui, Strathclyde and Central
Blawhorn Moss, Lothian
Braehead Moss, Strathclyde
Caenlochan, Tayside
Caerlaverock, Dumfries and Galloway*
Cairngorms, Highland*
Cairnsmore of Fleet, Dumphries and Galloway
Claish Moss, Highland
Clyde Valley Woodlands, Strathclyde
Coille Thocabhaig, Highland
Corrieshalloch Gorge, Highland*
Craigellachie, Highland
Dinnet Oakwood, Grampian
Flanders Moss, Central*
Glasdrum Wood, Strathclyde
Glen Diomhan, Strathclyde
Glen Nant, Strathclyde
Glen Roy, Highland
Glen Tanar, Grampian
Gualin, Highland
Haaf Gruney, Shetland
Herma Ness, Shetland*
achnadamph, Highland*

Invernaver, Highland*
Inverpolly, Highland*
Isle of May, Fife*
Keen of Hamar, Shetland
Kirkconnell Flow,
   Dumfries and Galloway
Loch A'Mhuillin Wood, Highland
Loch Druidibeg, Western Isles*
Loch Leven, Tayside*
Loch Lomond,
   Central and Strathclyde*
Loch Maree Islands, Highland
Loch Sunart Woodlands, Highland
Milton Wood, Tayside
Monach Islands, Western Isles
Morrone Birkwoods, Grampian*
Morton Lochs, Fife*
Mound Alderwoods, Highland*
Muir of Dinnet, Grampian
Nig and Udale Bays, Highland
North Rona and Sula Sgeir,
   Western Isles*
Noss, Shetland*
Rannoch Moor, Tayside*
Rassal Ashwood, Highland
Rhum, Highland*
St Cyrus, Grampian*

St Kilda, Western Isles*
Sands of Forvie, Grampian*
Silver Flowe, Dumfries and Galloway
Strathfarrar, Highland
Strathy Bog, Highland
Taynish, Strathclyde
Tentsmuir Point, Fife*
Tynron Juniper Wood,
  Dumfries and Galloway
Whitlaw Mosses, Borders

England
Ainsdale Sand Dunes, Merseyside*
Ashby Scar, Cumbria
Arne, Dorset*
Aston Rowant, Oxfordshire
Avon Gorge, Avon
Axmouth-Lyme Regis Undercliffs, Devon
Barnack Hills and Holes, Cambridgeshire
Blean Woods, Kent*
Blelham Bog, Cumbria
Bovey Valley Woodlands, Devon*
Braunton Burrows, Devon*
Bridgwater Bay, Somerset*
Bure Marshes, Norfolk*
Castle Hill, Sussex
Castor Hanglands, Cambridgeshire
Cavenham Heath, Suffolk*
Chaddesley Woods, Hereford and
  Worcestershire*
Chartley Moss, Staffordshire*
Chippenham Fen, Cambridgeshire*
Clawthorpe Fell, Cumbria
Colt Park Wood, North Yorkshire*
Coom Rigg Moss, Northumberland
Cothill, Oxfordshire
Cotswold Common and Beechwoods,
  Gloucestershire
Dendles Wood, Devon
Derbyshire Dales, Derbyshire
Ebbor Gorge, Somerset
Forge Valley Woods, North Yorkshire
Gait Barrows, Cumbria*
Fyfield Down, Wiltshire
Glasson Moss, Cumbria
Hales Wood, Essex
Ham Street Woods, Kent
Hartland Moor, Dorset
Hickling Broad, Norfolk*
High Halstow, Kent*
Holkham, Norfolk*
Holme Fen, Cambridgeshire
Kingley Vale, West Sussex*
Knocking Hoe, Bedfordshire
Leigh Marsh, Essex*

Lindisfarne, Northumberland*
Ling Gill, North Yorkshire*
Lizard, Cornwall*
Lullington Heath, East Sussex
Moccas Park, Hereford and Worcestershire
Monks Wood, Cumbria
Moor House, Cumbria
Morden Bog, Dorset
Mottey Meadows, Staffordshire
North Fen, Cumbria
North Meadow, Wiltshire*
North Solent, Hampshire
Old Winchester Hill, Hampshire*
Orfordness – Havergate, Suffolk*
Park Wood, Cumbria
Parsonage Down, Wiltshire
Pewsey Down, Wiltshire*
Prescombe Down, Wiltshire
Ribble Marshes, Lancashire and Merseyside
Rodney Stoke, Somerset*
Rostherne Mere, Cheshire*
Roudsea Wood, Cumbria*
Rusland Moss, Cumbria
Saltfleetby – Theddlethorpe Dunes,
  Lincolnshire*
Scar Close, North Yorkshire*
Scolt Head Island, Norfolk*
Shapwick Heath, Somerset
Stodmarsh, Kent*
Studland Heath, Dorset*
Swanscombe Skull Site, Kent
Swanton Novers Woods, Norfolk
The Swale, Kent*
Thetford Heath, Suffolk
Thursley, Surrey*
Tring Reservoirs, Hertfordshire*
Upper Teesdale, Durham
Upwood Meadows, Cambridgeshire
Walberswick, Suffolk*
Weeting Heath, Norfolk*
Westleton Heath, Suffolk
Winterton Dunes, Norfolk
Woodwalton Fen, Cambridgeshire
Wren's Nest, West Midlands
Wylye Down, Wiltshire
Wynbunbury Moss, Cheshire
Wychwood, Oxfordshire
Wye, Kent*
Wyre Forest, Hereford and Worcestershire
Yarner Wood, Devon*

Wales
Allt Rhyd y Groes, Dyfed
Cader Idris, Gwynedd*

Coed Camlyn, Gwynedd*
Coed Cymerau, Gwynedd
Coed Dolgarrog, Gwynedd
Coed Ganllwyd, Gwynedd*
Coed Gorswen, Gwynedd
Coed Rheidol, Dyfed
Coed y Rhygen, Gwynedd
Coed Tremadoc, Gwynedd
Coedydd Aber, Gwynedd
Coedydd Maentwrog, Gwynedd
Cors Caron, Dyfed
Cors Erddreiniog, Gwynedd
Cors Tregaron, Dyfed*
Craig Cerrig Gleisiad, Powys*
Craig y Cilau, Powys*
Cwm Clydach, Gwent*

Cwm Glas Crafnant, Gwynedd
Cwm Idwal, Gwynedd*
Dyfi, Gwynedd and Powys*
Gower Coast, West Glamorgan*
Morfa Dyffryn, Gwynedd*
Morfa Harlech, Gwynedd*
Nant Irfon, Powys
Newborough Warren, Gwynedd*
Ogof Ffynnon Ddu, Powys
Oxwich Bay, West Glamorgan*
Rhinog, Gwynedd*
Skomer, Dyfed*
Stackpole, Dyfed*
Stanner Rocks, Powys
Whiteford Burrows, West Glamorgan
Y Wyddfa, Gwynedd*

R.S.P.B. reserves APPENDIX 4

(An asterisk indicates that the reserve is described in this book.)

Scotland
Balranald, Western Isles
Birsay Moors, Orkney
Culbin Sands, Highland
Dale of Cottasgarth, Orkney
Copinsay, Orkney*
Fetlar, Shetland*
Forth Islands, Strathclyde*
Fowlsheugh, Grampian
Handa, Highland*
Hobbister, Orkney
Inchmickery, Strathclyde
Insh Marshes, Highland
Ken/Dee Marshes, Dumfries and Galloway
Killiecrankie, Tayside
Loch Garten, Highland*
Loch of Kinnordy, Tayside*
Loch of Spiggie, Shetland
Loch of Strathbeg, Grampian*
Lochwinnoch, Strathclyde
Lumbister, Shetland
Marwick Head, Orkney
Mull of Galloway,
    Dumfries and Galloway*
North Hill, Orkney*
North Hoy, Orkney
Noup Cliffs, Orkney*
Papa Westray, Orkney
Ramna Stacks, Shetland
The Loons, Orkney
Vane Farm, Tayside*
Yellow Sound Islands, Shetland

England
Arne, Dorset*
Aylesbeare Common, Devon
Barfold Copse, Surrey
Bempton Cliffs, Humberside*
Blacktoft Sands, Humberside*
Blean Woods, Kent*
Chapel Wood, Devon
Church Wood, Bucks
Coombes Valley, Staffs*
Dungeness, Kent*
Eastwood, Greater Manchester
Elmley Marshes, Kent
Fairburn Ings, West Yorkshire*
Fore Wood, East Sussex
Fowlmere, Cambridgeshire
Gayton Sands, Cheshire
Havergate Island, Suffolk*
Hornsea Mere, Humberside*
Langstone Harbour, Hampshire*
Leighton Moss, Lancashire*
The Lodge, Bedfordshire
Minsmere, Suffolk*
Morecambe Bay, Lancashire*
Nagshead, Gloucestershire*
Nene Washes, Cambridgeshire
Northward Hill, Kent
North Warren, Suffolk
Ouse Washes, Cambridgeshire*
Radipole Lake, Dorset*
Rye House Marsh, Hertfordshire
St. Bees Head, Cumbria*

Snettisham, Norfolk
Stour Wood and Copperas Bay, Essex
Strumpshaw Fen, Norfolk
Tetney Marsh, Lincolnshire
Titchwell Marsh, Norfolk
West Sedgemoor, Somerset
Wolves Wood, Suffolk

Wales
Corngafallt, Powys
Grassholm, Dyfed*
Gwenffrwd and Dinas, Dyfed*
Llyn Vyrnwy, Powys*

Mawddach Woods, Gwynedd
Point of Air, Clwyd
Ramsey Island, Dyfed
South Stack, Gwynedd*
The Skerries, Anglesey
Ynys-hir, Dyfed*

Northern Ireland
Castlecaldwell, Co. Fermanagh*
Green and Blockhouse Islands,
   Co. Down
Loch Foyle, Londonderry
Rathlin Island, Co. Antrim*
Shanes Castle, Co. Antrim*

Major conservation and wildlife organizations of Britain APPENDIX 5

Association for the Study of Reptilia and Amphibia, Reptile House,
   Cotswold Wildlife Park, Burford, Oxfordshire OX8 4JW.
This association aims to promote an interest in reptiles and amphibians
among the public, and to provide an information service on matters
concerned with reptiles and amphibians. Members are also concerned with
the captive breeding and conservation of reptiles and amphibians. The
Association produces a regular journal and holds meetings for its members.

Botanical Society of the British Isles, c/o Dept of Botany, British
   Museum (Natural History), Cromwell Road, London SW7 5BD
The Society is a voluntary association of amateur and professional botanists
whose principal interests are British flowering plants and ferns and the
promotion of plant conservation. The Society also organizes surveys of
British plants and publishes a regular journal, newsletter and other
publications.

British Butterfly Conservation Society, Sternes, York Road, Beverley,
   East Yorkshire HU17 7AN
This society is a voluntary charity whose objectives are to protect British
butterflies both by field conservation and captive breeding and release, as
well as to encourage interest among the general public.

British Deer Society, The Mill House, Bishopstrow, Warminster,
   Wiltshire BA12 9HJ
The British Deer Society is an offshoot of the mammal society. Its main aims
are to study deer in Britain and to promote the spread of knowledge in all
aspects of deer biology and management. The Society produces a variety of
publications and holds regular outdoor meetings.

British Lichen Society, Dept of Botany, British Museum (Natural
    History), Cromwell Road, London SW7 5BD
The British Lichen Society exists to encourage interest in the study of
lichens. It produces a regular newsletter and magazine, and holds
conferences for members and lichen enthusiasts.

British Museum (Natural History), Cromwell Road, London SW7 5DB
The main buildings of the museum are situated in south-west London and
there is also a branch at Tring, Herts. It holds the national collection of
natural history specimens and, in addition, undertakes a great deal of
research into various aspects of natural history, provides educational
facilities and will answer queries on natural history. A series of striking
exhibitions are also on view.

British Pteridological Society, 42 Lewisham Road, Smethwick, Warley,
    West Midlands B66 2B5
The British Pteridological Society exists to encourage interest in British
ferns and their allies, and to promote their study and conservation. It
produces a regular bulletin and magazine, and runs occasional conferences
for fern enthusiasts.

British Trust for Conservation Volunteers, 26 St Mary Street,
    Wallingford, Oxfordshire OX10 0EU
This charitable organization encourages young people (16 +) to participate
in practical conservation work on nature reserves and other rich wildlife
sites by inviting them to join regular work parties at local reserves where
management work is needed. It co-operates closely with the RSNC, local
authorities and other bodies concerned with wildlife conservation.

British Trust for Ornithology, Beech Grove, Tring,
    Hertfordshire HP23 5NR
The British Trust for Ornithology (B.T.O.) is a voluntary research
organization whose members collaborate with a team of professional
biologists to increase knowledge of the bird life of Britain. Field surveys are
carried out nationwide, the distribution of birds is investigated and ringing
studies arranged. The Trust produces a quarterly journal and newsletter.

The Field Studies Council, 9 Devereux Court, The Strand,
    London WC2R 3JR
This is a voluntary educational body which manages a collection of study
centres in various parts of the country, where it runs courses for those who
are interested in wildlife and various other aspects of life in the
countryside. Many of its study centres are set in the most interesting
surroundings, however, and are managed so as to encourage wildlife.
Therefore they are, in effect, nature reserves.

Forestry Commission, 231 Corstorphine Road, Edinburgh EH12 7AT
The principal function of the Forestry Commission (F.C.) is, of course, to grow timber, and to this end it has bought and planted immense areas of the country, especially in the north and west. In its early days the Commission aroused the wrath of a great many wildlife enthusiasts by single mindedly planting blocks of fast-growing exotic conifers with little regard for their effect on the landscape or indigenous wildlife. Since the war, however, the Forestry Commission has been rather more enlightened in its policies, and is now very conscious of public opinion. Whenever possible the policy now is to conserve old existing hardwoods, to encourage wildlife, and to open its forests for public amenity use. The result has been the establishment of what is, in effect, a series of wildlife sanctuaries.

National Trust, 42 Queen Anne's Gate, London SW1H 9AS, and
National Trust for Scotland, 5 Charlotte Square, Edinburgh EH2 4DU
The oldest voluntary conservation body in Britain. The National Trust (N.T.) was started in 1894 by three public spirited and enlightened conservationists who were anxious that as much as possible of Britain's national heritage should be kept in trust for the future. Today, the National Trust is the largest private landowner in the country, and it owns about 1 per cent of our total land area and 10 per cent of our coastline. Most of its properties are historic buildings, monuments and so on, but it also owns a huge acreage of land where the scenery and wildlife are the prime interest. The majority of the Trust's properties are open to the public free of charge, and the Trust is financed by voluntary support and the subscriptions of its members.

Nature Conservancy Council (English H.Q.), Calthorpe House,
    Calthorpe Street, Banbury, Oxon OX16 8EZ
Nature Conservancy Council (Scottish H.Q.), 12 Hope Terrace,
    Edinburgh EH9 2AS
Nature Conservancy Council (Welsh H.Q.), Plas Penrhos, Penrhos Road,
    Bangor, Gwynedd LL57 2LQ
The Nature Conservancy Council (N.C.C.) is the official government body which is concerned with wildlife and nature conservation. It was set up by Royal Charter in 1949 with the aims of undertaking research into various aspects of wildlife and ecology, advising on conservation problems, and establishing and maintaining a series of nature reserves.

It has succeeded admirably in all its aims. Backed by public funds, it has been able to secure some of the finest wildlife sites in the country and has declared them as National Nature Reserves (N.N.R.). Not all N.N.Rs are actually owned by the Council, but many are leased to it and others are managed by the Council with agreement from the owners. Wherever possible the public are allowed to visit these N.N.Rs., although in some cases it has been necessary to deter too many casual visitors, large numbers of which might damage delicate ecosystems and cause unnecessary disturbance. To deal with this problem, the Council has instituted a permit system whereby bona fide naturalists may obtain a permit from the local Nature Conservancy Council headquarters prior to their visit. (The addresses are given, where applicable, in the text.)

In addition to N.N.Rs the Council has also scheduled a great many areas as Sites of Special Scientific Interest (S.S.S.I.). These are not actually managed as nature reserves, but the Council endeavours to protect them by co-operating with the landowners and discouraging them from undertaking any activity which might adversely affect the wildlife interest.

Royal Entomological Society, 41 Queen's Gate, London SW7 5HU
This society exists to encourage the study of, and stimulate interest in, insects. It holds regular meetings and symposiums, produces several publications (including a series of identification guides) and encourages communication between entomologists, amateur and professional alike.

Royal Society for Nature Conservation, The Green, Nettleham,
    Lincoln LN2 2NR
1926 saw the birth of a small local club of wildlife enthusiasts known as the Norfolk Naturalists' Trust, one of the aims of which was to try to protect as much of Norfolk's wildlife as possible by establishing nature reserves. No-one could have foreseen at that time, however, just what far-reaching consequences the birth of that small society was to have on nature conservation. Soon, the Trust became so successful in achieving its aims that other counties followed the example and established similar trusts of their own. The idea continued to gain popularity until today the whole of England and Wales is covered by a series of over 40 similar bodies; Scotland and Ulster each have their own.

Later, the County Naturalists' Trusts joined forces both with each other and with another conservation body – the Society for the Promotion of Nature Reserves (S.P.N.R.). The S.P.N.R. actually started a long time before the County Trusts – in 1912 in fact. It quickly became a most influential body, but the real turning point in its fortunes came in 1950 when it established a special committee to represent the County Trusts. Since then, the S.P.N.R. has changed its name and has become the Royal Society for Nature Conservation (R.S.N.C.). The Society and local Trusts between them now have over 140,000 members and manage about 1400 nature reserves – far more than any other conservation body in the country.

Membership of the County Trusts is still growing apace, and prospective members may obtain details of their local trust from the R.S.N.C.

Royal Society for the Protection of Birds, The Lodge, Sandy,
    Bedfordshire SG19 2DL
The Royal Society for the Protection of Birds (R.S.P.B.) is Britain's biggest

voluntary body entirely concerned with nature conservation. It was founded in 1889, although it did not receive its Royal prefix until 1904. It now has over 360,000 members and maintains an impressive collection of nature reserves throughout the country. Although the emphasis is on birdlife, most of the reserves harbour a great deal of other interesting wildlife as well.

Most of the Society's reserves are open to both members and non-members alike, although the latter generally have to pay a small admission charge for their visit. Members pay an annual subscription fee which entitles them to visit most of the reserves free and, in the long run, it is often cheaper to join the Society than not.

Scottish Wildlife Trust, 25 Johnston Terrace, Edinburgh EH1 2NH.
This is the national body concerned with the conservation of wildlife in Scotland. It works in close liaison with government and with landowners. The Trust arranges lectures and produces the journal *Scottish Wildlife*.

Wildfowl Trust, The New Grounds, Slimbridge,
  Gloucestershire GL2 7BT
The Wildfowl Trust was set up by Peter Scott in 1946 in order to study and conserve wildfowl. It began by establishing a wildfowl refuge at Slimbridge on the Bristol Channel, and since then it has expanded considerably and now has several sites where wildfowl and other birds are encouraged to put down and, hopefully, stay during the course of their migrations. The birds are attracted by large shallow lagoons and plenty of food, and bird enthusiasts are made equally welcome by the provision of hides, wildlife exhibitions and, at most of the sanctuaries, collections of captive exotic waterfowl. Indeed, the Trust now has the most comprehensive collection of wildfowl anywhere in the world, and has achieved major successes in breeding over the years.

All this, of course, costs a great deal of money and so the Trust charges admission to its reserves. Wildfowl enthusiasts will find it cheaper to join the Trust.

Biological suppliers   APPENDIX 6

Longworth Instrument Co. Ltd, Radley Road, Abingdon,
  Oxford OX14 3PH

Philip Harris Ltd, Lynn Lane, Shenstone, Staffordshire SW14 0EE

Watkins and Doncaster, Four Throws, Hawkhurst, Kent TN18 5ED

Worldwide Butterflies Ltd, Over Compton, Sherborne, Dorset DT9 4QN

Bibliography APPENDIX 7

The following is a selection of the many useful books which can be purchased, or borrowed from the library, to help increase your knowledge of natural history and assist in identification.

A Day in the Country by John Gooders (Andre Deutsch)
A Nature Conservation Review by D. Ratcliffe (Cambridge University Press)
Birds by John Andrews (Hamlyn nature guides)
Butterflies by Paul Whalley (Hamlyn nature guides)
Britain's Green Mantle by Sir Arthur Tansley (Allen & Unwin)
Finding Wild Flowers by R.S.R. Fitter (Collins)
Guide to Animal Tracks and Signs by Preben Bang & Preben Dahlstrom (Collins)
Guide to Birdwatching by R.S.R. Fitter (Collins)
Nature Conservation in Britain by Sir Dudley Stamp (Collins New Naturalist)
Nature Photography – its art and techniques by Heather Angel (Fountain Press)
Plant Life by C.T. Prime (Collins)
R.S.P.B. Guide to British Birds by David Saunders (Hamlyn)
The Amateur Naturalist by Gerald Durrell (Hamish Hamilton)
The Atlas of Breeding Birds in Britain and Ireland by J.T.R. Sharrock (British Trust for Ornithology)
The Making of the British Countryside by Ron Freethy (David & Charles)
Where to Watch Birds by John Gooders (Andre Deutsch)
Wildflowers by Helen Pursey (Hamlyn nature guides)

Further details of many of the organizations listed in Appendix 5, as well as many other organizations, National Parks, etc. can be found in *Environmental Education – sources of information* (H.M.S.O.)

Index

Page numbers in *italic* refer to illustrations